ENDORSEMENTS

I congratulate Dr. Candice Smithyman on her book, *365 Prophetic Revelations from the Hebrew Calendar*. I found it to be very insightful and I learned things that I had never been acquainted with previously. I recommend this very inspiring work!

Patricia King
Founder, Patricia King Ministries

One of the most amazing discoveries I've made in my walk with the Lord is that God has His own calendar! God's calendar is clearly given to us in the Bible, but most Christians have never paid much attention to it. The ancient Jews followed God's calendar, and the early church did also. In the dark ages, under pressure from the Roman government, the church switched to a "Christianized" version of the pagan Roman calendar. We need to realize however, that *we* switched... *God didn't!* God is *God*, and He uses His own calendar! So, if we want to understand what God is doing, it's important that we know where we are in God's calendar. God's calendar has great prophetic significance. Each year has its own meaning. Each month is a new prophetic season. God's calendar is made up of special "appointed times" and seasons. I've found that if we align our lives with God's times, we can prosper in every season. If you sincerely desire to align your life with Heaven's prophetic timeline, I believe *365 Prophetic Revelations from the Hebrew Calendar* can be a valuable resource. In this book, Dr. Smithyman pulls together a vast amount of information! She draws from the Bible, Jewish tradition, and church history. She includes the major and minor biblical feasts, Sabbaths, and new moon celebrations. Then she walks you day by day through the Hebrew calendar to reveal how it all fits together, adding prophetic insights along the way. If you have been seeking a way to better understand God's calendar, I believe this book is for you!

Dr. Robert Heidler
Apostolic Teacher
Glory of Zion International Ministries

Our God is supernatural in all His ways. He designed a supernatural calendar for the Jewish people whom He chose to carry His name and represent Him to every nation on earth. Within that calendar God embedded spiritual feasts and holy days which He created to function along with the natural, normal agricultural and weather cycles of the planet. He still follows that calendar to this day. Dr. Candice Smithyman has done the body of Christ a great favor by summarizing and contextualizing the heavenly rhythms of God contained in His supernatural calendar in a series of 365 divine vignettes. I have no doubt you will find these essays revelatory and encouraging. By aligning yourself with Heaven's rhythm, you will also become naturally attuned to the supernatural ways of God.

Joan Hunter
Author/Evangelist
Host of *Miracles Happen!* TV Show

365 Revelations from the Hebrew Calendar by Dr. Candice Smithyman is a wonderful deep dive into God's heart for His people through the appointed times and seasons according to the Hebrew calendar. This book teaches us that God desires to intimately connect with His sons and daughters daily. This book will encourage every believer in Jesus to seek the Lord with more passion as they experience the multidimensional goodness of God.

Dr. Rob Covell
Wagner University

Throughout the centuries our Jewish brothers and sisters have been the stewards of the *moadim* of the Hebrew calendar, which belongs to the body of King Jesus as a whole. As a prophetic voice in my life, I know that when Dr. Candice brings a revelation, it is truly from the Lord. In her book *365 Prophetic Revelations from the Hebrew Calendar,* Dr. Candice walks you through setting yourself up for divine appointments with the Lord on a day-to-day basis. She is an authority on this subject and has my highest endorsement!

Troy Brewer
Senior Pastor of OpenDoor Church
Burleson, Texas

Realignment and attunement with the appointed times and seasons of God is critical for the hour we live in. Through research and revelation, Dr. Candice Smithyman does a brilliant job of not only giving insight into the Hebrew Calendar, but the Lord's calendar. *365 Prophetic Revelations from the Hebrew Calendar* shifts you into understanding the ways of God. God's way applied is the wisdom of God lived, which is the key to release blessings, acceleration, and advancement into your life. I highly recommend this book!

Tony Kim
Vice President, Harvest International Ministry
Senior Leader, Renaissance International,
Roar Collective, Roar Academy
Tony Kim Ministries

There is a great realignment happening in the church today, a returning to our Jewish roots. With it a great revelation is dawning, one that is giving us wisdom concerning God's calendar, times and seasons. Now in this new book of amazing insight by Candice Smithyman we are receiving and recovering once hidden but now found fresh prophetic biblical revelation for every day. Morning by morning He opens my ear to listen—wow! This is so significant.

Lou Engle
Founder, Lou Engle Ministries

Candice Smithyman has created an amazing book that gives believers tools to discerning the times and seasons using God's calendar—the Hebrew calendar! If you want to be aligned with God's perfect timing, it makes sense that you pay attention to His prophetic timeline. This book is a devotional for every day of the year, a study of the biblical feasts (God's appointed times), and will help you to understand more deeply what God is saying and doing in these Last Days. It is critical, now more than ever, to discern what you are seeing day to day as the end time unfolds. Every believer should have this book! Lori and I are pleased to recommend this book—put it in your end times library!

Jim and Lori Bakker
Founders, Jim Bakker Show

Historically Israel's times and seasons are something almost all Christians have ignored as irrelevant. However in this season, Israel's calendar is emerging with great significance as to how we live and interpret the times. Candice Smithyman comprehends the significance and lays the Jewish calendar out in an understandable and profound way for us. This is a must-read!

Barbara J. Yoder
Founding and Overseeing Apostle
Shekinah Christian Church

1 Chronicles 12:32 says "of the sons of Issachar who had under-standing of the times ..." I believe Dr. Candice Smithyman has an Issachar anointing and has blessed the Body of Christ with a Profoundly Prophetic Tool in her new book, *365 Prophetic Revelations from the Hebrew Calendar*. This book is so prophetic and practical that it is sure to become an everyday Manual in the hands of believers around the world!

Dr. Joshua Fowler
Author of *Daily Decrees for Accessing Abundance*
and many other anointed books!
Apostle of AwakeTheWorld.org
Dallas, Texas

Contemporary church history highlights what the Holy Spirit is currently doing to restore to believers, those eternal things designed for and designated to the church. However, the church has suffered from spiritual memory loss and subtle drift for cen-turies. Thankfully, biblical truths are being restored one by one; holiness, baptism of the Holy Spirit, divine healing, deliverance, healing of memories, gifts of the Spirit, fivefold ministry, and now the Hebrew roots to historic Christianity. From within the depths of these restored truths Dr. Candice sounds the "shofar" of Revelation.

Central to the fresh, biblical, and prophetic revelation of the contributions of our ancient Hebrew ancestors is an amazing understanding of how God views time and sequences. God's Masterplan includes unveiling a deeper appreciation for the feasts and festivals of ancient Israel. Understanding the prophetic nature of these feasts and their sequences matters! Dr. Candice beautifully explains and illustrates why these feasts are critical to navigating our future and interpreting our present. Her detailed work on the significance of these celebrations is remarkable and inspirational. This book will radically transform you. Understand-ing God's timetable will surely adjust and realign your spirit-man to God's sense of time, sequence, and eternity. This volume is an excellent read for those seeking to know what is on God's mind and written in His Day-planner!

Rabbi Ed Bez
Congregation Zerah Avraham

If there was ever a time on planet earth that demanded that we understand the times and seasons of God, it is now! In her new book, *365 Prophetic Revelations from the Hebrew Calendar,* Dr. Candice Smithyman unlocks the mystery of how to synchronize what is happening in the heavens with the earth.

Isaac Pitre Ministries
2Kings Global Network

Discovering the Bible's Hebrew roots is like opening a spiritual time capsule, illuminating scripture with remarkable clarity and bridging the millennial gap between our modern religion and its divine genesis. By shedding light on the depth of the Hebrew feasts and their relevance to Christians in the present day, Dr. Candace Smithyman builds a bridge between ancient customs and our contemporary religious walk. As you turn each page, you'll find yourself immersed in a daily encounter with God's Word, His appointed times, and His prophetic timeline. This is not just a book; it's a divine invitation to align your life with Heaven's rhythm. If you're interested in the prophetic importance of the Hebrew calendar and developing a more intimate relationship with God, this book is a must-read.

Bishop Alan Didio
Founder, Encounter Ministries
Host, Encounter Today

365 PROPHETIC REVELATIONS FROM THE HEBREW CALENDAR

OTHER DESTINY BOOKS
BY CANDICE SMITHYMAN

*Releasing Heaven: Creating a Supernatural
Environment Through Heavenly Encounters*

*Angels of Fire: The Ministry of
Angels in End-Time Revival*

*Releasing Heaven's Atmosphere
into Chaos, Crisis, and Fear*

365 PROPHETIC REVELATIONS FROM THE

HEBREW CALENDAR

EXPERIENCE THE POWER, BLESSING,

AND ABUNDANCE OF ALIGNING

WITH GOD'S TIMES AND SEASONS

CANDICE SMITHYMAN

DESTINY IMAGE® PUBLISHERS, INC.
P.O. Box 310, Shippensburg, PA 17257-0310
"Publishing cutting-edge prophetic resources to supernaturally empower the body of Christ"

This book and all other Destiny Image and Destiny Image Fiction books are available at Christian bookstores and distributors worldwide.

For more information on foreign distributors, call 717-532-3040.

Reach us on the Internet: www.destinyimage.com.

ISBN 13 TP: 978-0-7684-7531-9

ISBN 13 eBook: 9780768475326

For Worldwide Distribution, Printed in the U.S.A.

2 3 4 5 6 7 8 / 28 27 26 25 24

ACKNOWLEDGMENTS

I acknowledge my husband, Adam Smithyman, for his continued support of the ministry as I am writing and traveling to share the messages that God gives me for the body of Christ. My children, Alexandria, Nicholas and daughter-in-law Avery, and Samantha and son-in-law Hunter. My grandbabies, Asher, Lily, Addy, and Leighton as they bring me so much joy! My mother Joan Rainsberger and stepfather Daniel Rainsberger with their faithful support, and my sister and brother-in-law, Debra and Rob Hodgson.

A special thank you goes to my intercessory team, which has been overseen by Maria DiSebastiano for many years. Without these treasured women, I would not be able to move forward in any vision or endeavor. Elisa Andrews, who faithfully ordered all these devotional entries as the manuscript was prepared. Debbi Shon, who has been with my ministry for years and is always encouraging us and sacrificing her time to meet ministry needs where necessary. All of my friends who endorsed the book and continued to encourage me forward to finish. Especially the team at Destiny Image of Larry Sparks and Tina Pugh who saw instant potential in this to bring forth blessing in the Kingdom. And production/editorial staff: Shaun Tabatt, Katie Rios, and Angela R. Shears.

Sid Roth and his team, whom I credit with helping expand my message through media, as well as Sid's desire to see One New Man and Glory happen on earth today. My producer, Connie

Janzen of *Your Path to Destiny* on ISN, It's Supernatural Network, and Marian Duffee who are faithful friends who see the vision and help me make it plain in video and in prayer. To my friends and family at Christ the Messiah Church, Rabbi Ed and Rabbanit Rachel Bez, and my faithful Glory Road Community Mentees, Dream Mentors Teachers, Students, and Partners who monthly support this ministry and keep us going forward.

CONTENTS

FOREWORD

Dr. Candice Smithyman hosts, *Your Path to Destiny,* which is seen on the It's Supernatural Network (ISN). She and I personally share a great love for the glory of the Lord and seeing His glory be made manifest on earth in these last days. I believe this book, *365 Prophetic Revelations from the Hebrew Calendar,* will be a tool God will use to unite both Jews and Gentiles alike in the revelation of the One New Man as we approach the return of Yeshua. This manual will help those who know nothing about the Hebrew calendar to be encouraged prophetically to know the times and seasons of the Lord. It will also help those who do know the Hebrew calendar to understand how it correlates monthly with the Gregorian calendar. As we approach the return of Yeshua and the release of golden global glory on earth, it is important for us all to understand the overlap in the calendars so we can be ready as one and united in our faith in Yeshua. I believe this book will be a great asset prophetically now, and in the years to come.

Sid Roth
Founder, Messianic Vision
Host, It's Supernatural Network

PREFACE

As most Christians, I know you want to have a closer relationship to the Lord, which includes knowing the times of an open heaven to experience a deeper connection to God. When you understand the Hebrew calendar, you can walk in the open heaven that comes monthly during *Rosh Chodesh,* the first day on each Hebrew calendar that is sanctified holy by God.

These daily prophetic revelations will keep you excited about what God will do each day based on His calendar. In each daily devotional, you will grow in understanding more of who God is and how He thinks. You will learn the ways of God. Moses knew His ways and knew His calendar!

You will learn how to coincide the Gregorian calendar (today's common calendar with 12 months based on a solar dating system—position of the sun) with the Hebrew calendar (based on a lunisolar dating system—positions of the sun and moon). I hope this will be a lifelong resource and manual for understanding the Hebrew calendar and learning to apply God's truth daily.

This book does not have a specific Gregorian year attached, this way you can return to it year after year for encouragement. The Hebrew month is cited plus each day is numbered, which is biblical (Nisan 1, Nisan 2, etc.). So no matter the Gregorian year or Hebrew year you are in, you will have prophetic words relevant to you every day in every year. (Numerous Internet sites offer Gregorian/Hebrew date converter calendars.)

This book will also help you connect with God daily through prophetic revelations that will guide you to God's very own heart for you. You will see from history and biblical Scriptures where God revealed Himself in the past—and how He is revealing Himself now in the present to His people. God has not stopped using His calendar; and when you get on His calendar and times and seasons, you will know His heart and mind. This will cause you to become excited by what you are seeing around you in the earth realm, as you see God in the relevancy of the Hebrew calendar and the new moons. This will give you confidence to prophesy correctly based not only on the Word, but also on the times and seasons.

The Hebrew calendar is as relevant yesterday as it is to today! Why? Because God is the same yesterday, today, and forever! (See Hebrews 13:8.) The enemy does not want you to know these truths. It says in Daniel 7:25 (NASB) that satan will *"speak out against the Most High and wear down the saints of the Highest One, and he will intend to make alterations in times and in the law; and they will be handed over to him for a time, times, and half a time."* The enemy succeeds in duping the people of God about the power of the Hebrew calendar; but it is time now for us—the chosen ones of the inheritance—to know the proper times and seasons and God's heart through His Hebrew calendar that is timeless and based on eternal time!

INTRODUCTION

This book was designed to share the heart of God from His very own prophetic calendar. I am blessed to share these insights with you as God has revealed them to me over many years. The prophetic revelation I have received from God has come as a result of supernatural encounters I have had with Him during certain months on the Hebrew calendar, in which God would reveal prophetically what was happening in the spirit realm and He would take me to the month it was happening and the dates on the Hebrew calendar—these encounters accurately matched up with Scriptures in the Torah for those months.

These spiritual encounters and supernatural prophetic revelations first began to come together for me in wisdom and revelation concerning the Hebrew calendar during the spring feast months of March-April, summer feast months of May-June, fall feast months of September-October, and again in December and January. I began to understand how the certain feasts or appointed times of God on His Hebrew calendar revealed more about the Christian events we were celebrating on the Gregorian calendar.

For example, Easter made more sense as Passover, and Pentecost came alive when I understood the Feast of Shavuot, and Rosh Hashanah when I understood how it was a celebration of the beginning of creation, and how the Day of Atonement was really a day to remember the AT-ONE, Yom Kippur, or the atoning blood of our Savior Jesus. With these and other dates and times, the Lord would grab my attention in the spirit. The more I studied, the more I could see prophetically how the earth would rejoice, mourn, experience warfare, favor, and overall blessing and prosperity. Then as I felt these things prophetically and in the spirit realm, I would check the Hebrew calendar—and at that same date and time something significant was happening. Each time God gave me new prophecy, I checked its accuracy with the scriptural Word of God; then I studied the Hebrew calendar for those same dates. The things God was speaking to me about what prophetically was happening was matching up to the Hebrew calendar.

Over many years of this prophetic revelation from the Lord and its repeated accuracy, I began to see how God was sharing with His prophetic church the significance today of His Hebrew calendar and how He is still living by it. We abandoned it at the First Council of Nicaea in the year 325, but God did not.

Today God still talks strategically through His Word and specific acts on earth prophetically, according to the Hebrew calendar. Another revelation came when my husband, Adam, and I began to gain wisdom in the area of sowing seed offerings in accordance with the special feasts of the Lord. We learned to honor God when He wants to be honored and to receive the overflow of financial prosperity. As a result, as an act of worship, we biblically sow during each Feast of Passover, Pentecost, and Tabernacles according to Deuteronomy 16:16-18 and many other Scriptures that reveal this, plus we sow on firstfruits according to our Gregorian calendar.

The following is a chart that may help you determine the difference between the Hebrew calendar and the Gregorian calendar:

Jewish Months	Civil	Religious
Tishri	1	7
Heshvan	2	8
Kislev	3	9
Tevet	4	10
Shevat	5	11
Adar	6	12
Nisan	7	1
Iyar	8	2
Sivan	9	3
Tammuz	10	4
Av	11	5
Elul	12	6

In this book, I reveal to you these keys to the Kingdom revealed to us in Scripture and proved by the months and dates on the Hebrew calendar. I have researched a variety of publications to pull forth the historical dates that are in this book.

The book also includes special dates specific to the Jews and the Hebrew calendar, such as: *Rosh Chodesh* or new moons of every Hebrew month; special Shabbatot that are on or around those dates as they change slightly based on actual Sabbath days each year; major and minor religious holidays; minor fasts;

and modern holidays exhibited in Israel relative to Israelis. We also have included the constellation in the sky over that month, which of the 12 tribes of Israel conventionally is relative to that month and the constellation in the night sky, and the corresponding gemstone in Aaron's breastplate that concurs with which of the 12 tribes of Israel for that month. This information is given so that you may know the times and seasons as stated in Genesis 1:14 (KJV), *"And God said, Let there be lights in the firmament of the heaven to divide the day from the night; and let them be for signs, and for seasons, and for days, and years."*

In regard to the prophetic revelations you read in the devotionals, these are what God gave me personally as I would seek Him monthly for them in prayer, and then He showed me where they matched up with Scriptures.

Christians believe Yeshua will return to rule and reign on earth one day. He is returning for a bride (the Church) who knows the times and seasons to worship Him and bring Him offerings. My prayer is this book will help prepare the bride of Christ for our Messiah's return to earth and we will know the times and seasons and be a bride ready. This is one resource to prepare our hearts as we get closer to His return.

May your relationship with God overflow with blessing as you learn the power of God's prophetic calendar and the keys to accurate daily prophecy on earth today!

WHY THE HEBREW CALENDAR?

This book is manual for those who want to draw close to the heart of God using His Hebrew calendar as a basis for understanding the Father and His love for His people. This is not an exhaustive theological look at the differences between the Hebrew and Gregorian calendar. This is for those people who prophetically want to know what God is doing in the universe daily according to His Hebrew calendar. Psalm 19:1 (NIV) says, *"The heavens declare the glory of God; the skies proclaim the work of his hands."*

The Hebrew calendar is a resource that gives you God's daily desire and reveals where He is speaking and working to grow you into the likeness of Jesus. This book helps readers who know nothing about God's Hebrew calendar to come into alignment with who He is and where He wants us to join Him daily in knowing ourselves and knowing Jesus more.

As a prophet of the Lord, I believe God wants His people to know the times and seasons practically and logically so they are not overcome with legalistic details that don't further their relationship with Him. We must be biblically sound, but we don't need details that overrule our relationship with God by not giving Him a chance to speak to us personally. This book is designed to grow your relationship with God and His heart for you. If you want more exhaustive resources you can find them as stated;

but I believe the Lord wants humankind to develop into One New Man (Humanity)—both Jew and Gentile.

In Ephesians 2:11-22 (NIV), the apostle Paul shares:

> *Therefore, remember that formerly you who are Gentiles by birth and called "uncircumcised" by those who call themselves "the circumcision" (which is done in the body by human hands)— remember that at that time you were separate from Christ, excluded from citizenship in Israel and foreigners to the covenants of the promise, without hope and without God in the world. But now in Christ Jesus you who once were far away have been brought near by the blood of Christ.*
>
> *For he himself is our peace, who has made the two groups one and has destroyed the barrier, the dividing wall of hostility, by setting aside in his flesh the law with its commands and regulations. **His purpose was to create in himself one new humanity out of the two, thus making peace, and in one body to reconcile both of them to God through the cross, by which he put to death their hostility.** He came and preached peace to you who were far away and peace to those who were near. For through him we both have access to the Father by one Spirit.*
>
> *Consequently, you are no longer foreigners and strangers, but fellow citizens with God's people and also members of his household, built on the foundation of the apostles and prophets, with Christ Jesus himself as the chief cornerstone. In him the whole building is joined together and rises to become a holy temple in the Lord. And in him you too are*

being built together to become a dwelling in which God lives by his Spirit.

This book introduces both Gentile Christians and Jews who are unfamiliar with the power of the Hebrew calendar, by presenting a biblical and prophetic understanding of the Hebrew calendar and God's design for His people and His ways. This acquaints us all as one body with Yeshua and His love as we follow Him daily with a devotional revealing what He is doing in the universe. Since this book is based on the lunar calendar, you will become a researcher in how the moon is viewed out your window. How do you see the moon monthly? Is it hardly noticeable, a crescent in the night sky, or a full moon shining brightly?

When the sages tried to determine the first day of every month, they had to send the religious leaders out to look at the sky to see if it was a new moon, which is very pale and not well seen. I encourage you to do the same. Tonight you can look heavenward to see if there is a pale, faded moon which is new, a left crescent or a right crescent moon, or if it is full, which always happens around the 14th-16th of each Hebrew calendar month. Then you will know if you are at the beginning of a new month, or the middle, or near the end and it is about to turn again.

When the earth sits between the sun and moon, it is a *full* moon; when the moon sits between the sun and earth, it's a *new* moon. This is how they determined the months in days of old—and it is still this way today. This is a revelation of the synodic month, which you can observe every night.

My heart's desire for you is to learn to love God in the day and night sky and learn that He is the One who created the heavens and the heavens shall declare His name. Let us become practitioners of our daily faith walk and enjoy seeing what God is doing in the sky and in our hearts at the same time. Then we will know what He desires of us and where we should meet Him.

———————————

In John 4:34 (KJV), Jesus says, *"My meat is to do the will of him that sent me, and to finish his work."* Then again, in John 5:19 (NIV), *"Very truly I tell you, the Son can do nothing by himself; he can do only what he sees his Father doing, because whatever the Father does the Son also does."* We cannot meet Him where He desires every day if we don't know what He is doing in us and around us.

I pray this book opens the eyes of your heart to Him inside you and around you.

As we get closer to His return, I believe prophetically He will expect His people to know His special times, seasons, the feasts of the Lord, new moons, etc., so we as Jew and Gentile can celebrate who He is and His magnificence. This book will enlighten and draw you into that type of daily relationship with Him.

My prayer for you is that you come to love Him as much as He loves you through these encouraging daily prophetic revelations straight from His heart for His people.

RECEIVING THE MOST FROM THIS BOOK

Since the Hebrew calendar is God's original design and dates originally from the first day of creation, we are going to begin our monthly prophetic devotional readings by using the Hebrew calendar first and our Gregorian calendar will be subject to that. Back in the year 325, Constantine and the First Council of Nicaea introduced a 7-day week; and later in 1582, Pope Gregory XIII made additional adjustments due to the equinoxes for our Gregorian solar calendar, which has 365 days and its focus is the sun.

In contrast, the Hebrew Calendar is lunar-solar and its focus is the moon. It adjusts the solar to the lunar, which is 12 months and is 12 days shorter than the solar calendar. This 365-day prophetic declaration book is designed so you can look at the Hebrew calendar day starting with Nisan 1 on the first day of the new moon, which God says is the "first month of the year" and have a prophetic declaration for the corresponding month on the Gregorian calendar, which is adjusted to the vernal equinox or the sun. There will be 29-30 days of reflections each month.

Then there is the issue of the solar calendar having 365 days, vice roughly 360 lunar days. This issue is resolved when you simply follow the Hebrew calendar dates, which will overflow the other five or so days.

As far as leap year is concerned, move on to the Adar 2 prophetic declarations. Why? Because the Torah says that Passover, or Pesach, must be celebrated in the first lunar month, Nisan, when the solar and lunar calendars get out of sync; so a new Adar is added. The month Adar must always celebrate Purim, which is a joyous time of Jewish redemption remembering when Queen Esther offered her life to save her nation, and evil Haman was hung. So the true month of Adar each year is when Purim is celebrated. You will need to read the devotionals for Adar again when there is a leap year, which is 7 of every 19 years on the Hebrew calendar. When there is a need for two Adars, you will find Purim always in Adar 2 closest to Nisan.

My heart's desire is to draw you closer to Jesus through understanding the Hebrew calendar. A disclaimer: This book is not an exhaustive resource on the Hebrew calendar; it is an introduction to the power of the Hebrew calendar and its prophetic significance on earth today.

THE MOON AS A GUIDE

We will begin with the month of Nisan, which is considered to be God's first month on His calendar. In Exodus 12:1-2 (NIV), God spoke to Moses saying, *"The Lord said to Moses and Aaron in Egypt, 'This month is to be for you the first month, the first month of your year.'"* Now how do you know it's the first of the month? You need to look for a new moon.

The most practical way, with no help from any other means is to use your eyes and look up at the sky at night. First, you are looking for a full moon to help you navigate the middle of the month. Once you pass through seeing a full moon phase—which lasts about three days to the naked eye—then roughly 14 days later, the new moon will arrive, and this represents the first of the month. This moon will not be as bright as a full moon; it will be completely round, but pale in comparison. That is the easiest most natural means for daily calendar readers to use.

You will open this 365-day prophetic devotional on the first day of the new moon of the corresponding month on the Hebrew calendar. If it is springtime, you will be starting around March or April. It may be hard to know which exact Hebrew calendar month it is (March or April) without a little help from other sources. Many websites provide dates and moon phases, or you may choose to buy a lunar calendar that shows what phase of the moon is on certain days. I suggest you buy a Hebrew wall or desk calendar that has the year of creation on it as well as the Gregorian calendar year. These are sold in bookstores or online.

You can simply type into any Internet browser, *What day is it on the Hebrew calendar*, and up will come the day. Then you can begin here. Some smart phones can mesh the Hebrew calendar with your Gregorian calendar. Simply type, *How do I get my Hebrew calendar on my phone*, and instructions will pop up for you to set your phone.

Maybe you want to see the moon on your phone or on your watch if it is connected to your phone; choose the lunar moon option and the current moon view will be on your phone to watch daily. You can also type in, *What is the moon doing today*, and up will come pictures of the moon today so you will know if it is one of the two main options, a new moon (beginning of month) or full moon (middle of the month).

Then the cycle repeats itself every 29.5 days or 30 days as we will use for this book. These are easy practical ways in today's world to follow along in your 365-day prophetic revelations book. It is researched using a variety of sources but some dates could not be exactly recorded because this book is designed for use year after year. Due to the lunar calendar some calendar months will change from 29 to 30 days. I also left out exact days of specific

Shabbats, or Sabbaths, which go from Friday night at sundown to Saturday night at sundown, because of this reason too.

I have listed the special Shabbatot and Jewish holidays under the historical dates on each day but they are fluid and are only for generality, as technically they change based on the year and the laws set by the sages. There are some dates historically and even Shabbatot that could be missing based on the sources I used to gain my dates. All these dates are only given as a general guide.

Again, I encourage you to look at your technology resources and let them tell you exactly, and then read the prophetic declaration close to that day. Technically, as this book moves pro-phetically with the calendar, you will have a few days before and after each day that the declaration is relative to what is happen-ing in universe. The universe and its spiritual dominion is always flowing year after year in a circular motion through the months. Change happens every three months, about four times a year according to the calendar. You will prophetically in your life move through warfare, repentance, and promotion, and back again every three months as you move from glory to glory each year.

Now that you know how to match the Gregorian calendar day with the Hebrew calendar day, all you need to do is open your heart and begin to read the prophetic declaration for that day. Each Hebrew month consists of 29 to 30 days; you choose the month and day that it is and keep going. I encourage you to enjoy the beauty of this devotional by going outside a few times a month and look at the night sky. Learn for yourself when God is speaking through the declarations the heavens are making. Each month God has something to say and you can really con-nect with His heart and love for you if you see His message in the night sky.

The Word of God and Torah reveal the times that the new moons and feasts of the Lord were announced. God is very par-ticular about His new moons and feasts. They are His *moedim*,

Hebrew for "appointed times" and seasons. You will love to see in the Word when He is speaking to you in the heavens at the same time each month and what He is saying. Yeshua knew all of this too, and He practiced the feasts and knew when the new moons were. Luke 22:7-8 (NIV) refers to the Passover feast and says, *"Then came the day of Unleavened Bread on which the Passover lamb had to be sacrificed. Jesus sent Peter and John, saying, 'Go and make preparations for us to eat the Passover.'"*

Also, in Numbers 10:10 (NIV) the Lord speaks through Moses on the new moons and says, *"Also at your times of rejoicing—your appointed festivals and New Moon feasts—you are to sound the trumpets over your burnt offerings and fellowship offerings, and they will be a memorial for you before your God. I am the Lord your God."* These new moons are also called *Rosh Chodesh* and last about two days, as the new moons go for two-three days if you watch them in the night sky and are very special times on the Hebrew calendar when the portals of Heaven are open.

If you want to really be blessed, then you need to be able to recognize the *Rosh Chodesh* and new moon feasts as you prepare your heart with prayer and Bible reading. God speaks so clearly during the new moons and feasts times. It is a brand-new month and all the old of the last month is gone. Won't it be wonderful for you to know what God is saying each month to you in His Scriptures and the days it corresponds to what is written?!

Once I learned this, it changed my life so much, because I grew in knowing God's love for me and for His people every moment of every day. He knows everything about every day and wants us to fellowship with Him on those days through His Word. I pray this book helps you receive a special daily word just for you, direct from His heart; and as you look outside in the night sky, you will see His love in the moon as it bears down on you in the time and season of the life He ordained for you, even before your birth.

Two Hebrew New Years

There are two main seasons in each Hebrew calendar, these are called the religious season and the civil season, more well known as the religious calendar and the civil calendar. The differences lie basically in what we call the Hebrew new years. There are four Hebrew new years but only two are main, so we will stay here for the simplicity of this book. I mention the others during the daily devotionals, but basically the new years are broken up into the religious new year that begins in March or April at 1 Nisan, the first day of Nisan, which is the first month stated by God to Moses in Exodus 12:2 (NIV), *"This month is to be for you the first month, the first month of your year."* This is called the first of the religious calendar.

Now the civil calendar is 1 Tishri, the first day of the month of Tishri, which is around September or October each year. This new year is on the high holy day of *Rosh Hashanah,* which is the first day of the civil calendar. *Rosh Hashanah* is also called the "Head of the Year." More to follow on this as you read your devotionals, but you will see this is a special new year as well. Each month I tell you the month on the religious calendar and on the civil calendar.

As you start each new Hebrew month, you will learn the name of the month, what it means, its corresponding number month on the religious and civil calendars, and the basic Scripture for that month, then you will move forward reading each day. Now I offer a prayer for you as we begin this journey together through the Hebrew calendar.

Prayer for Your Journey

Lord, I ask You to bring divine revelation and Your sweet presence each day as my beloved friend reads the daily prophetic revelation. I thank You, Lord, that You wanted to draw closer to us, so You gave us the new moons, full moons, heavens in the sky, and all that was created on earth for us to know You more. You are the Creator of the universe; let us learn Your love for us as we grow more in your times and seasons. We want to be like You and meet You where You are, so please draw our hearts close to You in reflection as You bring forth this revelation daily of who You are in the Scriptures and the heavens.

We are grateful for Your Son, Jesus, who died to give us the chance to have relationship with You every day in Your Word and in the times and seasons of our lives. We worship You, Father, and are grateful for Your daily bread of the Word of God. We open our hearts to a word that will reveal You to our family, friends, city, state, and nations. We love You, Lord, and we lift our voices in adoration of Your name Jesus, Yeshua, the Christ Messiah. Thank You for uniting us to the Father and sharing with us Your heart!

SECTION 1

REVELATION
OF THE AGES

Before we jump into the daily prophetic revelations, I want to share important prophetic revelation for the years to come. This knowledge will help you grasp the heart of God for the "ages" to come. This revelation will advance your understanding of what year you are in today and how you must understand what we are approaching as our days draw near to Christ's return.

Presently we are in the years after 2000, but according to the Hebrew calendar we are in the years of 5700. It has been more than 5,700 Hebrew years since the birth of creation and the making of Adam and Eve in the Garden. The typical word "age" refers to roughly between 2,000 and 2,100 years. Although some argue it is only 1,000 years, and still to some only one age has passed and the second one is coming. No matter your position, we can all agree according to the Hebrew calendar, we are approaching 5,700 at the time of this writing and almost 6,000 years.

Matthew 24:3 (NIV) says, *"As Jesus was sitting on the Mount of Olives, the disciples came to him privately. 'Tell us,' they said, 'when will this happen, and what will be the sign of your coming and of the **end of the age**?'"* The Great Commission that Jesus spoke of says in Matthew 28:18-20 (NIV):

> *Then Jesus came to them and said, "All authority in heaven and on earth has been given to me. Therefore go and make disciples of all nations, baptizing them in the name of the Father and of the Son and of the Holy Spirit, and teaching them to obey everything I have commanded you. And surely **I am with you always, to the very end of the age."***

The apostle Paul speaks of the "ages" as in the end of one period and beginning of another and the wisdom of the Spirit. This was after the death of Jesus in between the years 55-56—a transition point in the new "age." Paul says in 1 Corinthians 2:6-16 (NIV):

*We do, however, speak a message of wisdom among the mature, but **not the wisdom of this age or of the rulers of this age**, who are coming to nothing. No, we declare God's wisdom, a mystery that has been hidden and that God destined for our glory before time began. **None of the rulers of this age** understood it, for if they had, they would not have crucified the Lord of glory. However, as it is written: "What no eye has seen, what no ear has heard, and what no human mind has conceived"— the things God has prepared for those who love him—**these are the things God has revealed to us by his Spirit.***

The Spirit searches all things, even the deep things of God. For who knows a person's thoughts except their own spirit within them? In the same way no one knows the thoughts of God except the Spirit of God. What we have received is not the spirit of the world, but the Spirit who is from God, so that we may understand what God has freely given us. This is what we speak, not in words taught us by human wisdom but in words taught by the Spirit, explaining spiritual realities with Spirit-taught words. The person without the Spirit does not accept the things that come from the Spirit of God but considers them foolishness, and cannot understand them because they are discerned only through the Spirit. The person with the Spirit makes judgments about all things, but such a person is not subject to merely human judgments, for, "Who has known the mind of the Lord so as to instruct him?" But we have the mind of Christ.

"Ages" mark changes and if we are to be a prophetic people destined to rule and reign as the royal priesthood and holy nation with Yeshua as our King, leading a one world government of Him on top, then we must know the age we are in and the ages to come. The demons have it right, there is a one world government coming, and all we see as earthly and all the disciples saw as earthly was the sickness that needed to be overcome by evil leaders. Today we have the same issues; however, the agenda of evil government is a one world force under the order of the enemy himself; however, Yeshua has sent us as His Kingdom rulers to usher in the shift of the age to come with Him as the Leader over all earthly governments. Because of His shed blood on the cross and His resurrection, we His church are now seated with Him in heavenly places (Ephesians 2:6).

We are called to rule and reign just as it was said in the first age when Adam and Eve were called of God in Genesis 1:26-28 (KJV):

> And God said, Let us make man in our image, after our likeness: and let them have dominion over the fish of the sea, and over the fowl of the air, and over the cattle, and over all the earth, and over every creeping thing that creepeth upon the earth. So God created man in his own image, in the image of God created he him; male and female created he them. And God blessed them, and God said unto them, Be fruitful, and multiply, and replenish the earth, and subdue it: and have dominion over the fish of the sea, and over the fowl of the air, and over every living thing that moveth upon the earth.

We are returning in the glory to do just this thing and we are transitioning now.

GOD'S GREATER REVELATION OF GLORY

God is now bringing forth a greater revelation of the glory of the Lord on earth. We are seeing the redemption of all things lost taking place spiritually. All things were redeemed by Jesus, and now we are called to activate this on earth. We are seeing a revelation of the redemption of time, understanding heavenly places, living in Heaven on earth when our bodies are not dead, a victorious mindset of the Lion of the tribe of Judah, and a release of the glory of God. As the Church or bride of Christ grows more in these truths, we will begin to dominate on earth, as we change the earth through our heavenly revelatory understanding. We are the ones taking the church into the year 6000 and the Lion of the tribe of Judah revelation of the ages. The heavens are declaring this truth (Psalm 19:1-6).

In understanding the ages we cannot leave out the revelation of the 12 Tribes of Israel as they are seen in the night sky represented by a specific constellation. These 12 Tribes each have a special place in Aaron's breastplate, in accordance with Exodus 39:14 (NKJV), *"There were twelve stones according to the names of the sons of Israel: according to their names, engraved like a signet, each one with its own name according to the twelve tribes."* Each month you read about in this book has a corresponding tribe of Israel along with its constellation in the night sky, along with the correct gemstone that represents that tribe from Aaron's breastplate. All of this points to the revelation of creation through to the tribe of the Lion of Judah and the great ROAR that His people are bringing forth in His authority today.

_____

WHAT AGE ARE WE IN NOW?

The Scriptures relate to this shift from the law to grace when the author of Hebrews prophesies what is to come. This is the revelation of the Church today. The Torah or law on Mount Sinai was the revelation of who God is and His demands to worship Him only and the setting up of the law, which we read of in the Hebrew month of Sivan, only to have Jesus meet the whole law and now propel the Church to Mount Zion, a heavenly Jerusalem. As more Christians see the Lord in His majesty from His throne room and have heavenly encounters, we are now in the age of the release of the glory on earth and the roar of the Lion of the tribe of Judah.

As we properly take our place with Him and exude His glory, heavenly signs, miracles, and wonders will ensue. It will be a release of His Spirit presence and glory in more ways than we can see now. We will rule in authority as the ambassadors of the King!

The following Scriptures describe the Feast of *Shavout,* or Pentecost, the differences in the Law and the Spirit, both aspects of Jesus, who is the Word revealed in different ages (John 1). The author of Hebrews gives his best understanding of the differences between the years of 2000-4000 when the law was the prevalent system, and 4000-present when the law is met. Yet now we learn to rest as His royal children in heavenly places; and because of learning to live the ascended life with Jesus, in two places, both Heaven and earth daily, we will be the ones to usher in the glory.

Hebrews 12:18-29 (NIV):

> *You have not come to a mountain that can be touched and that is burning with fire; to darkness, gloom and storm; to a trumpet blast or to such a voice speaking words that those who heard it*

begged that no further word be spoken to them, because they could not bear what was commanded: "If even an animal touches the mountain, it must be stoned to death." The sight was so terrifying that Moses said, "I am trembling with fear."

But you have come to Mount Zion, to the city of the living God, the heavenly Jerusalem. You have come to thousands upon thousands of angels in joyful assembly, to the church of the firstborn, whose names are written in heaven. You have come to God, the Judge of all, to the spirits of the righteous made perfect, to Jesus the mediator of a new covenant, and to the sprinkled blood that speaks a better word than the blood of Abel.

See to it that you do not refuse him who speaks. If they did not escape when they refused him who warned them on earth, how much less will we, if we turn away from him who warns us from heaven? At that time his voice shook the earth, but now he has promised, "Once more I will shake not only the earth but also the heavens." The words "once more" indicate the removing of what can be shaken—that is, created things—so that what cannot be shaken may remain.

Therefore, since we are receiving a kingdom that cannot be shaken, let us be thankful, and so worship God acceptably with reverence and awe, for our "God is a consuming fire."

Messianic believers and Gentile Christians, it is time to open our eyes to the end of one age, and the revelation of another. We are moving into what I like to call the rulership of the children of the Lion of the tribe of Judah walking in a new Age of Glory! A release of the glory of the Lord into the earth made possible by Jesus's death, burial, resurrection, and the understanding of being in heavenly places as the Church raised and seated with Him responds from this seat on earth today. We are the releasers of the glory in the ages to come and the prophets called to share the news of the shift of the ages. We are ones crying out in the wilderness, *"Prepare ye the way of the Lord"* (Matthew 3:3 KJV). We are crying out a shift is here from one age to the next, and you are reading this book as the revelation of both.

This glory release will also cause a one world government not of evil, but of believers who are standing up in the glory with the King behind them to defeat powers of evil for good. The enemy now is hijacking our understanding of one world government by creating fear in believers. These terms are to be for the holy nation, but instead are hijacked by the enemy who stirs evil and robs God's people of their sovereignty and freedoms. This holy government under the headship of our Lord and King Yeshua Messiah, roars like Judah. It is a world where the One New Man (Humanity) exists and there is a revelation of both Jew and Gentile coming together.

This is why it is so important that we go back to the Garden of Eden in our hearts and minds as a replica of Heaven. We pray for Israel and a uniting of the nations for King Jesus. According to the resurrection and ascension of Jesus, we have returned there because He redeemed all things and this is where we live—ascended with Him now. We must be fruitful, dominate, subdue, replenish, and multiply the Kingdom as rulers with a ROAR, as His holy nation under the dominion of the King.

You are the key to the expansion of the glory in this new time of the coming Kingdom. We are the roaring prophets who declare a new age is coming and glory will be released. We are saying, "Kingdom people prepare yourselves." This is the voice of the "shift prophets" at work today on earth.

SECTION 2

SOWING IN
THE RIGHT SEASON
FOR A BLESSING

The understanding of the "ages" is a broader prophetic revelation to share with you about what will happen in the years to come, but now I would like you to know some important times and seasons within the revelation of the ages to sow properly to the King of kings, in order to bless the Lord and fully receive your blessing.

As you journey through the prophetic revelations, you will read specific times and seasons on the Hebrew calendar that are being eventuated for sowing. These required a bit more teaching and Scripture reference than you will find in the daily prophetic revelations. God wants you to receive the most from relationship with Him and know the proper times and seasons to sow into the Kingdom. You will forever be changed if you know when it is time on the Hebrew calendar to give to the Lord.

There are specifically three main feasts or *moedim* or appointed times of the Lord:

1. Feast of Unleavened Bread, also known as Feast of Passover (Pesach)

2. Feast of Weeks, also known as Feast of Shavuot or Feast of Pentecost

3. Festival of Tabernacles or Feast of Ingathering

These feasts occur throughout the year. There is one special time we can add that most Christian churches subscribe to on the Gregorian calendar, which is in the month of January when the principle of "Firstfruits" is practiced.

The command was given to Moses about the three appointed times or feasts of the Lord in Deuteronomy 16:16 (NIV): *"Three times a year all your men must appear before the Lord your God at the place he will choose: at the **Festival of Unleavened Bread, the Festival of Weeks** and the **Festival of Tabernacles**. No one should appear before the Lord empty-handed."* This is what we are should do every year. This is a holy ordinance. God tells Moses in Exodus 12:14 (NIV) about the Feast of Passover, *"This is a day you are to commemorate; for the generations to come you shall celebrate it as a festival to the Lord—a lasting ordinance."* That means it does not end, it is everlastingly celebrated.

What about the case of practicing the feasts, is this something that Gentile Christians should do? Of course, let us look to Jesus as One who practiced these feasts, but also fulfilled them as part of the law.

As a child Jesus practiced the feasts with Mary and Joseph. Luke 2:40-42 (NIV) says, *"And the child grew and became strong; he was filled with wisdom, and the grace of God was on him. Every year Jesus' parents went to Jerusalem for the Festival of the Passover. When* he was twelve years old, they went up to the festival, according to the custom."

Later we see Jesus honored His Father God by celebrating the feasts. In Luke 22:7-8 (NIV), Jesus says, *"Then came the day of Unleavened Bread on which the Passover lamb had to be sacrificed. Jesus sent Peter and John, saying, **"Go and make preparations for us to eat the Passover."***

In Luke 22:14-16 (NIV) we read, *"When the hour came, Jesus and his apostles reclined at the table. And he said to them, 'I have eagerly desired to eat this Passover with you before I suffer. For I tell you, I will not eat it again **until it finds fulfillment in the kingdom of God.'"*** He is referring to the ages to come. As you read more about this in the last chapter, you are now understanding the importance of this statement.

The Kingdom of God arrived when Jesus came and walked the earth, died, was buried and resurrected, and ascended. This feast is going on now in Heaven. Our job is to bring this Kingdom to fulfillment and completion as the sons and daughters of the King. Then we will have one great feast when He rules on earth.

Wouldn't He want us to practice now what will happen in the future when He comes to earth for the final time to rule?

Christians do not have to practice the feasts for salvation, but would they not want to do what Yeshua did—yet, He fulfilled the whole law. The freedom of choice is ours.

The apostle Paul knew this and chose to still practice the feasts after the resurrection and ascension of Jesus. He did not condemn those who did not, but he chose to continue. He was a practicing Jew; but as the main apostle to the Gentiles, Paul is our example and still chose to do it. This should tell us that in the ages to come we must know the importance of the feasts.

In Acts 18:18-22 (KJV) we understand the apostle Paul's desire to keep the Feast of Pentecost:

> *And Paul after this tarried there yet a good while, and then took his leave of the brethren, and sailed thence into Syria, and with him Priscilla and Aquila; having shorn his head in Cenchrea: for he had a vow. And he came to Ephesus, and left them there: but he himself entered into the synagogue, and reasoned with the Jews. When they desired him to tarry longer time with them, he consented not; But bade them farewell, saying,* **I must by all means keep this feast** *that cometh in Jerusalem: but I will return again unto you, if God will. And he sailed from Ephesus. And when he had landed at Caesarea, and gone up, and saluted the church, he went down to Antioch.*

Paul also expressed this same interest in Acts 20:16 (KJV) says, "*For Paul had determined to sail by Ephesus, because he would not spend the time in Asia: for he hasted, if it were possible for him, to be at Jerusalem the day of Pentecost.*"

Read in 1 Corinthians 5:8 (KJV) where he says, *"Therefore let us keep the feast, not with old leaven, neither with the leaven of malice and wickedness; but with the unleavened bread of sincerity and truth."* He is admonishing the people to keep it.

In Exodus 23:14-19 (NIV), God gives specifics concerning all three festivals unto the Lord. He says:

> *Three times a year you are to celebrate a festival to me.* **Celebrate the Festival of Unleavened Bread***; for seven days eat bread made without yeast, as I commanded you. Do this at the appointed time in the month of Aviv, for in that month you came out of Egypt. No one is to appear before me empty-handed.* **Celebrate the Festival of Harvest** *with the firstfruits of the crops you sow in your field.* **Celebrate the Festival of Ingathering** *at the end of the year, when you gather in your crops from the field. Three times a year all the men are to appear before the Sovereign Lord. Do not offer the blood of a sacrifice to me along with anything containing yeast. The fat of my festival offerings must not be kept until morning.* **Bring the best of the firstfruits of your soil to the house of the Lord your God.**

This passage of Scripture covers all three feasts plus the principle of firstfruits.

PRINCIPLE OF FIRSTFRUITS

Now in regard to Firstfruits, this is both a special day and a principle of living as well. Technically, the day of firstfruits on the

Hebrew calendar is Resurrection Sunday or the day we celebrate the resurrection of Jesus. On the Gregorian calendar it is a term referred to as Easter. Easter has roots back to the year 325 and the First Council of Nicaea. It is a term that has been used for years in certain church circles and was even used by pagans, but is technically not the correct term from a Hebraic principle. It is called the Day of Firstfruit.

If Resurrection Sunday is really the Day of Firstfruit, then why do we in Christian circles have a whole month at the beginning of the year dedicated to it? It is because as a church body we take time during our worldly endeavors to put God first in the first month of our calendar year. We honor Him by praying, fasting, and giving to the Lord during this time. This is really a principle, not just a special day each year. It is a season on the Gregorian calendar when we stop and say, "God, since this is the beginning of our calendar year, we want to honor You."

He accepts anytime we want to honor Him. The first is something holy and devoted unto God; and when we give to Him the first, then all other giving is sanctified throughout our Gregorian calendar year. Firstfruits also means a promise to come, first in chief rank and order. Jesus as our Firstfruit is the Promise for all of us of our hope and future, salvation for those who are seeking Christ Messiah as Savior.

This is the same as saying when we give God an offering on Resurrection Sunday, or Easter, the day He rose from the dead as the first of many brethren, we are confirming Romans 8:29 (NIV), *"For those God foreknew he also predestined to be conformed to the image of his Son, that he might be the firstborn among many brothers and sisters."* Jesus is the Firstfruit, the Promise to come, and we are the brothers and sisters after Him. He is holy and devoted and all who come after Him are sanctified by His death, burial, resurrection, and ascension.

The first is a whole thing, not a portion like the tithe. Tithe means 10 percent. The firstfruits is a foundation, and all the things that come off of that are now holy. We can see this principle of firstfruits being revealed. First Kings 17:8-16 (NIV) reads:

> Then the word of the Lord came to him: "Go at once to Zarephath in the region of Sidon and stay there. I have directed a widow there to supply you with food." So he went to Zarephath. When he came to the town gate, a widow was there gathering sticks. He called to her and asked, "Would you bring me a little water in a jar so I may have a drink?" As she was going to get it, he called, "And bring me, please, a piece of bread."
>
> "As surely as the Lord your God lives," she replied, "I don't have any bread—only a handful of flour in a jar and a little olive oil in a jug. I am gathering a few sticks to take home and make a meal for myself and my son, that we may eat it—and die."
>
> Elijah said to her, "Don't be afraid. Go home and do as you have said. But first make a small loaf of bread for me from what you have and bring it to me, and then make something for yourself and your son. For this is what the Lord, the God of Israel, says: 'The jar of flour will not be used up and the jug of oil will not run dry until the day the Lord sends rain on the land.'"
>
> She went away and did as Elijah had told her. So there was food every day for Elijah and for the woman and her family. For the jar of flour was not used up and the jug of oil did not run dry, in keeping with the word of the Lord spoken by Elijah.

In this passage the woman heard a request from the prophet Elijah; even in her fear of dying, she responded in faith and gave the prophet her last cake, which was really her first gift to the prophet. In this case, Elijah represents a giving over to God in faith. She didn't realize it was a firstfruits but since she gave the whole of what was requested by the holy man of God and in faith, her response led her to receive a blessing. Firstfruits involves an act of faith. The first of the whole we give to God is given by faith in a promise to come. This woman believed in the promise to come, which is that she would live and so would her son. Her obedience by faith opened a portal of continual blessing!

I know someone reading this right now has financial difficulty. Have you ever sown a firstfruits offering to the Lord. Firstfruits does not have to be only at the beginning of the year. We are actually called to give firstfruits at the beginning of our Gregorian calendar year, but also at the beginning of the Hebrew calendar year in a Passover offering, the beginning of God's religious calendar year, or as a representation of the resurrection of His Son Jesus on Firstfruit Day, also at Pentecost, which is all about waving the firstfruits of the offerings. We can also give God firstfruits on Rosh Chodesh or the first of every month of the Hebrew calendar year as some do also; this is in keeping with the principle that King Solomon followed for new moon celebrations (2 Chronicles 8:12-15).

Exodus 34:22-23 reads, "**Celebrate the Festival of Weeks with the firstfruits** of the wheat harvest, and the Festival of Ingathering at the turn of the year. Three times a year all your men are to appear before the Sovereign Lord, the God of Israel." In this passage we read of the Feast of Shavout, or Feast of Weeks or Pentecost, and God is asking for the firstfruits. Firstfruits here is the Hebrew word bikkur which is broken down to bakar, which means to burst the womb or bear or make early fruit, or to give a birthright.

This means when we give God the first and best of what we have, He will bless the rest because we believed in Him and His lovingkindness toward His people, and He will give us a harvest of blessing after this initial gift. We secure our hope and future—our promise to come from the womb of dreams!

Firstfruits for Today

Let me share with you practically what firstfruits would look like today. Proverbs 3:9-10 (NIV) says, "**Honor the Lord** with your wealth, **with the firstfruits** of all your crops; then your barns will be filled to overflowing, and your vats will brim over with new wine."

If we want to see the blessing of the Lord upon our homes, workplaces, churches, cities, states, governments, and nations, we must follow the principle of firstfruiting the Lord when we receive from Him. The principle of firstfruits is a lifestyle, not just a seasonal command. When God says our barns will be overflowing, this means our storehouses where we keep our wealth, or our homes for living, or our businesses. Then *wine* means new opportunity. If you want to keep seeing new opportunity for more wealth, learn to manage what you have by practicing the principle of firstfruits.

Let's say you have your first sale of a new business or job, or maybe you get your first hourly wage, first week's, first month's, first year's, whatever this is, it is the whole of the first of a blessing. This is not the tithe or 10 percent. It is the whole. This is something that we are to practice all year round. Anytime there is a first, there should be a handing over to God in holiness as the whole is devoted to Him.

If you want to see the blessings of God on all you do, practice the principle of firstfruits. It is a key that needs to be implemented. Firstfruits can bring with it protection from the enemy as well as progress into our promised destiny. To gain ground in the Kingdom, we as the body of Christ should be practicing firstfruits.

I remember one year I had a difficult lesson to learn from God about my giving over of firstfruits offerings to the Lord. This is when God was teaching me the principle.

Every January my husband and I give at least a whole month of our salary to sanctify all other offerings given throughout the year. One year we gave our whole year's salary. We have seen God bless us tremendously and the church we pastored as a result of practicing the principle of firstfruits. We have skyrocketed in our promised destiny each year as God trusts us with more territory because we hand over the holy and devoted things at the beginning of the year.

This also brings us confidence knowing we are keeping the principle, and it enables us to remember each month how we gave in obedience, which instills greater faith that God will indeed show up as He says because we have partnered with Him for our destiny and promise to come.

It takes a lot of faith to practice firstfruits because it is giving God the first. A lot of times it's not that we don't want to honor God, we are just so hungry to eat the first of something. Maybe you have not had a job for months and you finally get one, you are so hungry so you eat the whole firstfruit; you are afraid, so you don't give it all to God. Listen, we are human and this reveals what we believe to be true about God or not.

Do you believe He gives you all things or do you believe you earn all things? If you believe you are under covenant with God and He is the Giver all the time, you will give to Him no matter what. Remember the woman and Elijah—she was so afraid but she gave it all; she gave the promise to come, or firstfruits, to the prophet and the result is that she ate and lived and had enough for the future. Don't be so afraid that you eat the whole. The first-fruits is holy and devoted to God and requires faith to give it.

Even King Solomon dedicated the temple of the Lord with special offerings and during the New Moons or Rosh Chodesh, and three annual festivals. In this following passage we read how King Solomon honored the Lord:

> *On the altar of the Lord that he had built in front of the portico, Solomon sacrificed burnt offerings to the Lord, according to the daily requirement for offerings commanded by Moses for* **the Sabbaths, the New Moons and the three annual festivals— the Festival of Unleavened Bread, the Festival of Weeks and the Festival of Tabernacles.** *In keeping with the ordinance of his father David, he appointed the divisions of the priests for their duties, and the Levites to lead the praise and to assist the priests according to each day's requirement. He also appointed the gatekeepers by divisions for the various gates, because this was what David the man of God had ordered. They did not deviate from the king's commands to the priests or to the Levites in any matter, including that of the treasuries* (2 Chronicles 8:12-15 NIV).

Then it says is 2 Chronicles 8:16 (NIV), "*All Solomon's work was carried out,* **from the day the foundation** *of the temple of the Lord was laid until its completion. So the temple of the Lord was finished.*" Notice how this was done from the day of the foundation. The principle of firstfruits is a foundation principle focused on the whole as devoted or holy to be sanctified. King Solomon sanctified the whole of the temple and all that was given upon this whole was holy and devoted, sanctified unto the Lord.

First Kings 9:25 (NIV) also reads, *"Three times a year Solomon sacrificed burnt offerings and fellowship offerings on the altar he had built for the Lord, burning incense before the Lord along with them, and so fulfilled the temple obligations."*

FEAST OF SHAVOUT, WEEKS, PENTECOST

When God asks for the first sheaf during the Feast of Shavout (Weeks or Pentecost, same time), He does it so we will believe He is the supplier and will continue to supply. It is holy. It is in the land of promise where we give God the best of what He supplies to us and we receive more that is now holy and sanctified.

Leviticus 23:9-14 tells us:

> The Lord said to Moses, "Speak to the Israelites and say to them: '**When you enter the land I am going to give you and you reap its harvest, bring to the priest a sheaf of the first grain you harvest**. He is to wave the sheaf before the Lord so it will be accepted on your behalf; the priest is to wave it on the day after the Sabbath. On the day you wave the sheaf, you must sacrifice as a burnt offering to the Lord a lamb a year old without defect, together with its grain offering of two-tenths of an ephah of the finest flour mixed with olive oil—a food offering presented to the Lord, a pleasing aroma—and its drink offering of a quarter of a hin of wine. You must not eat any*

bread, or roasted or new grain, until the very day you bring this offering to your God. This is to be a lasting ordinance for the generations to come, wherever you live.'"

If you have violated this principle of firstfruits in the past, it is now time to take a few moments and ask God for forgiveness. What you don't know you can't be held liable for; but once we know we need to say, "Lord, I had no idea. Please forgive me. I want everything this year to be sanctified and holy before You."

Prayer for Firstfruits Giving

Lord, thank You for Your Son, Jesus Christ, who is firstborn of many brother and sisters of whom I am a part. I thank You, Lord, for loving me and supplying all my needs according to Your glorious riches in Christ Jesus. Forgive me, Lord, as I didn't know about the principle of firstfruits or I did know but I had not yet understood like I do now. I want all that You give me to be holy and devoted unto You, every day of the year. Lord, please give me revelation on how I can incorporate the principle of firstfruits in all year giving, anytime You give me something new in my destiny and I step into a new realm of living in the promise You have called me to on the earth. I want to honor You, Lord. I thank You, Father, for forgiving me; and I thank You that Your holy Son, Jesus Christ, gave His life that I may be forgiven always even when I don't know what I do wrong. Please teach me more, Father, so I can be holy and devoted unto You in all I do.

As we go forth during the *365 days of prophetic revelations,* I will reveal more about sowing during these special times and during the special appointed times God has set aside.

SECTION 3

DAILY
DEVOTIONALS
& PROPHETIC
REVELATIONS

THE MONTH
OF NISAN

Chodesh Ha-Aviv, which means the beginning of the spring months.

This is the first month of the religious calendar and the sixth month of the civic calendar.

It is also known by its Babylonian name *Abib.*

Exodus 12:1-2 (NIV) says, *"The Lord said to Moses and Aaron in Egypt, 'This month is to be for you the first month, **the first month of your year.'"***

Tribe of Israel (Conventional): Yehudah/Judah

Gemstone in Aaron's breastplate: Carbuncle/Garnet

Constellation in Sky/Hebrew name: Aries/Talch

NISAN 1
Rosh Chodesh Nisan!

Welcome to the wonderful Hebrew month of Nisan! Happy beginnings of God's New Year.

Tonight there is a new moon in the night sky.

Numbers 10:10 (KJV): *"Also in the day of your gladness, and in your solemn days, and in the **beginnings of your months**, ye shall blow with the trumpets over your **burnt offerings**, and over* *the sacrifices of your **peace offerings**; that they may be to you for a memorial before your God: I am the Lord your God."*

At the beginning of every new month, either one or two days will celebrate the minor holiday of Rosh Chodesh. Historically this is the day when God spoke to Moses and Aaron in Exodus 12:1-2. This is *"the first month, the first month of your year."*

According to Exodus 12:2, this is the time during which the Lord spoke to Moses and Aaron and the Israelites about preparing for the Passover. The heavens are open! New anointing, spiritual activations, and angelic assignments are coming upon you.

Isaiah 43:18-19 (NIV) reads, *"Forget the former things; do not dwell on the past. See, I am doing a new thing! Now it springs up; do you not perceive it?"*

I pray for you today, this first month of the new year, that God will open your eyes to His splendor, glory, and majesty—and you will see all things new for yourself as the Israelites did! As God released them from captivity this month—so He will you!

NISAN 2

When you sow into the heavens, you will reap from an open heaven.

Galatians 6:7-10 (NIV) tells us specifically how to sow a seed: *"Do not be deceived: God cannot be mocked. A man reaps what he sows. Whoever sows to please their flesh, from the flesh will reap destruction; whoever sows to please the Spirit, from the Spirit will reap eternal life. Let us not become weary in doing good, for at the proper time we will reap a harvest if we do not give up. Therefore, as we have opportunity, let us do good to all people, especially to those who belong to the family of believers."*

This passage contains some vital truths. What does it mean to sow into the heavens? It means to sow into things of the Spirit and not into the flesh. Are you sowing into the Spirit realms every day for breakthrough, or are you sowing into the soulish realms of your flesh and surroundings to gain? Sow into your faith this month of Nisan.

NISAN 3

In the appointed time of God you *shall* reap if you faint not!

Listen, you will not faint if you are sowing into the Spirit. Sowing into the Spirit is making a deposit into Heaven. It is a joyful deposit. It is a deposit where you give something to the Lord because you know He is about to release the blessings of Heaven upon you. When you do this, a new release of grain, wine, and oil will be poured out upon you. Grain represents revelation; wine represents new opportunities; and oil represents the anointing oil from Heaven (Hosea 2).

Thank God today that you have received new and fresh ideas, blessings from Him! Doing this will make you feel encouraged, uplifted, and radiant. Praise the Lord!

I see new, creative ideas—marketplace ideas and miracles—coming upon you today. God is giving you a fresh anointing. You will reap rapidly. Blessings are coming to your mind, will, emotions, health, body, family, church, community, and nation.

NISAN 4

Today, not only choose to give yourself as a living sacrifice to the Lord, but think about how you can sow a seed in faith which will position you in a realm of prosperity, and you will reap a harvest in the spirit. I know from experience that He will increase you when you sow. God doesn't play favorites. What He did for me, He will do for you too!

Just as the Israelites were told to spread the blood of the lamb on their doorframes so that the angel of death would pass over them at Passover, Jesus is the Passover Lamb of God, our Redeemer, and His blood is our covering. He is the complete and ultimate Sacrifice for sin and Victor over death and the grave. God did not hold back His offering of His Son, and we should not hold back in offering ourselves to God. We should celebrate Him with our time, talent, treasure, and testimony!

You have been called to live a life of dominion. Christ purchased this for you! Why don't you take some time this week to sit with the Lord in prayer, fasting, and giving (see Deuteronomy 16:16-17).

Let His grace manifest in your life today.

NISAN 5

Historically today is the day called *Ta'anit Bechorot;* only firstborns are required to fast on the Fast of the Firstborn.

We are approaching Passover, let us begin to reflect with humble hearts on the sacrifice God made in sending His beloved Son, Jesus Christ, as a sin offering to be our Lord and Savior. He is our Passover Lamb. He died, was buried, and resurrected to overcome sin, death, and the grave so the curse over us would be broken.

Not only have we entered into what the Lord calls "the first of the year," but we also entered into a time He calls the "spring rains." The spring rains last for six months and end at sundown the first month of Tishri. Then we step into the next six months, called the "fall rains," which take us then back to the month of Nisan and the double portion found in Joel chapter 2.

Thank the Lord today for the spring rains and double portion coming your way in the fall! Believe Him for great things because He loves you!

NISAN 6

Nisan is the month to march forward like the Israelites did out of Egypt. The Lord led them out of Egypt and took them across the Red Sea. They physically left Egypt, and then they had to leave Egypt again by shedding Egypt's way of thinking. This is why when they reached the Promised Land, they were not able to enter it for another 40 years. But God was with them in the desert. He allowed them to see, feel, and experience aspects of Heaven while they were there so that they would build their identity in Him alone.

The Lord has a special word for you for this season, and it's found in Deuteronomy 8:2-4 (NKJV):

> *And you shall remember all the way which the Lord your God has led you in the wilderness these forty years, in order to humble you, putting you to the test, to know what was in your heart, whether you would keep His commandments or not. And He humbled you and let you go hungry, and fed you with the manna which you did not know, nor did your fathers know, in order to make you under-stand that man shall not live on bread alone, but man shall live on everything that comes out of the mouth of the Lord. Your clothing did not wear out on you, nor did your foot swell these forty years.*

Start marching forward today as God has your every need covered as you believe in Him for fullness and prosperity!

NISAN 7

Can you imagine?! How powerful the Lord is to give the Israelites manna, their clothes did not wear out, and their feet did not swell at all during this time! The supernatural entered the natural while they were journeying those 40 years. God was removing the natural out of them, revealing how in their hearts they were murmurers, complainers, and that they had lived in bondage so long they had brought that bondage with them into their freedom.

The Israelites had entered into a realm where there was no decay; their mantles, or clothing, remained intact; their feet were able to withstand walking miles and miles; their bodies submitted daily to the desert conditions—and they received! They were completely covered and surrounded by Heaven even in the midst of what they were going through.

And just like they began to understand the supernatural in their wilderness season, you can too. Reflect today on how God might be tweaking your heart to repentance for things in your heart. God loves you and wants you to rely on Him! Honor the Lord today with a special offering from Deuteronomy 16:16-17 as we approach the Feast of Passover. Remember the earlier chapter on Sowing in the Right Season, so you know the special times to sow each year.

NISAN 8

The Israelites were fed a supernatural manna every day. Manna was honey flaked crackers or bread made with coriander seed that dropped from Heaven. This food from Heaven fed their natural bodies enough only for one day. Through it, the Lord was teaching them to trust and believe in Him, and that His provision comes directly from Heaven. Manna means, "What is it?" It's the bread of life. It's the Word of God every day that sustains you and enables you to walk in heavenly realms on earth.

Their clothes did not wear out. Clothing in Hebrew means their mantle. In other words, your mantle will not wear out when you walk in heavenly realms on earth. It will be strong. It will not be torn away from you, as it is part of who you are. The Lord wants you to know that the mantle He has given you is a covering that will last. Your mantle is the calling on your life and the supernatural provision in spiritual gifts to fulfill that call. It is a destiny God has placed in your heart!

What is your mantle? Do you know it? Can you communicate it to someone? Think on these questions this month as God is releasing you into a new level of authority and enlargement of territory.

NISAN 9

During this time, the Israelites' feet did not swell. The word *feet* in Hebrew is the word *regel* which means "to endure, journey, possess, time." It means "to walk along and a type of treading." It is putting one foot in front of the other. As you walk, you possess time, you endure and you move forward. Your feet will last because of God's provision. They will not decay or swell. You are not going to become overwhelmed with the walk. Everywhere you walk, you will possess what is before you! A foot possesses eternal time. There is only one thing that can refer to the "possession of time" or "eternal time"—walking in the heavenly realm.

This is very important to remember as you enter into a time of great awakening: The Lord is saying, "I am going to cause My people to walk in the heavenly realms." You are seated with Christ in heavenly places (Ephesians 2:6). You are a citizen of Heaven. You must operate on the earth from the heavenly perspective.

NISAN 10

Historically today is *Yom HaAliyah* (Aliyah Day), an Israeli national holiday commemorating the Jewish people entering the land of Israel in accordance with the Hebrew Bible.

Historically this holiday falls around the day of *Shabbat HaGadol* or the Great Sabbath as it is the Shabbat immediately before Passover.

The good news is that *right now* we can walk in Heaven on earth. That is why Jesus speaks to us in prayer, saying, *"Your will be done, on earth as it is in heaven."* The phrase *"on earth"* means like a movement of heaven actually making its place in the earth realm. *"On earth"* in the Greek means "superposition of time, place and order; a distribution over and above a place of rest and direction." So when we ask for Heaven to manifest in the earth realms, like Jesus taught in the Lord's Prayer (Matthew 6:9-13), what we are saying is, "Lord, superimpose Heaven on earth. Distribute rest and peace."

"In Heaven" means a "fixed position of place, time and state of rest." When we are walking in heavenly realms, Heaven comes upon us like a bubble. By faith we believe this; we understand it to be true not only because of the death, burial, and resurrection of Jesus, but because of His ascension. When He ascended, He sat next to the Father, and we are now seated in heavenly places with Him. That realm of Heaven is ours on earth.

Practice living in the realms of Heaven daily in prayer so you can live in prosperity and be a change agent in the earth. We manifest on earth what we believe to be true from a heavenly mindset.

NISAN 11

I believe you're going to see more signs, miracles, and wonders coming forth than you ever imagined. God is allowing His Spirit to come upon you. You are beginning to receive incredible grain from Heaven, incredible revelation about walking in heavenly realms on earth. You are getting ready to step into a brand-new revelation of walking in Heaven on earth.

Your clothes won't wear out, your feet won't swell, and you're going to have all the provision you need. You are wrapped in a heavenly realm. Blinders are being removed right now, in the name of Jesus. You are about to see the supernatural every day! You are about to engage with God right where you are, walking beyond time in eternity, a place where every need is met! You are about to receive manna from Heaven.

The Word of God is coming, enough to teach and train you in heavenly things every day! Tell someone about it! It's going to be an amazing season! As we approach Passover and then move into the Month of Iyar (the second month on the religious calendar), God is preparing our hearts for greater relationships with Him!

NISAN 12

Happy Passover! This week you will enter the great week of Passover. During this time, you can reflect and remember:

Israel's release from Egypt. This is a time to remember how the Israelites were released from their bondage when they killed a Passover lamb and put the blood on the doorpost. The angel of death, seeing the blood, passed over their homes. After this event, Pharoah finally released them to begin their journey to the Promised Land.

The Feasts of Passover. You can reflect on the Hebrew calendar, which shows that all these events took place during the Feast of Unleavened Bread and the Feast of Passover. Exodus 6:4-8 (KJV) reads: *"And I have also established my covenant with them, to give them the land of Canaan, the land of their pilgrimage, wherein they were strangers. And I have also heard the groaning of the children of Israel, whom the Egyptians keep in bondage; and I have remembered my covenant. Wherefore say unto the children of Israel, I am the Lord, and I will bring you out from under the burdens of the Egyptians, and I will rid you out of their bondage, and I will redeem you with a stretched out arm, and with great judgments: And I will take you to me for a people, and I will be to you a God: and ye shall know that I am the Lord your God, which bringeth you out from under the burdens of the Egyptians. And I will bring you in unto the land, concerning the which I did swear to give it to Abraham, to Isaac, and to Jacob; and I will give it you for an heritage: I am the Lord."*

God has a promise for you personally just as He did for the Israelites! Reflect on that promise today and write it down, so you can remember it and lift it up to the Lord! He will bring it to pass in His time, just have the faith to believe!

NISAN 13

On the Christian calendar this day is remembered as the Lord's Supper and is called Maundy Thursday.

This is the evening we remember how Jesus took His final Passover meal with His disciples. It was the night He was betrayed. It was the night He went to the Garden of Gethsemane and asked His Father to remove the cup from Him (Luke 22:42). This is also the night He ate and talked with His disciples, stating, *"And when the hour was come, he sat down, and the twelve apostles with him. And he said unto them, with desire I have desired to eat this passover with you before I suffer: For I say unto you, I will not any more eat thereof, until it be fulfilled in the kingdom of God"* (Luke 22:14-16 KJV).

But He had to go to the cross, for you and for me. *Take Communion in remembrance of Him!* Take time this week to remember these wonderful events with your family. Take the time with them to confess your sins and participate in the Passover by eating bread (unleavened or Matzah bread) and drinking from the cup (grape juice)—taking communion before the Lord. Set yourself apart in purification and consecration because you're coming into your promise.

Consider this day to *pray, fast, give and repent* of what you may be holding higher than God on the throne. Doing so will protect you from sickness. In Matthew 4:8, Jesus was tempted by the enemy and His response was that He worshipped God and served Him only! Are you worshipping God daily and serving Him only and not yourself? Ask God to reveal to you what He wants to change in this new season as you are crossing over here at Passover into the new season.

This is God's first month of His religious calendar year, and you want to be sanctified and holy for all He has for you! Pray this prayer with me, "Lord, today I recognize You entered the Garden of Gethsemane in much pain asking for the cup to be released from You; but You were willing to accept the cup of death and affliction on my behalf that I may have life and have it more abundantly. I thank You for giving Your life so that I might have mine. I want to serve You and worship You daily, please show me how. I love You! Amen."

NISAN 14

Tonight there is a full moon in the night sky.

Historically on the Christian calendar this is Good Friday if it falls on a Friday, but many times the Chrisitan calendar and the Jewish calendar do not match. That is why the day of Nisan 14 was Passover and Firstfruits was three days later is so important. The next three days have much research that debates the exact times of Jesus's Passover seder with His disciples, His crucifixion, His burial, and His resurrection.

Historically on the Hebrew calendar Nisan 14 is Passover or the Feast of Unleavened Bread.

Today is when we remember Jesus's death. His love for you was so great that He gave His life for you. This selfless act of obedience afforded you eternal life with Him if you will receive it. God was willing to send His only Son, and Jesus was willing to go to the cross. He experienced inexpressible pain that day, and by His stripes (wounds from whippings) you have been healed (Isaiah 53). Just as the Israelites were told to spread the blood of the lamb on their doorframes so that the angel of death would pass over them at Passover, Jesus is the Passover Lamb of God, our Redeemer, and His blood is our covering.

Exodus 12:13 (NIV) tells us, *"The blood will be a sign for you on the houses where you are, and when I see the blood, I will pass over you. No destructive plague will touch you when I strike Egypt."* Jesus is the complete and ultimate Sacrifice for sin and Victor over death and the grave.

"Get rid of the old yeast, so that you may be a new unleavened batch—as you really are. For Christ, our Passover lamb, has been sacrificed" (1 Corinthians 5:7 NIV).

Why don't you take some time this week to sit with the Lord in prayer, fasting, and giving (Deuteronomy 16:16-17). Let His grace manifest in your life today. You have been called to live a life of dominion. Christ purchased this for you! Bless the Lord today with a thank offering! Thank Him by blessing another!

NISAN 15

Because the Jewish calendar determines a day from sundown one day to the next, Nisan 15 would have been one day after Jesus's death to prepare Him for burial. Historically today on the Christian calendar, this marks the burial of Jesus.

Historically this is the day that Moses heard from God at the burning bush to go deliver Egypt. Exactly one year later, the people of God practiced Passover for the first time as they were delivered from Egyptian bondage. Moses ascended and descended the mountain of the Lord approximately eight times to meet with God as the mediator between Him and His people.

Take time to meditate today on how Jesus's death and burial mean that your old life is now gone. The apostle Paul reminds us in Romans 6:3-7 (NIV): *"Or don't you know that all of us who were baptized into Christ Jesus were baptized into his death? We were therefore buried with him through baptism into death in order that, just as Christ was raised from the dead through the glory of the Father, we too may live a new life. For if we have been united with him in a death like his, we will certainly also be united with him in a resurrection like his. For we know that our old self was crucified with him so that the body ruled by sin might be done away with, that we should no longer be slaves to sin—because anyone who has died has been set free from sin."*

Today, remember who you were and that person is now gone. Your sins are buried and you are resurrected as a new creature—alive in Christ! Thank Him for all He has done! Tomorrow we will take one more day to reflect on this truth.

NISAN 16

Today is when we remember Jesus's burial. The Seed of God was placed in darkness. It looked like all was lost, but really it had just begun! Jesus in the tomb reminds us that we have nothing to fear in the darkness because morning is coming! Resurrection is coming! This is a time we reflect on what the apostle Paul says in Romans 6:8-14 (NIV): *"Now if we died with Christ, we believe that we will also live with him. For we know that since Christ was raised from the dead, he cannot die again; death no longer has mastery over him. The death he died, he died to sin once for all; but the life he lives, he lives to God. In the same way, count yourselves dead to sin but alive to God in Christ Jesus. Therefore do not let sin reign in your mortal body so that you obey its evil desires. Do not offer any part of yourself to sin as an instrument of wickedness, but rather offer yourselves to God as those who have been brought from death to life; and offer every part of yourself to him as an instrument of righteousness. For sin shall no longer be your master, because you are not under the law, but under grace."*

We are now dead to sin and our transgressions, and we are called to bury this sin nature forever and become one with Him in baptism by death so we may have eternal life. Do you know when you are water baptized and go under the water as the outward sign of being a believer in Jesus, you are saying the old self or old sin nature is now gone and dead and buried. Then when you rise from the water you are saying you are a new creature in Christ—all the old is gone and the new has come!

Today represents that day. If you have not given your life to Jesus, you can do that now. You can ask for forgiveness of sin as your Passover Lamb took your punishments so you can live and remember that He was buried, and so are you by faith in what Jesus has done. You can live now and for eternity for Jesus!

Receive Him and what He has done, today!

NISAN 17

Historically today on the Christian calendar is Resurrection Sunday, or Easter! This would have been the early hours of the morning.

Historically today is *Sefirat HaOmer* (Counting the Omer) and begins today through all of the Month of Iyar until the Month of Sivan 6 or the Feast of Shavout, which is one day before Pentecost which is 50 days. This is a reciting of a blessing each day for 49 days. An *omer* is a measurement which is one-tenth of an ephah (which held about two quarts)—the container used to measure the manna (see Exodus 16:36). Exodus 16:18 (NKJV) reads, *"So when they measured it by omers, he who gathered much had nothing left over, and he who gathered little had no lack. Every man had gathered according to each one's need."* Since this begins the Counting of the Omer for 49 days, the Jews say a blessing every day! Count your blessings every day by continuing to read each day these prophetic revelations and declaring the blessings for you and your loved ones.

Historically today is the day Joshua brought the Israelites into Promised Land and they ate the fruit of the land (Joshua 5:10-12 NIV).

Historically today on the Christian calendar is when William Seymour received the baptism of Holy Spirit at Bonnie Brae house on April 9, 1906, which began the Azusa Street Revival.

Historically today Hezekiah cleansed the temple (see 2 Chronicles 28:3-5 NIV).

On this day you will celebrate the Feast of Firstfruits or Resurrection Sunday! It's a time of celebration and remembering how Jesus was once dead but is now *alive* and so are *you!* It's a day when your victory is proclaimed and declared. The resurrection stands as a monument declaring sin, death, and the grave have been overcome. Hallelujah! He has resurrected and so have we! *He is risen!*

NISAN 18

Historically this is the day when Pharaoh decided to go after the Israelites with his army. Exodus 14:8 (NIV) reads, "*And the Lord hardened the heart of Pharaoh king of Egypt, so that he pursued the Israelites, who were marching out boldly.*"

The Lord wants you to walk in mighty confidence, in the here and now. Hebrews 10:34-35 (NIV) says: "*You suffered along with those in prison and joyfully accepted the confiscation of your property, because you knew that you yourselves had better and lasting possessions. So do not throw away your confidence; it will be richly rewarded.*"

The author of Hebrews, who we believe is the apostle Paul, is speaking to givers and to those who showed him love during his difficult times. Now today, this passage is speaking to you.

God wants you to stand fast, stand firm, stand tall, and be a blessing. He has great things in store for you. But you have to step out in faith. Do not cast away your confidence. You have a right to walk in Heaven on earth—and God wants to make this happen for you!

Because of Jesus's resurrection, He became the first of many brothers. You, my friend, are part of the many brothers and sisters who come after Him. Now you will have fully stepped into your new year with the Lord. Great things will come forth. See your victory, healing, redemption, and wholeness. See your marriage being fixed, your children being saved. Whatever you're standing in faith for, see it! Expect these great things to happen! You are a new creature in Christ, seated with Christ in heavenly places—all because He was willing to die for you. The enemy has no more stronghold in your life. You have been set free. Who the Son sets free is free indeed! Let us lift up a praise! Stand firm and stand strong!

NISAN 19

Godly confidence comes from knowing who you are in Christ. Christ died, was buried, and resurrected to break the curse of sin, death and the grave. He ascended so we as a Church could be properly seated with Him in heavenly places. The Kingdom of Heaven arrived in Him so we could live in Heaven on earth. You have now been called to live life abundantly. Jesus says in John 10:10 (KJV), *"The thief cometh not, but for to steal, and to kill, and to destroy: I am come that they might have life, and that they might have it more abundantly."* You are now a new creature in Christ, called to live and abundant life. Think on that for a moment! You are called to live in the realms of prosperity every day in Him! How might you change your way of thinking knowing this is what God desires for you! This is why He paid the price, so He could give you a destiny!

Now that Passover is complete, it is time to begin living in the goodness in the mercy of the Lord every day and in His abundancy. This is the blessing of the children of the inheritance. That is you and me! See Psalm 27:13 and Psalm 34:8.

If you are feeling overwhelmed, weary, beat down, fearful, or ashamed, repent right now. Simply say, "Father, forgive me." The prayer is for restoration of fellowship, not salvation. However, if you have never received Jesus as your Lord and Savior, you first need to ask Him for forgiveness to obtain salvation. When you do this, you receive justification and step into the process of sanctification, which is the purifying of your mind, will, and emotions. Now you have begun the process of transformation into the likeness of Christ! This process of transformation is what gives us His life-giving power every day to overcome in every area! You are more than a conqueror because of what He has done!

NISAN 20

Historically today is the day that Pharaoh's army reached the Israelites at the Red Sea. Moses told the people: *"Do not be afraid. Stand firm and you will see the deliverance the Lord will bring you today. The Egyptians you see today you will never see again. The Lord will fight for you; you need only to be still"* (Exodus 14:13-14 NIV).

God loves you so much. He is a good Father and wants to see you walking in perfect fellowship with Him. Stand firm with the One True Living God. He has put His very own blood on your doorpost. Nothing can touch you! The angel of death that is coming to judge cannot take you out. So be encouraged!

This month is about you coming out of bondage and into your promise, out of a place of slavery to a place of freedom. You wear His blood on your forehead, and the angel of death shall pass over you. Your great reward is knowing what Jesus has done for you!

God is properly positioning you, and the enemy is not happy about this. He wants to push you back. Be bold! Look him square in the face and say, "I am not going to lose my confidence. I'm not going to cast it away. I will walk in the Kingdom of God. I will walk in Heaven on earth. I will walk in 'eternal time' while I am in the 'present earth time.' I will occupy the place and space that God has called me and given me."

Today, know that you're awesome, beautiful, amazing, and God has great things for you! Purpose to live a life of sanctification, purity, holiness, and fellowship with the Lord. Share this with a friend or two! Encourage them and be a blessing.

NISAN 21

Historically this is the day that the Red Sea was parted as Moses held his staff over the water.

Paul writes in 2 Corinthians 12:9-10 (NIV): *"But He said to me, 'My grace is sufficient for you, for my power is made perfect in weakness.' Therefore, I will boast all the more gladly about my weaknesses, so that Christ's power may rest on me. That is why, for Christ's sake, I delight in weaknesses, in insults, in hardships, in persecutions, in difficulties. For when I am weak, then I am strong."*

Grasp the importance of the concept, *"My grace is sufficient for you."* The word *grace* comes from the word *charis*, meaning "graciousness, acceptable, benefits, joy and pleasure." Jesus is saying to you, "My pleasure, My joy is sufficient for you!"

The word *sufficient* is from the word *arkeo*, which means "a barrier, to be content, to take away, raise the voice, suspend the mind, expiate in sin and to lift up and remove." Jesus is all-sufficient for you. Sufficiency is when we respond to who God is in His own pleasure and joy. Who He is and His joy is sufficiency—a barrier against sin. He has taken away your sin and positioned you to be an overcomer.

Now walk in that overcoming power today! Keep up with the pace of the Holy Spirit's grace in your life! Keep in step with Him!

NISAN 22

Did you notice? We stepped into a new land just as Passover finished! We now walk in a new spiritual authority that God has given us for where He is taking us! This is exciting!

Read for more understanding Exodus 23:20-33, which is cited in Nisan 25. They reveal that God has sent an angel to go before you to take you into this special land. Yes, you read that right:

there is a special angel assigned to you. Your angel has taken you into this new territory. Here God says that He will be an enemy to your enemies, and you will not be barren; you will bring forth fruit. He will take sickness away from you, give you a long life, and pour out a year of special blessings upon you!

Angels are with you every day! You have a guardian angel and angels assigned to you for God's plan and purpose for you on earth. God wants you to know the resources He has given you to rule and reign on earth, and one of those resources is the blessings of angels. Psalm 91:11 (KJV) tells us that God will: *"give his angels charge over thee, to keep thee in all thy ways."*

Ask the Lord to increase your faith for angelic encounters. Angels are all around you every day! I share this in my book *Angels of Fire: The Ministry of Angels in the End Time Revival.* Get a copy today and learn more about your guardian angel and angels assigned to you for your purpose and destiny.

God loves us all and assigned angels to all of us! I pray supernatural angelic encounters for you today!

NISAN 23

Your muscles are about to be flexed in a major way. God has positioned you spiritually. You are in a new space and place for His promise that is before you. However, beware of the devil's lurking there to ensnare you. Stay vigilant. You will overcome every enemy force in this new land. Every giant that comes against you will fall, in the mighty name of Jesus. No weapon that forms against you (or Christ in you) will prosper because of the resurrection power of Jesus we live in.

This also includes any form of witchcraft that tries to tempt or bind you. Stay alert! Temptation comes when we enter new places. No one is too spiritual to be exempt from temptation. Ask God to reveal to you any areas of temptation that you might be struggling with. What we know in this area is powerful enough to defeat the temptations that try to overcome us!

Ephesians 6:10-13 (NASB) reads, *"Finally, be strong in the Lord and in the strength of His might. Put on the full armor of God, so that **you will be able to stand firm** against the schemes of the devil. For our struggle is not against flesh and blood, but against the rulers, against the powers, against the world forces of this darkness, against the spiritual forces of wickedness in the heavenly places. Therefore, take up the full armor of God, so that you will be able to resist on the evil day, and having done everything, to stand firm."*

You are more than a conqueror and you have been given all you need to conquer the enemy and defeat Him by the blood of Jesus! Stand firm as the enemy prowls around seeking whom He can devour daily—but God has equipped you with the Word and His Spirit so you may stand strong and defeat evil and every plan of the evil one.

NISAN 24

You have everything you need in Christ. You must be secure in this truth in your heart and have it rooted in your mind. All the provision, protection, and acceptance you need has already been satisfied through your resurrection in Jesus Christ. Turn away from distractions and do not fear the giants. God is going to make you stronger so you can stay in this land for the next six months.

Then you'll step into the Feast of Tabernacles in the fall. God is going to double everything at that time. His name is a banner upon you. He will not allow you to fall to pieces; He has called you to be where you are right now. Stand firm, stand strong, keep going, keep praying, keep moving into what God has for you. It's a good land and it is prosperous; and through it, God is taking you to great places!

Let me pray over you today: "Father, I thank You for my friend reading this today. I ask You to cover them with Your power from Heaven. Release glory in their life, strengthen them against the giants of the land. Help them learn to walk in a new level of faith. Empower them for these new levels that You are taking them to. Cause them to stand up straighter and wear a crown firmly on their heads with the robe of righteousness secured in place. Shore up their feet so they may stand strong with the breastplate of righteousness and sword of the Spirit courageously placed. Help them to declare the Word of God and decree that this is a good, new land and that You will rule and reign in it. Lord, I thank You that You have placed us here for such a time as this. With You, we will rule this new land and bring glory to Your name. In Jesus's name, amen."

NISAN 25

You have crossed over! Passover, the Feast of Unleavened Bread and the Feast of Firstfruits, which was Resurrection Sunday, have all taken place. Now you have crossed over into your new journey to the Promised Land! New mantles and new assignments have arrived. God has even assigned an angel to you. It's truly an amazing time that will be full of blessings that come only when you cross over into new seasons like this. Let's look at Exodus 23 over the next few days to find out what they are!

Seven Blessings of the Passover

God tells us in Exodus 23:20-22 (NIV), "*See, **I am sending an angel ahead of you to guard you** along the way and **to bring you to the place I have prepared**. Pay attention to him and listen to what he says. Do not rebel against him; he will not forgive your rebellion, since my Name is in him. If you listen carefully to* *what he says and do all that I say,* **I will be an enemy to your enemies and will oppose those who oppose you.***"*

This is amazing! God is going to carry you into your Promised Land with the help of an assigned angel. You will prevail, just press into the promise!

NISAN 26

The first two blessings we cover today are from Exodus 23:20-22 that I referred to previously.

Blessing 1: *God will assign an angel to you.* **(verse 20)**

You are consecrated, set apart, and sanctified. You have prayed, fasted, and given your Passover offerings. You are ready to go! God has properly positioned you and you have a new mantle and a new angel assigned to protect you.

Blessing 2: *God will protect you and your family.* **(verse 22)**

God says, "With this protection for you and your family, I'm going to defend you." Hallelujah! That is amazing! God doesn't want you to dabble with idols or unclean things that you might meet in this new territory. Heed the warning and keep your guard up. Don't fall prey to worshipping any other gods—you are to remain pure, holy, and consecrated to Him.

These seven blessings are amazing and they are just for you! Hold fast the word as it will increase your faith and carry you through into God's mighty plan for you!

NISAN 27

Today is *Yom HaShoah* which is Holocaust and Heroism Remembrance Day, unless Nisan 27 falls on Shabbat which is a Friday to Saturday, then it is celebrated on Nisan 26.

What are some more blessings of the Passover? Let's look at Exodus 23:23-26 (NIV): *"My angel will go ahead of you and bring you into the land of the Amorites, Hittites, Perizzites, Canaanites, Hivites and Jebusites, and I will wipe them out. Do not bow down before their gods or worship them or follow their practices. You must demolish them and break their sacred stones to pieces. Worship the Lord your God, and his blessing will be on your food and water. I will take away sickness from among you, and none will miscarry or be barren in your land. I will give you a full life span."*

As you remain consecrated to God and worship Him, He promises to bless your food and water (provision) and take sickness away from you (health). God wants to make you productive and give you longevity and increase. He wants your life to count for something! I love how God says to us in Exodus 23:25 (NASB), *"And you shall serve the Lord your God, and He will bless your bread and your water; and I will remove sickness from your midst."*

Blessing 3: *God will give you prosperity.* **(verse 25)**

Blessing 4: *God will take sickness from you.* **(verse 25)**

Blessing 5: *God will give you a long life.* **(verse 26)**

Hallelujah! Everything that you gain between now and the Head of the Year—which is at Rosh Hashanah, the first day in the month of Tishri—will again be doubled! God is going to clear out your Promised Land and make space for you to thrive in it.

Get excited and thank God for all He has done for you! He has given us His great and precious promises for a new way of life. He has given us His precious son, Yeshua Messiah, who shed His blood on a cross, died, was buried, and resurrected that all of these seven promises are possible for us today!

_____

NISAN 28

God says in Exodus 23:30 (NIV): "*Little by little I will drive them out before you, until **you have increased** enough to take possession of the land.*"

Blessing 6: *God will cause increase to come to you.* **(verse 30)**

This increase is often considered to be nonwage prosperity obtained through position; however, I'm believing that you will get a financial blessing and prosperity in position, an increase of authority! Because you have been faithful to God in doing this last season, He is ready to establish your borders and give you a special blessing. But He wants you to stay consecrated and sanctified in your new land.

Exodus 23:31-33 (NIV) says, "**I will establish your borders** *from the Red Sea to the Sea of the Philistines, and from the desert to the River. I will hand over to you the people who live in the land and you will drive them out before you. Do not make a covenant with them or with their gods. Do not let them live in your land, or they will cause you to sin against me, because the worship of their gods will certainly be a snare to you.*" Take comfort in these verses: He is going to drive out anything causing you problems in this blessed season of your life!

Blessing 7: *God will give you a special blessing for the year.* **(verse 31)**

You have stepped into a season of victory! Celebrate it! Then share this with friends. They need to hear the good news too—and they need to have the faith to step into their own Promised Lands!

The seven blessings are complete and ready to be realized now in this season of your life! Rejoice today and share this with a friend. Sow a seed in thanksgiving to the Lord today!

NISAN 29

Jesus gave His only life that you may be saved, healed, redeemed, and reconciled to the Father. That's what we just celebrated on Resurrection Sunday and that's what we celebrate with Passover and the Seven Blessings!

Now the Lord is properly positioning you to have the same attitude as Christ Jesus. His mindset was a mindset of prosperity. He is the Lover of souls and the Giver of all things. You are called to live likewise, in connection with God, in the place of overflow with Him. You have also been properly positioned to be a giver in every aspect of your life.

The word *attitude* is the Greek word *phroneó,* and it means "to exercise the mind, to be mentally disposed in a certain direction, to set affections on one and the same." Jesus set His affection, His thoughts, His mind, and His heart on God, and that devotion couldn't help but overflow on us all!

Now that you are a new creation in Christ, with a new "mind skin," you can do the same! Think different and act different and you will see the blessings of the Lord sustained upon your life!

NISAN 30

The only way you can live like Jesus is to live knowing that the Lord will supply all your needs according to His riches. Your attitude must reflect your relationship with the Father—knowing that He sent you, He provided you with wholeness and fullness, and nothing is missing or broken in your life. Shalom peace is yours through the Prince of Peace. Do not lose your confidence. Do not cast it away. Endeavor to walk in the Kingdom of God as Heaven on earth. Make it a point to occupy the place and space that God has called you and given you!

Tell that enemy who sabotages your faith that He has no authority and you will not listen to him. Tell him that he cannot talk to you that way and you will live by faith! If you have not blessed the Lord with a Passover offering from Deuteronomy 16:16-17, remember to honor Him before the month is complete.

Today, know that you're awesome, beautiful, amazing and God has great things for you! Purpose to live a life of sanctification, purity, holiness, and fellowship with the Lord. As we end the month of Nisan, get ready for a new fresh Month of Iyar, a month of radiance and light, where you will learn more about what God is doing on earth through His prophetic Hebrew calendar.

THE MONTH
OF IYAR

This is referred to as the month of radiance and light or blossom or glow.

The Month of Iyar is the second month of the religious calendar and the eighth month of the civil calendar. The Babylonia name for this month is *Ziv.*

> *And it came to pass in the four hundred and eightieth year after the children of Israel were come out of the land of Egypt, in the fourth year of Solomon's reign over Israel, in the month Ziv, which is the second month, that he began to build the house of the Lord* **(1 Kings 6:1 NKJV).**

> *And the Lord spake unto Moses, saying, "Speak unto the children of Israel, saying, If any man of you or of your posterity shall be unclean by reason of a dead body, or be in a journey afar off, yet he shall keep the passover unto the Lord. The fourteenth day of the second month at even they shall keep it, and eat it with unleavened bread and bitter herbs. They shall leave none of it unto the morning, nor break any bone of it: according to all the ordinances of the passover they shall keep it"* **(Numbers 9:9-12 KJV).**

Tribe of Israel (Conventional): Issachar

Gemstone in Aaron's breastplate: Amethyst

Constellation in Sky/Hebrew name: Taurus/Shor

IYAR 1
Rosh Chodesh Iyar

Tonight there is a new moon is in the night sky.

You have now entered into the second month of the Hebrew religious calendar, the month of Iyar. This is the month of radiance and light! It's also a bringing forth of the fullness, majesty, and splendor of God.

Do you remember how the Israelites were freed from 400 years of bondage in Egypt? Their freedom came after they obeyed God's direction to place blood from a sacrificial lamb on their doorposts. This caused the angel of death to pass over their homes. Pharaoh's son, however, was not spared; so after that tragedy, Pharaoh finally let them go. They were set free!

After the Lord released the Israelites from bondage, they ended up in the wilderness. Here they came across water that was bitter. Moses threw a piece of wood into the water, and the water became sweet. In a similar way, Jesus can make the things that are bitter in our life turn sweet.

It was during the month of Iyar when the Israelites encountered God in the wilderness through the supernatural. He performed many miracles and healings on their behalf.

For instance, as they continued their journey, they found it difficult to find food to eat. In His goodness, the Lord supplied them with quail and a special type of bread called "manna," which rained down from Heaven. Manna was made from a very special crushed coriander seed. Each day, the Israelites were instructed to take just enough for that day. The only day they were to take a double portion was the sixth day of the week, so that they could rest on the Sabbath, the seventh day. If they hoarded the manna, it would turn into maggots. Trust God today as He is the fullness of provision in your life.

IYAR 2

I feel a shift in the atmosphere today. God is releasing things to us from Heaven. He is giving strategies for the new places where He is taking you. I saw very clearly in the spirit realm that specific strategies pertaining to the enlargement of your territory are coming to you. First Chronicles 4:10 (NASB) says, *"Now Jabez called on the God of Israel, saying, 'Oh that You would greatly bless me and extend my border, and that Your hand might be with me, and that You would keep me from harm so that it would not hurt me!' And God brought about what he requested."* I want you to be encouraged today. What God did for Jabez, He will do for you!

Cry out to the Lord for greater territory. Right now, in this very moment, cry out for a release in the supernatural. The spirit realm is bringing an advancement of territory. Angels are being released to give you God's ideas on how you can acquire new borders and experience increase. God is taking you to new places of understanding and showing you the specifics behind things.

"Father, we thank You right now for new territory, just as Jabez prayed. We are in agreement. Enlarge our borders and allow us to enter into the very place that You have called us to inhabit. God, we thank You for enlarged territory and influence. Help us to be able to fit into that plan with new wine and new strategies. We declare that this year will be a great year, despite all the crushing and the difficulties that we have gone through as a nation and world. I decree, right now in the mighty name of Jesus that my friend is going to get into alignment with You. They will step into this new territory with faith. God, we give You glory, honor, and praise! In Jesus's name, amen."

IYAR 3

This is *Yom HaShoah,* Holocaust Remembrance Day, which is a national memorial day for the six million Holocaust victims and five million others who perished during the Holocaust.

In this Month of Iyar, we remember the story of Moses in Exodus 15:22-26 (KJV): *"So Moses brought Israel from the Red Sea, and they went out into the wilderness of Shur; and they went three days in the wilderness, and found no water. And when they came to Marah, they could not drink of the waters of Marah, for they were bitter: therefore the name of it was called Marah. And the people murmured against Moses, saying, What shall we drink? And he cried unto the Lord; and the Lord shewed him a tree, which when he had cast into the waters, the waters were made sweet: there he made for them a statute and an ordinance, and there he proved them, and said, If thou wilt diligently hearken to the voice of the Lord thy God, and wilt do that which is right in His sight, and wilt give ear to His commandments, and keep all His statutes, I will put none of these diseases upon thee, which I have brought upon the Egyptians: for I am the Lord that healeth thee."*

Jesus was crucified on a wooden cross made from a tree. He was crucified for our sins and transgressions. He redeemed the curse that we might be saved, healed, and delivered. Everything bitter in our life is redeemed and made whole by His stripes. Our God is Healer and He will heal you today in your body! Rest in this truth and meditate on how God made all provision for the Israelites this year while they were in the wilderness.

IYAR 4

Around today is *Yom HaZikaron,* a day to remember the fallen soldiers who died during the war of independence and other wars including national terrorism. This day of remembrance may change if there's a conflict with Shabbat.

In the passage cited yesterday, Exodus 15:22-26, in essence God says to Moses, "Listen, this could be a very prosperous time for you. Hold on to the fact that I am good. My goodness is always there for you. I love you intently. I have led you into this place and I am going to take care of you. I know that you might be afraid after you saw the ten plagues take place. But you also saw that I fought for you. I split the Red Sea and I brought you over. Now you have come to a place of despair where there is bitter water, but I'm going to make it sweet." Isn't that amazing?

Moses was instructed by the Lord to throw a tree into the waters of Marah, and the bitter waters would be made sweet! From the New Testament perspective, the tree represents the cross that Jesus died upon. This is the Tree of Life in Jesus. He is the Passover Lamb who shed His blood for you!

Here, God is defining Himself as the Lord. He wanted a personal relationship with Israel and He wants a personal relationship with you! I encourage you to know the Lord today. Taste His goodness. Taste the sweetness of a relationship with our Father and spend time in fellowship with Him.

IYAR 5

Around today is *Yom Ha'atzma'ut,* or Independence Day, a national holiday declaring Israel's independence in 1948. This day changes on the calendar if it conflicts with Shabbat.

In Exodus 15:26 (NIV), we see the Lord defining Himself as the Healer. We see this when He spoke to Moses, *"If you listen* carefully to the Lord your God and do what is right in his eyes, if you pay attention to his commands and keep all his decrees, I will not bring on you any of the diseases I brought on the Egyptians, for I am the Lord, who heals you."

As Christians, we know Jesus as our Messiah. He fulfilled the Scripture in Isaiah 53:5 (KJV) that says, by *"his stripes we are healed."* You may have bitter water in your life right now. You may have resentment, difficulties, anger, guilt, and condemnation. But because of Jesus, you can now live a sweet life, one filled with walking in His commandments and living in a place of prosperity.

Take time today to position yourself to live a life of prosperity. In 3 John 2 (NASB) we are told, *"May you prosper and be in good health even as your soul prospers."* To prosper is to have fullness, wholeness, completion; nothing is missing and nothing is broken. Jesus made a way for you to live in wholeness and completeness! He will take your bitterness and make it sweet.

May you live this life of prosperity and be in good health, both in your soul and your body. May you have increase here on earth! Hallelujah! The curse has been broken!

IYAR 6

In Exodus 16:8 (KJV), Moses says, *"This shall be, when the Lord shall give you in the evening flesh to eat, and in the morning bread to the full; for that the Lord heareth your murmurings which ye murmur against him: and what are we? Your murmurings are not against us, but against the Lord."*

Even though the Lord supplied their every need, the Israelites still complained; and as a result, they wandered in the wilderness for forty years. God used this time to work out of them the bondage mindset of Egypt, along with their trauma and poverty thinking. It was difficult for them to have the right mindset of who God really is. Because of this, God had to transform their mindset and get them to a place where they could know and understand that He is a prosperous God who loved them very much.

What do you believe to be true about God? Is God the generous Giver? Will He give to you and supply all your needs? Read Exodus 16 to see how much God loved them and ultimately loves you! Then put into practice what you have read and begin to walk out your promise.

IYAR 7

Historically this is the month when the walls of Jerusalem were dedicated, nearly 88 years after their destruction by Nebuchadnezzar.

The Lord calls Himself the One who heals (see Exodus 15:26). He is also the One who supplies all needs according to His riches in Christ Jesus (see Philippians 4:19). Just like God taught the Israelites, He is teaching you that with Him is fullness in every way.

We can learn so much about how great God is through the Israelites' wilderness journey to the Promised Land.

Jesus is our sacrificial Lamb, and His blood redeems us from sin, death, and the grave. When you come to know Jesus as your Lord and Savior, you step into a time of sanctification.

It's time for you to grow and develop in God's holiness, prosperity, and the understanding of who our Lord is. He wants you to learn how to walk in these realms on a daily basis. Each day, you can enter into your Promised Land of peace and joy in Him. All you must do is check your heart and respond in repentance. Repentance is not a dirty word, it is a blessing from the Lord and a way of life for the believer in Yeshua Messiah.

Share this with a friend who needs to know today is a wonderful day to begin walking in the prosperity of who God is!

IYAR 8

Luke 2:52 (KJV) says, *"Jesus increased in wisdom and stature, and in favour with God and man."* This verse doesn't just say that He grew in favor with man. He also grew in favor with God, His Father. This is what the Lord wants for you and me as well: He wants us to grow in favor with Him.

How do we grow in favor with God? We need to mirror Jesus's example of cultivating a relationship with God. Favor is based on relationship and intimacy with Him. Favor is understanding that nothing can separate you from the love of God. It's knowing that He has made a way for you to prosper in your soul with Him.

The Bible tells us in 3 John 2 (NASB), *"Beloved, I pray that in all respects you may prosper and be in good health, just as your soul prospers."* You need to stay mindful of the order that God has set. Once you have gained favor with God, you will then find favor with people, opportunities, provision, protection, acceptance, and all you need to accomplish the will of God on earth. In other words, favor opens doors of opportunity for you in every area of your life.

Why is that so important? Because prosperity of soul and the favor of God are synonymous. Jesus had a prosperous soul. When you have a prosperous soul, your mind, will, and emotions are expanded. You think prosperously, without lack. You think heavenly, not earthly. You think eternally, not within the confines of time as we know it.

Determine to become prosperous in your soul, and you will also have prosperity of health. Learn how to position yourself to receive the favor of God. Remember, it is accomplished through relationship. Build your relationship with God, and His favor over your life expands!

IYAR 9

There is nothing more valuable than your relationship with your heavenly Father.

If you have doubts, fears, sickness in your body waiting to be healed, maybe something is holding you back or something is clouding your belief in God's goodness, which can affect your identity. If it affects your identity, it certainly can affect your soul. It can cause you to wonder, *Who am I? Why is this happening? And why would God allow this to happen?*

Here's what I want you to say to yourself instead, especially in a time of sickness: "Wait a minute. I'm called to be prosperous and to have a prosperous soul. I'm not going to think lack. God is good and causes all things for my good. He is the Lord who heals me according to Exodus 15!"

The four Gospels talk about how God is the Healer and how He is willing to heal. We need to know and understand that just because we don't have our healing in this moment or have great things happening around us, it doesn't mean that we should adapt to our environment. Don't adapt to the world; adapt to having a prosperous soul! Only then will you see your circumstances change!

When you have a prosperous attitude, you will bounce back quicker when faced with trials and difficult circumstances. That, my friend, is the favor of God! That is what He wants you to grow in. When you grow in favor with God, everything else is going to work out. I want to encourage you to continue to flourish daily as God transforms your soul.

If you would like to learn more, I have an amazing course called Soul Transformation. In it, you will understand how prosperity of soul leads to living an abundant life and a life of ascension with transformative power. You will be empowered to step into the victories that God has assigned to you! Simply go to my website at www.candicesmithyman.com and get a copy today!

IYAR 10

This is Herzl Day, an Israeli national holiday for Theodor Herzl and the impact he made on helping establish Israel as a Jewish state.

Historically, this day is the anniversary of the death of the priest Eli (see 1 Samuel 4:17:18 NIV).

God is such a great Giver! Not only did He show the Israelites how much He loved them by freeing them from Egypt, but He showed them how much He wanted to give them by leading them to the Promised Land. Today, I believe God is revealing His heart to you just like He did to the Israelites. He has a Promised Land for you as well!

Deuteronomy 8:3 (NIV) speaks powerfully to us: *"He humbled you, causing you to hunger and then feeding you with manna, which neither you nor your ancestors had known, to teach you that **man does not live on bread alone but on every word that comes from the mouth of the Lord.**"*

In this verse, we discover how we can live even if we are in the middle of the desert or in our own wilderness experience. We survive by the Word of God! Every word that is spoken out of His mouth teaches us how to live. Jesus was faced with the same test regarding the word of God in Matthew 4:3-4 (NIV): *"The tempter came to him and said, 'If you are the Son of God, tell these stones to become bread.' Jesus answered, 'It is written: "Man shall not live on bread alone, but on every word that comes from the mouth of God."'"*

You can stop being concerned about what you will eat, what you will wear, where you will live, and other concerns of this world. God has taken care of everything! He cares about what you care about—and He has already taken care of it! Simply believe these truths by faith and watch the miracles happen!

IYAR 11

The word *mouth* in Hebrew is *peh*. *Peh* means "portion, mind, and two-edged sword." God has set you up to live out of every word that He speaks and has spoken. God's mouth reveals His mind. He wants you to know His divine heart and intention toward you. His heart is to give. He blesses, and He is a blessing.

Hebrews 4:12 (NKJV) says, *"For the Word of God is living and powerful and sharper than any two-edged sword, piercing even to the division of soul and spirit, and of joints and marrow, and is a discerner of the thoughts and intents of the heart."*

This is so important. Read Hebrews 4:12 again. God's mind proceeds out of His mouth. He wants you to obey His commandments, learn His heart, listen to His voice, and do what He says.

He is saying to you today, "Trust Me! Know that I love you! I love to give to you, and I want to bless you in so many ways!"

God cares so much for you. Jesus's blood has already been shed so you could be saved, healed, redeemed, set up for success, and able to receive all that you need from Him. Don't be shy today. Reach out to your Savior and declare His Living Word! Grab a friend and speak the Word over them too!

IYAR 12

Recently, I heard the voice of God. He said to tell you, "It's time to start moving. A shift has taken place, and it's time for Kingdom advancement." And, listen, it's the Kingdom of God that starts any kind of move from the Lord. It's the body of Christ moving when He says to move that creates change in the world.

The Lord reminded me of Joshua. In Joshua 3 we see the Lord giving him instructions. He was told, "It's time to cross the Jordan River. When the priests carrying the Ark of the Covenant begin to move, tell the people to set out and follow after it." I believe the Lord is urging us to begin moving today. There's been a shift in the spirit realm, and now is the time to begin making plans to move forward. The Lord wants us, like Joshua and the Israelites, to start crossing over, to inhabit the place He has called us to inhabit.

I know during this season we have had to press pause in some areas, but God is nudging us to begin moving again, to pursue and to advance. Don't allow yourself to be confused. The Kingdom of God, from Heaven to earth, rules the world. The rulers of this world do not call the shots—God does. We are His people, and we must listen to our King's command.

As the prophet of the Lord, I declare and decree now a shift in the atmosphere. We, the people of God, must begin to advance. Find out what your role is in this advancement—in your home, town, and current situation. Whoever you are influencing, speak the Word of God and say, "Let's get moving!" Press forward. Pentecost and the Feast of Shavuot are coming. What a wonderful time to remember that we are moving forward and stepping into the power of the Holy Spirit to do miracles, signs, and wonders!

Let me pray this over you: "Father, thank You for stirring Your Spirit in Your church. Stir every believer to start getting up early, just like Joshua did in chapter 3 when he was ready to receive Your instruction. We, Your people, will start moving. Thank You for the deposit and release of the joy of the Lord upon the earth. A fresh excitement for Kingdom advancement! Father, I thank You right now for calling us to advance Your Kingdom. Begin to move in our lives, in the mighty name of Jesus. The power of Your Holy Spirit goes with us, angels go with us, and You are dispatching us to go and do signs, miracles, and wonders. Your Kingdom is on the move! In Jesus's name I pray, amen."

IYAR 13

Have you been experiencing huge pushback from the enemy? I have seen so much spiritual warfare lately. It began right after Resurrection Sunday. The enemy is mad and cannot do anything about the resurrected Jesus! He cannot do anything about you being resurrected with Christ or being properly ascended and positioned with Him. Instead, the enemy is trying different forms of trickery to push you and get you to question your beliefs. But what he doesn't realize is that his pushback is proving that what is inside you is greater than him!

Ephesians 6:12-13 (KJV) says, *"For we wrestle not against flesh and blood, but against principalities, against powers, against the rulers of the darkness of this world, against spiritual wickedness in high places. Wherefore take unto you the whole armour of God, that ye may be able to withstand in the evil day, and having done all, to stand."*

That word *withstand* is the Greek word *anthistémi*, which translates into our English word anti-*histamine*. Your mind and body may need some anti-*histamine* receptors to fight the battle. Get out your Bible, the Word of God, and begin today to take every thought captive to His Word throughout the Scriptures! You will see victory today in Jesus's name!

IYAR 14

Tonight there is a full moon in the night sky.

Historically this day is *Pesach Sheni,* the second chance Passover for individuals who were impure or missed the first Passover on Nisan 14, according to Numbers 9:11.

Isn't that interesting? Let's look again at what the apostle Paul wrote, *"Take unto you the whole armour of God, that ye may be able to withstand in the evil day, and having done all, to stand"*

(Ephesians 6:13 KJV). In other words, you have natural histamines that help your natural body fight; but the word *withstand* also represents a spiritual histamine that fights back against the attacks of the enemy. The whole armor of God is your spiritual histamine.

Today, the Lord is saying to stand. No matter what you are going through—even if your body or soul is responding, even if you are dealing with things that are very difficult—keep standing against the powers and principalities of darkness, not against your flesh-and-blood situation.

That word *anthistémi* is a fight word. In the same way, the Lord is saying, "I want you to just stand right now. Stand and see the deliverance of the Lord. Stand and see that I'm going to come rescue you. I'm going to bring about an outcome that is remarkable. I know you are losing faith right now. You're discouraged, questioning things. Just stand no matter what you see going on around you, no matter how aggravating or difficult it is. Stand in the midst of it!"

You fight against the enemy with the Word and with the faith of God. Today, agree with what God says. Adjust how you think! Agree with His voice and partner with Him and He will give you the strategy to withstand your enemy. God is doing something great and wants you to be on His team! Stand with the full armor of God upon your soul!

Share this with a friend who needs to be empowered to break free from the enemy.

IYAR 15

Jesus listened to every word that came out of the mouth of His Father. It was His food. He was led by the Lord in everything He did. The same should be true for you and me. No matter how much we hunger and thirst in this world today for actual food, our food should be to do the will God. The Word of God is His will. John 4:31-34 (NIV) says, *"Meanwhile his disciples urged him, 'Rabbi, eat something.' But he said to them, 'I have food to eat that you know nothing about.' Then his disciples said to each other, 'Could someone have brought him food?' 'My food,' said Jesus, 'is to do the will of him who sent me and to finish his work.'"*

Jesus told His disciples to obey His commands. You need to realize that what you do in this world isn't important—doing the will of the Lord is what is important. Are you following after His Word? Are you taking time to get in it? Are you studying it? Are you setting yourself apart for His purposes? Jesus wanted His disciples to see that He operated on a different plane of existence. Jesus was not only 100 percent man, He was 100 percent God too. He had flesh just like us, so yes, He had to partake of natural food; but what He was trying to explain to them is that doing the will of God was His nourishment.

Is your food to do the will of Him who sent you? Do you hunger and thirst after His Word and His righteousness? If you want more passion to hunger for God, just ask Him. It is a simple request that He wants to answer today for you! Say, "Lord, give me a hunger for You in the Word of God. I want more of You!" Then watch supernaturally what He does to bring this out in your life. Watch closely—things will change!

IYAR 16

Historically this is the first day that quail and manna came from Heaven to feed the Israelites.

Exodus 16:12-13 (NIV) says, *"I have heard the grumbling of the Israelites. Tell them, 'At twilight you will eat meat, and in the morning you will be filled with bread. Then you will know that I am the Lord your God.' That evening quail came and covered the camp, and in the morning there was a layer of dew around the camp."*

Over the past month as we have discussed the Israelites' journey across the desert to the Promised Land, the word *manna* has come up multiple times.

Natural manna smells like honey and is made from crushed coriander seeds. Coriander seeds are white with black stripes. Who does that remind you of? Who bore stripes on His back and took your infirmities and transgressions, according to Isaiah 53? Jesus!

He is your Manna from Heaven! Your Bread of Life! He is the Bread of Life who you should hunger and thirst for every day! Seek the Lord and watch Him give you that hunger for more of Him! Your intimacy with Yeshua is going to the next levels! I can see it in the spirit realm now. As you humble yourself He will meet your needs for Him and Him alone!

IYAR 17

Historically today is from the day the rain stopped in Noah's time. Genesis 8:1-4 (KJV) tells us:

*"And God remembered Noah, and every living thing, and all the cattle that was with him in the ark: and God made a wind to pass over the earth, and the waters assuaged; The fountains also of the deep and the windows of heaven were stopped, and the rain from heaven was restrained; And the waters returned from off the earth continually: and after the end of the hundred and fifty days the waters were abated. And **the ark rested in the seventh month, on the seventeenth day of the month,** upon the mountains of Ararat."*

This was the seventh month on the civil calendar, not the religious calendar because Exodus came after Genesis and so there was no religious calendar yet.

Your soul is hungry and thirsty for the Manna from Heaven, the Word of God. A relationship with God is what makes a difference in your life. I encourage you to tap into that kind of relationship with Him. Listen to His Word and do what He says.

Tell the Lord today that you want a deeper relationship with Him: "Father, I confess right now that I need more of You. I need more understanding of the Word. Enlighten my heart. Open my heart that I might know Your Word and hear Your voice. May I revel in and understand Your beauty and Your majesty. May I rest in Your pleasure, and may Your grace be sufficient for me. Keep me away from sin and empower me to overcome even my flesh by the power of Your Word. Amen."

Today is your day to dive deep into your relationship with the Lord. Encourage a friend to dive in too!

IYAR 18

Historically today is *Lag BaOmer,* the 33rd day of the Omer count, a 49-day period between Passover and Shavuot.

Are you counting—your blessings? God says, "I have a destiny for you! You have crossed over! Rise up. Stand up. Get to the place I have called you to be. You are a new creature in Christ. Yes, you are! All the darkness, all the old has gone away and all the new has come!"

In 1 Peter 2:9 (NIV) we find Peter encouraging the church, *"You are a chosen people, a royal priesthood, a holy nation, God's special possession, that you may declare the praises of him who called you out of darkness into his wonderful light."*

God is raising you up! You have received mercy as a child of God. He is restoring your foundation and is bringing you into greater places. The key is to position yourself in His will by faith. You must maintain this position! This position is in the realms of prosperity. You are seated with Him in heavenly places!

IYAR 19

We are a victorious church. Don't believe the lie that we are beaten down from the happenings in the world today. He has moved us up, and we live victoriously in Him! We need to know this is our place in the heavenly realms and stand firm in this truth. We are people of God, called to be royal, holy, and set apart. Embrace the fact that God has called you! This is a great place to be!

I want you to rest, hear the voice of the Lord, and listen to Him speaking to you. You can be victorious, no matter what is going on in your life right now. Just stay in the heavenly realms. This is above the warfare. When we allow the glory to come to earth, the glory will change everything in your environment.

Know that I've been praying for you. I pray that your spiritual ears will be open and that you will hear God speak clearly. I pray that He will give you words of knowledge, words of wisdom, and tell you how He is meeting your need. I pray that you will hear the sound of angels and trumpets in the spiritual realm as they declare and decree that He is King! I speak life and blessings over you. Prosperity, increase, healing, transformation, spiritual sight, hearing, smell, taste and touch will be parts of your abundant life. God will show you the increase that you are coming into, in His mighty name! Praise Him for it!

IYAR 20

Historically this is the day the Israelites left their camp at Mount Sinai after one year and twenty days; when the glory cloud lifted and they began their journey to the Land of Canaan around 1312 BC.

Numbers 10:11-12 (KJV), *"And it came to pass on **the twentieth day of the second month, in the second year**, that the cloud* was taken up from off the tabernacle of the testimony. And the children of Israel took their journeys out of the wilderness of Sinai; and the cloud rested in the wilderness of Paran."

In 2 Corinthians 8:9 (NKJV), the apostle Paul says, *"For you know the grace of our Lord Jesus Christ, that, though He was rich, yet for your sakes He became poor, that you through His poverty might become rich."*

That word *rich* means *to become wealthy in every sense.* This is not just financial wealth but the wealth of your soul. This is not only possessions, abundance, bestowment; it is broken down to another word, *pletho,* which means "to fill, influence, supply." It is to literally fulfill time.

Jesus was rich but was made poor so that you might become rich in the fulfillment of time. Lack was broken at the cross when sin, death, and the grave were defeated. Why is this important? Because when you live your life with an understanding of the Word of God—that it is faithful, true, specific—you will have a prosperous soul. The Lord wants this for you. He wants your soul to be full of wealth and prosperity! With this understanding, you will bring about the blessings of the Kingdom.

IYAR 21

Let me show you a church that had that understanding talked about yesterday. Paul writes in 2 Corinthians 8:1-5 (NIV): *"And now, brothers and sisters, we want you to know about the grace that God has given the Macedonian churches. In the midst of a very severe trial, their overflowing joy and their extreme poverty welled up in rich generosity. For I testify that they gave as much as they were able, and even beyond their ability. Entirely on their own, they urgently pleaded with us for the privilege of sharing in this service to the Lord's people. And they exceeded* our expectations: *They gave themselves first of all to the Lord, and then by the will of God also to us."*

A trial always represents lack, pain, and disappointment. The Macedonia churches were about to fight through their poverty to bring forth a rich, generous blessing and inheritance. Let me tell you what is so amazing about this passage of Scripture: No matter what you are going through—loss, disappointment, trial, confusion or sickness—there is a place inside you where you can break through to wealth and abundance!

Listen to me, I'm not just talking about finances. I'm talking about what we bring forth out of our hearts. If you have a rich heart, you can bring forth a blessing because of your prosperous soul. You cannot outgive God. You can bless the Lord in every way, even if you think you have nothing. You may be flat-out broke, busted, and disgusted. You are sick of your sickness. You're tired and wasted. You've lost relationships. Hear this again: right now there is a place inside you that is ready to burst forth! From this place God is bringing forth blessings, in the name of Jesus, I declare and decree it today! Get up and fight! Let your faith lead the way!

IYAR 22

Historically today is the day the children of Israel arrived at the rock that would bring forth the water in the wilderness.

Exodus 17:1 (NKJV) tells us, *"Then all the congregation of the children of Israel set out on their journey from the Wilderness of Sin, according to the commandment of the Lord, and camped in Rephidim; and there was no water for the people to drink."*

You are stepping out of poverty into prosperity. You are stepping out of the earth realm into the eternal realm. You are stepping out of a place of pain into a place of purpose. Be encouraged today! The enemy can't do anything to you that wasn't already done to Jesus. Because of His resurrection, you now have the grace of exceeding riches, grace beyond measure. Just like the Israelites receiving water out of a rock—a miracle is here!

I'm getting excited! I can feel the presence of the Lord! I want you to lift your hands as I pray over you:

"I see the vats of Heaven opening for you right now, gold and silver treasure. Financial blessing is coming to you. Rent is going to be paid right now, in the mighty name of Jesus. Go out to your mailbox: there are some checks waiting for you. God is bringing someone out of extreme poverty. Why? Because He already did it, and now you are seeing the manifestation of it on earth. He loves and cares for you. He broke the curse of poverty over your life, the curse of lack. I know your mind is going to what you don't have, but listen right now, in the name of Jesus—that is broken! You have it right now! The Lord is good. Let that glory fall upon you right now in the name of Jesus. Receive fire, in the name of Jesus, receive impartations for spiritual gifts. Glory!"

Thank the Lord right now. Thank Him for the provision that's coming from Heaven to you. Thank Him for opening the vats and pouring them down upon you. Thank Him for new opportunities, new revelation, new anointing! It's yours, in the mighty name of Jesus!

Through Jesus's death, burial, and resurrection, you have been made rich. So grab hold of the faith of God, as shared in Galatians 2:20. That's when you will receive all these things from Heaven. You can live in prosperity!

IYAR 23

Our God is a covenant-keeping God! He keeps His promises from generation to generation. He wants you to be faithful to Him and keep your covenants too. God wants you to be a child that walks in the covenant He has given you through being a child of the most High God!

In one week we will approach the Hebrew month of Sivan. This is the month when the Lord came upon Mount Sinai and gave the Ten Commandments. It's an important time to understand that the Word of God is representative of who God is.

On Mount Sinai, the Lord shared His flawless character, who He is. He is a God of justice, righteousness and love. He longs for you to follow after the covenant commandments He gave.

Exodus 19:3-6 from the New Living Translation says, *"Then Moses climbed the mountain to appear before God. The Lord called to him from the mountain and said, 'Give these instructions to the family of Jacob; announce it to the descendants of Israel: "You have seen what I did to the Egyptians. You know how I carried you on eagles' wings and brought you to myself. Now if you will obey me and keep my covenant, you will be my own special treasure from among all the peoples on earth; for all the earth belongs to me. And you will be my kingdom of priests, my holy nation." This is the message you must give to the people of Israel.'"*

You are a member of a holy nation and a kingdom of priests—meditate on this truth today! God wants you to live as a child of the inheritance—walking in all the blessings of the Kingdom!

IYAR 24

God has not changed. He gave us His Word. He gave us The Word, Jesus Christ, who walked the earth. He keeps His covenants!

When you know the Word, you know more of who God is and how faithful He is. We should model this faithfulness. How can we do that? By keeping His commandments. He often speaks to us in Scripture about how our joy will be complete as we keep His commandments.

The world sees you and me as children of the King when we keep covenant with God. They see a pure faith and commitment to being all God called us to be.

I want you to know you are loved. You are His treasure, part of a holy nation, and a kingdom of priests unto the Lord. Now it's time for you to know who God is. Press in to know Him. If you doubt this truth, simply wash your mind in the word until you begin to believe this covenant truth that will empower you every day!

IYAR 25

Historically this day is *Mem B'Omer*, the 40th day of the Omer count.

God provided for the Israelites quail, manna, and water in the desert. He supplied their every need and gave of Himself in so many ways. And He is committed to doing the same thing for you.

I'm also sensing, as the month of Sivan gets closer, that this may be a time in which you are tested in keeping your contracts or covenants, your binding agreements. If you are under a specific binding agreement, now is the time to determine to keep your contract and walk in righteousness. I understand that some contracts cannot continue because seasons have changed. If this is the case, pray and ask the Lord for the wisdom to renegotiate or even release you from the contract. Go talk with those to whom you are bound. Do not be afraid.

The enemy gets a foothold and develops a stronghold when you aren't doing what you should be doing or fulfilling your contracts. This allows an open door that allows demonic forces to come in and affect your sleep and cause fear, anxiety, and depression. Don't open any doors for the enemy to enter your life. Close them! If you need to move on from some contracts, then move on! If you need to renegotiate your commitment to a contract, have faith that God will help you step into your destiny. The battle belongs to the Lord!

You are called to be faithful unto God. Share this with a friend who needs to be encouraged to keep moving forward.

IYAR 26

This day is a Jewish holiday established as the Day of Salvation and Liberation in honor of the rescue of European Jews from the threat of total destruction in World War II on May 9, 1945.

Today, I hear the Lord saying, "Rise up. Stand up. Get to the place I have called you to be. You are a new creature in Christ. Yes, you are! All the darkness, all the old, has gone away and all the new has come!"

In 1 Peter 2:9 (NKJV) we find Peter encouraging the church, *"You are a chosen generation, a royal priesthood, a holy nation, His own special people, that you may proclaim the praises of Him who called you out of darkness into His marvelous light."*

God is raising you up! You have received mercy as a child of God. He is restoring your foundation and is bringing you into greater places. The key is to position yourself in His will by faith. You must maintain this position! Change your thinking—you are indeed royalty!

IYAR 27

Historically today is Ascension Day, which is 40 days after Resurrection Sunday. This is the day that Jesus would have ascended into Heaven after appearing for 40 days after His resurrection to His disciples.

Acts 1:8-9 (NIV) tells us: "'*But you will receive power when the Holy Spirit comes on you; and you will be my witnesses in Jerusalem, and in all Judea and Samaria, and to the ends of the earth.' After he said this, he was taken up before their very eyes, and a cloud hid him from their sight.*"

Historically this day is *Ta'anit Tzadik,* which remembers the death of the prophet Samuel with a fast and pilgrimages to his tomb.

The Lord is doing amazing things! I'm so filled with joy! I've seen Him do so many miracles this week! Wow! Our God is good!

People have and are being released from the power of death today. The Lord has asked the dispatching of angels to go forth.

God is healing you right now. The angels of fire are being released. Hebrews 1:7 (NIV) reads, *"In speaking of the angels he says, 'He makes his angels spirits, and his servants flames of fire.'"* You are called to participate with angels. You have a guardian angel with you all the time, but God has also assigned angels to you so that you can accomplish the purposes He has for you in the new territories He is taking you. (For more understanding on angels and their fire properties, get a copy of my book, *Angels of Fire: The Ministry of Angels in the End Time Revival,* which is a manual on angels and how God wants you to work with them for healing and Kingdom advancement.)

IYAR 28

Historically today is *Yom Yerushalayim,* an Israeli national holiday commemorating the reunifying of Jerusalem and taking back control of the Old City in 1967. This is also a religious holiday expressing thanks to God for victory in the Six Day War and answering the prayer of Next Day Jerusalem for 2000 years.

The power of sin, death, and the grave was broken when Jesus shed His blood and resurrected. He was the Sacrifice to bring you back into the place of sovereign rulership and dominion under the King of Heaven. But in order for you to see *dunamis,* which is *the miracle-working power of God*, you have to know and understand the word *kratos.*

Hebrews 2:14-15 (KJV) reads, *"Forasmuch then as the children are partakers of flesh and blood, he also himself likewise took part of the same; that through death he might destroy him that had the power of death, that is, the devil; and deliver them who through fear of death were all their lifetime subject to bondage."*

The word *power* in this passage of Scripture is *kratos,* the dominion power of God. The *kratos* power was repositioned because of what Jesus did for us. All the sovereign power of the enemy over your life is gone—it is now in the hands of the Lord. The devil no longer has dominion over your life. If you have received Jesus as your Lord and Savior, the dominion power has gone to the true Sovereign King and you are completely delivered.

IYAR 29

Again, the word *kratos* is the dominion power of God, and it releases you from the hold of the enemy. The miracle-working power of God is able to come forth because of the dominion power of God that came back into the earth realms during Jesus's resurrection. This is when Jesus took the keys from the enemy.

Now, if you want to be a miracle worker and see amazing things happen, you have to understand the difference between *kratos* power, *dunamis* power, and *exousia* power. I know its Greek, but they all mean different things. We already mentioned the meaning of *kratos* and *dunamis*. The word *exousia* means authority or delegated authority.

Both *dunamis* and *exousia* spring off the foundation of the *kratos* power. This is extremely important. Some are being overcome by the spirit of death, but death has already been defeated! Anything that is coming against you to overcome you, don't agree with it. If your family members have the spirit of death over them, don't agree with it. Instead, I want you to declare life over yourself and over them, in the mighty name of Jesus and dispatch the healing angels—God has given you the power to be His voice on earth today. You have His Spirit and His word and you have His *kratos* power. He gave us all these tools, now let us advance His Kingdom and be the agents of change.

We are approaching the third Hebrew month, Sivan; and as we close this month of Iyar, let us remember to live not on bread alone but every word, His voice, that proceeds from His mouth—then we will live each day to the fullest.

THE MONTH
OF SIVAN

This is referred to as the month of revelation.

Sivan is the third month of the religious calendar and the ninth month of the civil calendar. Sivan is an Assyrian name and means joy or month of harvest and ripening of grain.

Exodus 19:1-2 (KJV): *"In **the third month**, when the children of Israel were gone forth out of the land of Egypt, the same day came they into the wilderness of Sinai. For they were departed from Rephidim, and were come to the desert of Sinai, and had pitched in the wilderness; and there Israel camped before the mount."*

Tribe of Israel (Conventional): Zebulon

Gemstone in Aaron's breastplate: Citrine

Constellation in Sky/Hebrew name: Gemini/Te'omim

SIVAN 1
Rosh Chodesh Sivan

Tonight there is a new moon in the night sky.

Historically this was the day when Moses ascended up the mountain the second time to get the Ten Commandments. His first ascent was when God called to him from the burning bush.

It is said he went up and down about eight times as a mediator between God and the people.

Exodus 19:3-5 (KJV) reads, *"And Moses went up unto God, and the Lord called unto him out of the mountain, saying, Thus shalt thou say to the house of Jacob, and tell the children of Israel; Ye have seen what I did unto the Egyptians, and how I bare you on eagles' wings, and brought you unto myself. Now therefore, if ye will obey my voice indeed, and keep my covenant, then ye shall be a peculiar treasure unto me above all people: for all the earth is mine."*

You have now entered into the brand-new Hebrew month of Sivan! Not only did the Lord bring the Torah to the people during Sivan, He brought forth the power of His Holy Spirit in the upper room. In one day, 120 people received the power of the Holy Spirit! (See Acts 2.)

Now is the time for the people of God to understand the importance of *living by faith!* The Greek word for *faith* is *pistis*. *Pistis* means "to have a reliance upon Christ." You need to recognize that God's Word is constant, it is the code and substance by which you must live. The word *substance* is the Greek word *hupostasis*, and means "a setting under, a support, a concrete resolve (subjectively or objectively)." It is confidence. Have God-confidence and live by faith every day!

SIVAN 2

Historically today is *Yom Hameyuchas* which means the day of distinction in which the people of God accepted the Torah and prepared themselves with consecration

Exodus 19:6-8 (NIV): *"'You will be for me a kingdom of priests and a holy nation.' These are the words you are to speak to the Israelites."* So Moses went back and summoned the elders of the people and set before them all the words the Lord had *commanded him to speak. The people all responded together, 'We will do everything the Lord has said.' So Moses brought their answer back to the Lord."*

When the Lord spoke to Moses and said in Exodus 19:10-11 (NIV), *"And the Lord said to Moses, 'Go to the people and consecrate them today and tomorrow. Have them wash their clothes and be ready by the third day, because on that day the Lord will come down on Mount Sinai in the sight of all the people.'"*

Today, you have God's Word and His Spirit. The Spirit of the Lord works in you according to His Word. You have more than enough faith to be strong, to step out and to impact the world around you. Hebrews 11:2 (NKJV) says, *"For by it the elders obtained a good testimony."* The elders lived by the Word of God, which strengthened their souls. These individuals were honored by God because they lived by faith.

Your job as a Kingdom citizen is to live by FAITH just like they did! In our world right now there is so much going on. It's all about sight—what you see as you hear, touch, smell, and taste. But this is not how the Lord expects His children to live. God says, *"Live by faith and not by sight."* Practice living by faith today and every day as that is what pleases the Lord.

SIVAN 3

Historically this day begins the Three Days of Separation: *Sheloshet Yemei Hagbalah.*

Exodus 19:11-15 (NKJV): *"'And let them **be ready for the third day.** For **on the third day** the Lord will come down upon Mount Sinai in the sight of all the people. You shall set bounds for the people all around, saying, "Take heed to yourselves that you do not go up to the mountain or touch its base. Whoever touches the mountain shall surely be put to death. Not a hand shall touch* *him, but he shall surely be stoned or shot with an arrow; whether man or beast, he shall not live." When the trumpet sounds long, they shall come near the mountain.' So Moses went down from the mountain to the people and sanctified the people, and they washed their clothes. And he said to the people, '**Be ready for the third day**; do not come near your wives.'"*

Then three days later the Ten Commandments came down.

This principle is so important. Today's culture will tell you what is right and wrong, yet most don't even know the difference between the two. They don't know the truth! Only God knows what is right and what is wrong, and it's written in *His Word!* His Word is infallible. It stands today and forever. If you want to increase your faith and step out to do the things that God has called you to do, you must increase your understanding of the Word! Get into your Bible. Read it every day. Meditate on it. Ask God to reveal its truth to you in your prayer time. And base every decision you make in life upon the Word and God's truthfulness.

Encourage a friend today! Let them know they have everything they need to advance in their calling and defeat the enemy. It's found in God's Word and through His Spirit!

SIVAN 4

Historically this day was considered to be the birth of David around 1000 BC.

Entering the Hebrew month of Sivan is such an exciting time! This month, we remember that the Torah was received on Mount Sinai for the Israelites and that we as believers received the power of the Holy Spirit at Pentecost.

Recently, the Lord took me into an ascension place with Him. He reminded me how important it is for His Church to maintain their position of ascension with Him. The apostle John tells us in

Revelation 4:1 (NKJV), *"After these things I looked, and behold a door standing open in heaven. And the first voice which I heard was like a trumpet speaking with me, saying, 'Come up here, and I will show you things which must take place after this.'"*

I want to remind you to come up to where God is. We know that when the disciples received the baptism of the Holy Spirit, they were in the Upper Room (Acts 2). We must position ourselves "up" with Him. It is in this place that we have protection, covering, connection, power, the ability to access the glory realms, and the power of the Lord that can change environments. You have access to live in these realms every day by faith, so endeavor to do so! If you are having trouble doing this, simply ask the Lord and He will help you reposition yourself by faith.

SIVAN 5

Another thing we should remember this month is found in Hebrews 12:18-29. Mount Zion is called the heavenly Jerusalem, *"where the myriad of angels dwell in joyful assembly."* God is calling us to come up to Mount Zion. Our place is to be on this mountain, not with an earthly perspective but with a supernatural one. Though shaking may continue on this earth, we need to stay in the place that He has called us to be. Meet with Him in your upper room and go deeper with Christ. You are just a visitor here on earth. The Lord has placed His power and presence right in your spirit, which is housed in your earthly body. Cultivate His presence and watch Him change your environment.

I see supernatural provision coming down from Heaven. I see great things being released into the earth, and I'm praying for you, that you too will receive supernatural provision. That the vats of Heaven will be released and gold and silver will come to you, and wine! I see wine being poured out as a symbol of opportunities coming to you, in the mighty name of Jesus!

We are approaching the Feast of Shavout tomorrow and this is a time in accordance with Deuteronomy 16:16-18 (NIV) which reads: *"Three times a year all your men must appear before the Lord your God at the place he will choose: at the Festival of Unleavened Bread* [Passover], *the Festival of Weeks* [Pentecost] *and the Festival of Tabernacles. No one should appear before the Lord empty-handed: Each of you must bring a gift in proportion to the way the Lord your God has blessed you."*

Give the Lord what is due Him. Render Him praise! Share this word with a friend and bless someone today!

SIVAN 6

Historically this is the second Feast of the year called the Feast of Shavout or Festival of Weeks which 49 days after the Exodus. *Shavout* means *weeks* or *oath*. The Hebrews took an oath to obey God as a chosen people. Today begins *Sefirat HaOmer* a time of reflection to receive the Torah. It is now 49 days since Passover or the Counting of the Omer. This marks the conclusion of the Counting of the Omer.

Historically this is also called *Atzaret Pesach,* which means a day of redemption for the Jewish people because this marks the day they received the Torah or Law of God. Historically this is the day Moses reascended Sinai for 40 days to get the rest of the Torah. (See Exodus 20:1-17.)

This is also ten days after Ascension Day on the Christian calendar. This is also Pentecost on the Christian calendar when the promised Holy Spirit or *Ruach Ha-Kodesh* was given to those who waited in the upper room.

Historically today was the death of King David.

Right now we are in the Hebrew month of Sivan, ending the Feast of Shavuot and nearing the Feast of Pentecost (starting on May 23rd). At the Feast of Shavuot, the Jews waited at Mount Sinai in dedication and consecration. It was a very important time. The Lord spoke to them about setting themselves apart. He was going to meet the people and reveal His fullness to them in the Torah (Exodus 19). For Christians, this is a time to remember the God-fearing Jews who went to the upper room and waited on the Holy Spirit to come. He came during the Feast of Pentecost and they received the fullness of the Holy Spirit and began speaking in other tongues.

The Feast of Pentecost took place in Acts 2 after Jesus had resurrected and ascended. Not only did He send the Holy Spirit, the Comforter and the Fullness of God, to be with those in the upper room. He sent the Holy Spirit for you! He sent the Holy Spirit for those who believe in Jesus as Lord and Savior and waited for the power and presence of the Holy Spirit.

SIVAN 7

Historically the Feast of Shavout or Festival of Weeks continues today. Historically this was the day that Moses was found in the water as a baby when he was 3 months old and brought to live in the house of Pharaoh.

In both Exodus and Acts we read that the Lord came to speak to those whom He had called, set apart, anointed and appointed. You are called to be a Kingdom priest and a holy nation. God has written His laws on your heart, mind, and soul. You are called, set apart, anointed, and appointed. When you believe in Jesus as your Lord and Savior, He then deposits His Holy Spirit inside you. At this moment you have *dunamis* power, the power that comes from *kratos* power, *the sovereign dominion power of God*.

Remember, the will of God was accomplished when Jesus died, was buried and then resurrected. The dominion of sin was broken, and now you are positioned to receive the power of God, the miracle-working, *dumanis* power of God.

If you haven't already, choose today to believe in Jesus as your Lord and Savior. Confess your sins and receive His forgiveness. Then take time this week to consecrate yourself. Position and set yourself apart to be in a place of complete dedication to the Lord. Jesus is the Passover Lamb, and by His shed blood you are saved, healed, redeemed, and forgiven. You are called to receive the power and the presence of the Holy Spirit!

Share this with a friend who you want to experience this powerful season of Holy Spirit impartation!

SIVAN 8

We just passed through the Feast of Pentecost, which is also known as the Feast of Shavuot. This is a special time for the Jewish people, a celebration of the unity between the people of God and His Word.

For Christians, we celebrate the Feast of Pentecost. During this feast Jesus told the disciples to go to the upper room and wait. There, 120 men waited for the power of the Holy Spirit to come. Then the power of God fell upon them, and they all received tongues of fire and began to speak in other languages. This was the Spirit of God baptizing them in the power of the Holy Spirit!

Ephesians 1:11-14 (NKJV): *"In Him also we have obtained an inheritance, being predestined according to the purpose of Him who works all things according to the counsel of His will, that we who first trusted in Christ should be to the praise of His glory. In Him you also trusted, after you heard the word of truth, the gospel of your salvation; in whom also, having believed, you were sealed with the Holy Spirit of promise, who is the guarantee of our inheritance until the redemption of the purchased possession, to the praise of His glory."*

The Lord is calling His people to Himself and purifying them in holiness and righteousness. He is baptizing us with His fire and Holy Spirit, the promise of our inheritance. You can read more about the baptism by fire if you go to the prophetic revelations on Sivan 13 and Sivan 15. This whole month is a celebration of the power of the Word and His Spirit coming together.

SIVAN 9

If you have felt great loss, confusion, grief, and depression in this season, as if spiritual assaults are taking place around you, there are three possible causes.

The first one is because God is cleansing the body of Christ. When a fire revival comes, it first starts with the Baptism of Fire like we read about in Acts 2. Exodus 19 also talks about how the fire of God came with thunder and lightning on the mountain when He brought forth the Ten Commandments. Jesus Christ is your Mediator of the New Covenant, and He will unite you with God in such a way that you will no longer fear the thunder or the fire.

Hebrews 12:22-24 (NIV): *"But you have come to Mount Zion, to the city of the living God, the heavenly Jerusalem. You have come to thousands upon thousands of angels in joyful assembly, to the church of the firstborn, whose names are written in heaven. You have come to God, the Judge of all, to the spirits of the righteous made perfect, to Jesus the mediator of a new covenant, and to the sprinkled blood that speaks a better word than the blood of Abel."*

You have come to Mount Zion, a heavenly Jerusalem, and God wants to use you mightily in His grace!

SIVAN 10

If spiritual assaults are taking place around you here is reason number two.

This is a time of chastening on the Hebrew calendar and you are being chastened. Remember, you are part of God's family, and He will bring discipline to His sons and daughters. God may be chastening you to get you into alignment with Him and His Word as He shares in Hebrews chapter 12. God has great things in store for you!

At the end of this month, we will move into the Hebrew month of Tammuz, which is connected to new mantle assignments. God is opening the heavens to release these into your life. For now, remember that God disciplined the Israelites because He loved them. They were a chosen people set apart to be a holy nation and royal priesthood.

Exodus 19:3-6 (KJV) reads: *"And Moses went up unto God, and the Lord called unto him out of the mountain, saying, Thus shalt thou say to the house of Jacob, and tell the children of Israel; Ye have seen what I did unto the Egyptians, and how I bare you on eagles' wings, and brought you unto myself. Now therefore, if ye will obey my voice indeed, and keep my covenant, then ye shall be a peculiar treasure unto me above all people: for all the earth is mine: And ye shall be unto me a kingdom of priests, and an holy nation. These are the words which thou shalt speak unto the children of Israel."*

Allow God to transform you into a royal child of the inheritance.

SIVAN 11

The third reason why spiritual assaults maybe taking place this time of year is because you are experiencing a suffering of Christ as in 1 Peter 4:12-14 (NIV) says, *"Dear friends, do not be surprised at the fiery ordeal that has come on you to test you, as though something strange were happening to you. But rejoice inasmuch as you participate in the sufferings of Christ, so that you may be overjoyed when his glory is revealed. If you are insulted because of the name of Christ, you are blessed, for the Spirit of glory and of God rests on you."*

If you haven't done anything wrong, you just might happen to be stuck in the crossfire in a war between others. You may simply be in the middle of difficult situations that are taking place around you.

Listen, God will use these things to purify you and bring you to a place of knowing who you are in Christ and what He has done for you. You are being tested and purified by fire and you will come out shining like silver refined!

SIVAN 12

The apostle Peter also talks about temptations and trials in 1 Peter 1:7-9 (NIV): *"These have come so that the proven genuineness of your faith—of greater worth than gold, which perishes even though refined by fire—may result in praise, glory and honor when Jesus Christ is revealed. Though you have not seen Him, you love Him; and even though you do not see Him now, you believe in Him and are filled with an inexpressible and glorious joy, for you are receiving the end result of your faith, the salvation of your souls."*

Your faith is being tested. God is allowing you to be a living sacrifice on His altar where He can reveal more of Himself to you. No matter how the purification comes, it is with the goal of bringing you closer to Him and more in alignment with Him.

Your faith is going to shine forth more precious than gold! There are times when the trials and difficulties of life cause you to develop a greater faith. That's what God wants! He wants your faith to increase! He wants to reward you for your great faith!

No matter what you are going through, no matter what you are fighting, just humble yourself before God. When you go to the next levels, you learn another aspect of God being your Source. Focus on the good that will come out of this season. It will help you to bear up under the weight of it.

Share this with a friend who needs to keep their focus on the Lord during this time of purification as well.

SIVAN 13

God is releasing glory and a new sound from Heaven right now. Hallelujah! We have celebrated Pentecost. This was the first time in the new decade that we positioned ourselves to receive from Heaven during Pentecost.

Acts 2:1-4 (NASB) says, *"When the day of Pentecost had come, they were all together in one place. And suddenly a noise like a violent rushing wind came from heaven, and it filled the whole house where they were sitting. And tongues that looked like fire appeared to them, distributing themselves, and a tongue rested on each one of them. And they were all filled with the Holy Spirit and began to speak with different tongues, as the Spirit was giving them the ability to speak out."*

We know that the noise Paul was talking about was a heavenly sound of a heavenly release. The word *sound* actually means "fame coming to the earth." God was revealing Himself to His people and bringing them into unity. He is the famous One, and you are chosen to be a member of His royal priesthood and holy nation. A child of the inheritance.

SIVAN 14

Tonight there is a full moon in the night sky.

Now is the time for us to remember the outpouring of His Spirit and position ourselves to receive it. We are called to do the same as those in the book of Acts and go forth ministering the gospel and the message of Jesus Christ. People need to hear that Christ is the overcomer and resurrected to bring us power.

Transition is taking place. A crossover is happening. A change in our mindset from an Egypt harvest to Promised Land prosperity is occurring. We know that at the Feast of Shavuot there were two loaves of wheat bread. Not only do they represent the Jew and the Gentile, but they also represent prosperity. God is showing us that we have entered into a prosperous time, and wherever His glory and release of new sound is, new things have come.

You have to ask God to give you the new. You are called to be a victorious overcomer and move beyond obstacles and block-ades and into the new plan and purpose that God has for you for the remainder of this year.

Let me pray with you: "Father, I thank You so much, in the mighty name of Jesus. We thank You, Father, for this release of glory from Heaven. The release of power. The release of a new sound. A new sound for this decade coming just as it did at Pentecost more than 2,000 years ago. We have a new sound in this year. Father, help us tune our ears, spiritual ears and spiritual hearing, to this new sound that is coming forth so that we can recognize Your voice and strategically respond to You and what You want to do in the atmosphere. Father, we give You glory, honor, and praise. We thank You that we are all participators in this great move, amen."

SIVAN 15

You have been sent into the world as God's representative. You have His authority (*exousia* authority) and His power (*dunamis* power) combined to impact the world for Kingdom transformation. You are called to bring forth the Kingdom and cause others to come into alignment with the rule of the King. You are a "sent one" with governmental authority. You have this authority because of Christ and His defeat of the dominion of death, which opens up realms for His *dunamis*, miracle-working power, that will bring change to the nations. You also have *exousia* power, *delegated authority,* the jurisdiction of the King who is telling you to, "Go forth and conquer. Conquer the earth realms with the Kingdom of Heaven."

In Acts 1:1-8 (NIV) we read: *"In my former book, Theophilus, I wrote about all that Jesus began to do and to teach until the day he was taken up to heaven, after giving instructions through the Holy Spirit to the apostles he had chosen. After his suffering, he presented himself to them and gave many convincing proofs that he was alive. He appeared to them over a period of forty days and spoke about the kingdom of God. On one occasion, while he was eating with them, he gave them this command: 'Do not leave Jerusalem, but wait for the gift my Father promised, which you have heard me speak about. For John baptized with water, but in a few days you will be baptized with the Holy Spirit.' Then they gathered around him and asked him, 'Lord, are you at this time going to restore the kingdom to Israel?' He said to them: 'It is not for you to know the times or dates the Father has set by his own authority. But you will receive power when the Holy Spirit comes on you; and you will be my witnesses in Jerusalem, and in all Judea and Samaria, and to the ends of the earth.'"*

Just open your mouth and the utterance of Heaven and the baptism by fire is going to come forth today and upon your life! Activation of spiritual gifts in this season for God's glory on earth.

SIVAN 16

Acts 1:1-8, the passage you read yesterday, was written after Jesus's death, burial, and resurrection, but before He ascended. The word *kingdom* here is the word *basileia,* meaning royalty or a realm of royalty. It is also broken down to the word *basileus,* which means a foundation of power, the sovereign power of God. It also references things of the Kingdom that are backed by the sovereign power of God. That's much like *kratos,* the word that I have been teaching you concerning the dominion power of God.

You now live in a realm of dominion (*kratos, basileus*). That is a very important realization! With the dominion of sin, death, and the grave broken, you are positioned to live in the realm of life! You have a new identity in Christ. Don't participate in death or the process of death. You are called to bring life to every situation you walk into!

Share this with a friend, and go forth bringing life to those you meet!

SIVAN 17

Pentecost is behind us, and we have successfully crossed over into a new season! The Lord showed me that a great, effectual door in Heaven has been opened. As we access this heavenly portal, we are going to be the change in the earth that the people need us to be.

God is calling *you* to be the change. How? You become the change by staying seated with Christ in heavenly places and having a pure heart. I encourage you to get in your private space, secure with the Lord. Make it a daily activity to go to the throne room and ask Him to reveal His will and way to you. Ask Him to keep your heart pure. Ask Him to give you the baptism of the Holy Spirit and fire if you have not received this gift from Him. All you have to do is ask.

Luke 11:10-13 (KJV) reads, *"For every one that asketh receiveth; and he that seeketh findeth; and to him that knocketh it shall be opened. If a son shall ask bread of any of you that is a father, will he give him a stone? or if he ask a fish, will he for a fish give him a serpent? Or if he shall ask an egg, will he offer him a scorpion? If ye then, being evil, know how to give good gifts unto your children: how much more shall your heavenly Father give the Holy Spirit to them that ask him?"*

As you remain seated with the Lord with a pure heart, a heavenly portal will open to you and miracles will come forth. God is going to show you that *you* are the portal on earth and teach *you* how to bring Heaven to earth.

SIVAN 18

In this new season you're going to feel and sense His love for people, sense what He is doing in the earthly realms, and be able to be that change by opening yourself up first to the heavenly portal. This great heavenly portal is effectual and a place of rest. When you are resting in the Lord and sitting in His presence, you become more like Him. This is what brings change on earth. No matter what turmoil is going on, you have chosen Heaven first and earth second. This decision releases God's glory upon us and we become glory-carriers to those around us.

Heaven is waiting for you to tap into that place with Christ and get ready to be the one He uses to release His glory. Receive His love, forgiveness, and righteousness today. Position yourself to make a difference, be a shining light, and show His love to those around you who may be stressed or discouraged. God placed it in your heart to be this glory portal, and He is empowering you in this season to do His will.

SIVAN 19

Shifting and transition is here! I saw it taking place in the spirit realms. This shifting is actually quite normal for this time of year, as the Hebrew calendar rolls into the fourth month of Tammuz in just 11 days.

God is shifting His people! Many job shifts and new opportunities are taking place right now. You may have exciting things coming into your life that will cause you to feel stretched. Yes, you will be stretched! God is calling you to greater things. You'll have to stretch to access them!

Any time we shift into a new season, we must expect that a stretching will come with it. Whether your stretching comes from a financial standpoint or from opportunities that stretch you emotionally, intellectually or physically, you must increase your faith and embrace the stretching!

I see this stretching like playdough. When you pull on playdough, it stretches out. I remember as a kid pulling it and thinking, *Wow, how far can this thing go?!* Well, that is what God is doing right now. Stand firm in faith through the stretching because He is making you more beautiful every day.

SIVAN 20

Some of your stretching may simply be how well you have positioned yourself in the realm of glory, in eternal realms, and purposed to live with joy, righteousness, and peace in the earthly realm.

You may even be stretching as a result of being persecuted for the good and right things you are doing. Your enemies may be coming out to push you back. Even when it's hard, you need to make sure you respond in love. Jesus says in Matthew 5:43-45 (NIV), *"You have heard that it was said, 'Love your neighbor and hate your enemy.' But I tell you, love your enemies and pray for those who persecute you, that you may be children of your Father in heaven."*

Be encouraged today! If you're beginning to feel there are new opportunities ahead of you and you're being stretched in your faith—just go for it! This is the time! This is the season! Go for the greater. It will be worth it all!

Share this with a friend who may need to understand why they're feeling stretched today!

SIVAN 21

God is doing so much in your life and in the lives of those around you. God is bringing forth an increased faith and an understanding that you are changing addresses—from living on Mount Sinai to living on Mount Zion!

Mount Zion, the heavenly Jerusalem, is where Jesus mediates the New Covenant. Praise God for His provision of the New Covenant to us! Praise Him that we can abide in that New Covenant freely! All our fears, doubts, shame, guilt, and all that prevented us from stepping into His purpose and destiny for our lives have been removed. We have a new inheritance!

Maintain faith in His Word and His Spirit as He is carrying you into a greater territory as we approach the month of Tammuz. You will want to hang on to what you learned in this month. Go back and review some of the days so you can be familiar again of all that has happened.

SIVAN 22

The apostle Paul shares with us in Philippians 4:19 (KJV), *"But my God shall supply all your need according to his riches in glory by Christ Jesus."*

Because Jesus is our Mediator, it doesn't matter how hard or how easy your situation is today. He will provide what you need to get through.

The Greek word for *need* is *chreia. Chreia* means "employment, occasion, demand or requirement, destitute area."

To make it even easier to understand, God will take care of anything that is a necessity, anywhere you have lack, and any-place you have need or want.

So stop! Stop being concerned and fearful about where your supply is going to come from. Nothing is too big for Him to handle. Keep your eyes on His Word. Put your faith in Him, and know that He has you safely in the palm of His hand.

SIVAN 23

Historically today is the day that Esther and Mordecai sent letters to warn the Jews of the pending annihilation by Haman, which was scheduled to be on Adar 13.

Sometimes we are so focused on the challenges around us that we don't see the Lord is using these challenges as opportunities to prune us and speak to us. God wants to tell you things about your calling, employment, and the places His provision is waiting for you, so that you can follow the vision He gave you!

Hear me today: God *will provide* wherever you are in need, including feeling destitute, abandoned, or alone!

You serve a supernatural God. He will come and touch you with His provision. You don't have to know what is going to happen next. Let your faith rise up, and completely trust Him for every area of your life. You are in a perfect place for your faith in action to move mountains!

SIVAN 24

There's been a shifting and a shaking in the atmosphere, and it's continuing to happen all around us. I heard the Lord say from Zechariah 1:3, *"Tell the people to return to Me and I will return to them."* God wants to bring forth a great outpouring onto the earth. It will start with His outpouring upon our hearts.

God says, *"Return to Me."* In other words, "Put your eyes on Me. See Me. Stop focusing on what's going on around you. Get back to the place of focusing on who you are in Me. Return to Me and I will return to you." Friend, this should be our stabilizer in the midst of all the turmoil and chaos, in the midst of this global shifting and shaking we're experiencing right now.

We need to be in a place where our hearts are in deep and intimate relationship with Him. Your identity is who you are in Christ. Stand on that identity. That's who you are! That's the identity that will open pathways and release the heavenly blessings God has ordained for you! When you hold your position, when you repent and turn to Him with your whole heart, you will release your flesh, anger, frustration, jealously, and identity crisis, and you'll take on the identity He has given you in Jesus Christ. Then the blessings will come.

SIVAN 25

This is a month of covenant remembrance. We are to remember that we are in covenant with God and He is a covenant-keeping God. Covenant means you are child of the King. He wants you to rest in who He is and what He has done on the cross. All things have been redeemed and our job now is to walk as such.

Deuteronomy 8:2-3 (NKJV) reads, *"And you shall remember that the Lord your God led you all the way these forty years in the wilderness, to humble you and test you, to know what was in your heart, whether you would keep His commandments or not. So He humbled you, allowed you to hunger, and fed you with manna which you did not know nor did your fathers know, that He might make you know that man shall not live by bread alone; but man lives by every word that proceeds from the mouth of the Lord."*

The Lord is chastening us this month so we will listen and our hearts will turn to Him and Him alone for truth and provision. We want to be smarter than the enemy, so God must reveal to us what is in our hearts so we can follow Him more closely. What has God shown you this month in your own heart? Think on it and write it down. God will minister to you in this place.

SIVAN 26

As God humbled the Israelites night and day in the wilderness, as He made provision in every way for them, He was opening ways for them to understand the revelation of His word. He wanted them to live not only by the bread of provision filling their stomachs but by the precious word that proceeded from His mouth.

One way He pulled this out of them was to restrict them daily on their provisional intake. You can read this in Exodus 16. When manna began to fall from Heaven, they only could take so much for each day; and if they took too much, it turned to maggots. If they took more than they should because of fear that He would no longer provide, there were consequences.

How closely do you walk with God on a daily basis? Are you consistently challenged by a spirit of fear that says God will not provide. Think for a moment about how God might be weaning you of this fear and instead teaching you that you are a child of the inheritance and He supplies all of your needs!

SIVAN 27

In Deuteronomy 8:16-18 (NKJV) the Israelites were reminded not to forget the one "*who fed you in the wilderness with manna, which your fathers did not know, that He might humble you and that He might test you, to do you good in the end—then you say in your heart, 'My power and the might of my hand have gained me this wealth.' And you shall remember the Lord your God, for it is He who gives you power to get wealth, that He may establish His covenant which He swore to your fathers, as it is this day.*"

We are called not to say that the power of our hands made who we are or what we have, but all things come from the Lord. Because human pride holds us hostage after the fall, we are inclined always to strive for what we have. As a child of royal inheritance, you are called to receive what is given you, not strive to gain. If you would like to enter the state of rest that God calls us to enter into as redeemed children of the King, we must constantly repent of not believing God and His provision and always trying to make our own way.

Rest today and lift up all the ways you are not resting in the Lord so God can make you aware, and then remove these obstacles from you. He loves you and wants you to live as His covenant child.

SIVAN 28

God is expecting His people to get in proper position. He's done everything for us. We are resurrected in Him. Now we need to apply His truth. We need to return to Him. When we do, He will stabilize and bless us. He will send the favor and provision we need for the assignments He's given us.

Don't get distracted from the plan and purpose of God for your life by what's going on around you. Open your spiritual eyes. See through the Spirit first. Let us be people of purpose and destiny, and let us stay focused on who we are in Him. God is getting ready to promote you and give you a new mantle. Be steadfast as He leads you in these new truths for victory and assignment.

Share this with a friend who may feel as though they don't know who they are today. Be an encouragement! You'll be encouraged yourself as you do!

Embrace the good news of who you are in Christ!

SIVAN 29

God is releasing new mantles. Now that you have come through the month of Sivan you are more prepared to walk in new mantle assignments.

Prophetically this new mantle will affect your identity just like it affected Elisha in 1 Kings 19:19 (NIV), *"So Elijah went from there and found Elisha son of Shaphat. He was plowing with twelve yoke of oxen, and he himself was driving the twelfth pair. Elijah went up to him and threw his cloak around him."* Elijah's act of distributing his cloak or mantle changed the course of Elisha's life. He had to get a mental and spiritual handle on the exchange.

We read in 1 Kings 19:20-21 (NIV), *"Elisha then left his oxen and ran after Elijah. 'Let me kiss my father and mother goodbye,' he said, 'and then I will come with you.' 'Go back,' Elijah replied. 'What have I done to you?' So Elisha left him and went back. He took his yoke of oxen and slaughtered them. He burned the plowing equipment to cook the meat and gave it to the people, and they ate. Then he set out to follow Elijah and became his servant."*

Get your mind ready to walk in some new mantles and the challenges surrounding your promotion time.

SIVAN 30

A mantle can change many aspects of your life as well! You will have to learn how to walk in the new mantle. You will have to learn how to walk away from old things, even things that are good, to take on the new which is better but unfamiliar. You may have to say goodbye to the ways you used to do things and even certain relationships of the past because the new is on the horizon.

You have changed your clothes when you put on a new mantle. It is like wearing a tuxedo when you are used to wearing jeans. That requires a mind shift for a while. However, God will grow you in wisdom, stature, and favor with Him and others, and you will carry this mantle well by *Rosh Hashanah* in September-October of this year. Then you will be running with your tuxedo on.

Over the next three months, shift your mind to the Word of God. You will see that the eternal time frame has already been shifted because we are in the latter months of the spring rains, which happen in the Hebrew months of Tammuz, Av, and Elul—and that is why these mantles are coming forth. God is giving you a little taste now so you can be ready for the bigger promotion in the fall season!

Today, purpose to position yourself on a strong foundation and be ready to receive great things from the Lord! We are moving into the month of Tammuz with its revelation and challenges—and God is getting you ready!

THE MONTH
OF TAMMUZ

*This is referred to as the season of summer
and is a time of repentance.*

This is fourth month of the religious calendar and tenth month of the civil calendar.

Tammuz is named after a Babylonia god as a remembrance of the pain suffered by the Jewish people when they chose to worship false gods.

Exodus 32:7-8 (NKJV), *"And the Lord said to Moses, 'Go, get down! For your people whom you brought out of the land of Egypt have corrupted themselves. They have turned aside quickly out of the way which I commanded them. They have made themselves a molded calf, and worshiped it and sacrificed to it, and said, "This is your god, O Israel, that brought you out of the land of Egypt!"'"*

Tribe of Israel (Conventional): Reuben

Gemstone in Aaron's breastplate: Carnelian/Blood Red Translucent

Constellation in Sky/Hebrew name: Cancer/Sartan

TAMMUZ 1

Rosh Chodesh Tammuz

Tonight there is a new moon in the night sky.

Tammuz is the month when we remember the destruction of our relationship with Father God when the Israelites chose to worship a golden calf instead of the one true God.

It is characterized as a time of sorrow in Israel. The word *Tammuz* represents a Babylonian god. Israel mourned at this time as they remembered their worship of idols. They never forgot that after Moses went up on Mount Sinai and received the first tablets of the Ten Commandments, he ended up breaking them in anger because he saw them worshipping a golden calf.

As you continue to understand your new and fresh identity in Christ, these mantles will come. Now you need to start asking the question, "Who am I in Christ?" It can be easy to idolize the things God has given you, but you must keep your focus on Him, not on the provision He gives. God wants a pure and authentic heart, open to His direction and discipline. Don't forget who you are as your promotion is upon you. Let us begin this month with a heart of repentance, looking closely at our relationship with Father God. Our Father in Heaven is loving, kind, and long-suffering with us!

This month in the United States we celebrate Father's Day on the third Sunday in June. Tammuz is a month fitting for us to remember God our heavenly Father's love for us and acknowledge Him for it. Remember Matthew 6:9-13, when Jesus was teaching the disciples how to pray. God *is* our Father, and it's fitting that we declare His Kingdom, power, and glory. This is what we as a Church will grow in this month of Tammuz.

TAMMUZ 2

Many people struggle with their relationships with their earthly fathers. But you have been adopted by the King of kings. No more orphan spirit for you! He has given you so much. You are an heir in His family. You are a favored child, the head and not the tail, above and not beneath. You sit at the King's table. You have received His inheritance—His crown of righteousness, His breastplate of righteousness, and His robe of righteousness. And now you can decree what the King decrees. When you speak God's will, He comes and changes atmospheres and environments. That's powerful!

I hope you will get to know your heavenly Father today. He is beautiful, lovely, amazing, full of glory, and has great things in store for you. He has a purpose and a destiny for you. He wants to bless you, not harm you. So no matter what you are going through or how difficult things look right now, remember to keep your eyes on Him because He is a good, good Father. He is going to bring you into the land that He has promised you.

You have great favor upon your life. Rest in His favor, receive it and record it! Walk in it and speak this same favor over other people's lives. Then watch it return to you!

How beautiful it is that we can call the King of the universe our Father!

TAMMUZ 3

Historically this is the day that Joshua stops the sun in Joshua 10:1-15.

Joshua 10:12-14 (NIV) says, *"On the day the Lord gave the Amorites over to Israel, Joshua said to the Lord in the presence of Israel: 'Sun, stand still over Gibeon, and you, moon, over the Valley of Aijalon.' So the sun stood still, and the moon stopped, till the nation avenged itself on its enemies, as it is written in the Book of Jashar. The sun stopped in the middle of the sky and delayed going down about a full day. There has never been a day like it before or since, a day when the Lord listened to a human being. Surely the Lord was fighting for Israel!"*

We have even the favor of God upon us that we can move Heaven and earth to accomplish the will of God. As God fought for Israel, He will fight for you! Ask Him to move earthly things to make room for victories from Heaven.

TAMMUZ 4

God is for us! He is for you in this month of Tammuz which can be very difficult. Tammuz is the beginning of the summer months on the Hebrew calendar and many times it is a season when God works on our hearts. The enemy is fiercely attacking, but God is using it as a time to remind us of who we are in Him! You have God on your side in the midst of every storm.

Romans 8:31-33 (NASB): *"What then shall we say to these things? If God is for us, who is against us? He who did not spare His own Son, but delivered Him over for us all, how will He not also with Him freely give us all things? Who will bring charges against God's elect? God is the one who justifies."*

God is justifying you and standing with you! Continue to be holy and righteous and have a heart of repentance—and God will continue to reveal strategies this month to move you into your destiny.

TAMMUZ 5

Historically this is the day Ezekiel received a vision concerning the chariots of fire.

Ezekiel 1:1-4 (NKJV) reads, *"Now it came to pass in the thirtieth year, in the **fourth month, on the fifth day of the month**, as I was among the captives by the River Chebar, that the heavens were opened and I saw visions of God. On the fifth day of the month, which was in the fifth year of King Jehoiachin's captivity, the word of the Lord came expressly to Ezekiel the priest, the son of Buzi, in the land of the Chaldeans by the River Chebar; and the hand of the Lord was upon him there. Then I looked, and behold, a whirlwind was coming out of the north, a great cloud with raging fire engulfing itself; and brightness was all around it and radiating out of its midst like the color of amber, out of the midst of the fire."*

Fire angels were ever present in this vision. Fire angels are God's angels designed not only to help us today but also for the ministry of end-time revival. If you continue to read Ezekiel 1:25-28, we find that the glory of the Lord is revealed.

We need to understand the angels that have been assigned to us daily to help us accomplish the plans and purposes of God. God revealed to Ezekiel and is revealing to us today His great sovereignty and love for His universe as He has assigned angels to not only worship Him but to care for His creation. To learn more about Angels of Fire and this vision, I suggest you read my book, *Angels of Fire: The Ministry of Angels and the End Time Revival.*

TAMMUZ 6

In Tammuz we have the favor of God as His children. Jesus had God's favor upon Him!

Today's word is from Luke 4:18-19 (NIV), which is the same word found in Isaiah 61:1-2. In it, Jesus arrives on the scene as the Messiah and says, *"The Spirit of the Lord is upon Me, because He has anointed Me to preach the gospel to the poor; He has sent Me to heal the brokenhearted, to proclaim liberty to the captives and recovery of sight to the blind, to set at liberty those who are oppressed; to proclaim the acceptable year of the Lord."*

Jesus is our Messiah, and He has come to live, rule, and reign in the temple inside us. The Jewish people will begin mourning on Tammuz 17 to commemorate the destruction of the temple. But we, as the people of God who know the Messiah today, are not in a place of mourning. We know our Father as our Comforter, One who frees the captives and brings liberty to those in need. He is the Messiah who lives and reigns in our temple today!

Your temple holds the power and the presence of the Holy Spirit. How exciting! Give Him a praise because He has come on the scene to set you free and to use you to set others free. Today is a good day in the Lord, and we should give Him all the praise!

TAMMUZ 7

Romans 8:15 (KJV) reads, "For ye have not received the spirit of bondage again to fear; but ye have received the Spirit of adoption, whereby we cry, Abba, Father."

Today, the Lord wants you to know that He has given you an inheritance straight from Heaven, directly for you! Maybe you have never received an inheritance in the natural realm, but I want you to know—you are a recipient of God's inheritance! It is far greater!

If you receive an inheritance from a family member, you know you didn't pay the price for it. It came to you at the time of their passing, and you simply benefited from it. Your inheritance was based on relationship.

The same goes for the heavenly realms. Your inheritance is based on who God is and the covenant that you have with Him as your heavenly Father. You don't have to work for it. Jesus shed His blood to allow you to become part of the family of God and be adopted into His inheritance. It's an aspect of who He is. He wants to see you blessed.

TAMMUZ 8

Part of this inheritance is that you are called to walk in God's authority in every aspect of your life!

You are called, anointed, appointed, set apart, consecrated, and one of His peculiar people and treasured possessions. He has a special anointing being released to you so you can understand your inheritance in Christ.

In this month of Tammuz, you must understand that you are a child of the King. If you are still concerned about your identity, the Lord is saying you need to step into knowing Him and who you are in Him as your identity. You need to let go of the things of old.

God is tearing down false identities, idols, false structures, inauthentic masks that you've been wearing, and wrong things that you have allowed to build up in your life. He wants every area that you have been trying to cover up to come out into the open. God wants you to rise up, stand on His strong foundation, and be ready for this promotion.

Hebrews 12:7-8 (NIV): *"Endure hardship as discipline; God is treating you as his children. For what children are not disciplined by their father? If you are not disciplined—and everyone undergoes discipline—then you are not legitimate, not true sons and daughters at all."*

TAMMUZ 9

Historically this is when Jerusalem's walls were breached in by Nebuchadnezzar II, recorded in 2 Kings 25:3-5 (NKJV): *"By the ninth day of the fourth month the famine had become so severe in the city that there was no food for the people of the land. Then the city wall was broken through, and all the men of war fled at night by way of the gate between two walls, which was by the king's garden, even though the Chaldeans were still encamped all around against the city. And the king went by way of the plain. But the army of the Chaldeans pursued the king, and they overtook him in the plains of Jericho. All his army was scattered from him."*

If you are in a place where you feel your soul, your family, your job, your church is under siege and being attacked, it is time to stand up and fight. Put on the full armor of God and begin to actively pray and seek the Lord for a strategy. God is with you and He will deliver you! Though times get tough, He will give you His favor to surround you as a shield.

Psalm 5:11-12 (NKJV): *"But let all those rejoice who put their trust in You; let them ever shout for joy, because You defend them; let those also who love Your name be joyful in You. For You, O Lord, will bless the righteous; with favor You will surround him as with a shield."*

TAMMUZ 10

New mantles are being released to fulfill your purpose. The new mantles that are coming are assignments built upon His inheritance. A mantle is a raiment, a clothing, a covering that comes directly from God. It comes with His righteousness and His holiness.

Now is the time for impartation, for receiving His righteousness. Walk in favor, wisdom, and stature—just like Jesus did in Luke 2:52. It is yours to access. Everything that God has and is will be imparted into you. He will make provision for you in every circumstance of your life.

I declare over you today that no matter what's gone on in your life, where you have been or the hardships you have faced, you will carry this inheritance upon your life, in the mighty name of Jesus.

Share this with a friend who needs to let go of the past and start walking in their full, God-given inheritance.

TAMMUZ 11

This past week the Lord gave me a dream where I was receiving favor every day. I knew this was a word for His people. This is a time on the Hebrew calendar for favor to flow on earth. There is a portal in Heaven open now until the 17th day of Tammuz. Now until then, God will pour out His favor immeasurably upon His people for advancement of the Kingdom.

This is not unusual, as when God wants things done on earth He will pour forth His favor. Why? Because the favor of God opens doors that no human can open themselves. We know favor opened doors for many, including Esther, David, Moses, Joseph, Daniel, and even our Lord and Savior, Jesus.

Esther 2:17 (NKJV), *"The king loved Esther more than all the other women, and **she obtained grace and favor in his sight** more than all the virgins; so he set the royal crown upon her head and made her queen instead of Vashti."*

As the people of God, we need favor active in our lives because favor divinely connects us to right relationships in season to accomplish God's purposes. Our God never sleeps and He is always working. We are called to join Him in His work. We as the people of God must let favor run its course. God is releasing favor at the same time He is reminding us of what needs to be torn down as He is getting us ready for promotion in the fall when Rosh Hashanah comes.

TAMMUZ 12

Why favor in Tammuz? This is the month in which the Israelites made the golden calf out of the wealth spoiled from the Egyptians. God had given them favor with the Egyptians and they took the spoils to travel with them as provision on their journey to the Promised Land. Favor was a portal to open the spoils of wealth. Favor was God's intention and design, but because they lacked their true identity, they squandered what they received and defiled God's holy name by taking the wealth and making it into an idol.

God's Word says in Exodus 32:7-10 (NIV): *"Then the Lord said to Moses, 'Go down, because your people, whom you brought up out of Egypt, have become corrupt. They have been quick to turn away from what I commanded them and have made themselves an idol cast in the shape of a calf. They have bowed down to it and sacrificed to it and have said, "These are your gods, Israel, who brought you up out of Egypt." I have seen these people,' the Lord said to Moses, 'and they are a stiff-necked people. Now leave me alone so that my anger may burn against them and that I may destroy them. Then I will make you into a great nation.'"*

Let us stand in our redemption as sons and daughters of the Most High God and thank Him for His favor. Let us not abuse it out of fear and lack mindsets as the Israelites did during this time.

TAMMUZ 13

In the month of Tammuz, we often face spiritual warfare to defend our souls, families, land, church, our spheres of influence. We face warfare because this was a time when the Israelites had sinned and they suffered great loss for their choices. God is patient and long-suffering with us, which reveals His favor to us as His royal priesthood. Yeshua Messiah is the One who suffered in His flesh to reunite us with the love of the Father. Let us remember Him today. He bought back all that we lost in the fall of man and all we continue to do daily that is from a heart of lack and fear.

Let's read Hebrews 10:11-17 (NASB), *"Every priest stands daily ministering and offering time after time the same sacrifices, which can never take away sins; but He [Jesus Christ], having offered one sacrifice for sins for all time, sat down at the right hand of God, waiting from that time onward until His enemies be made a footstool for His feet. For by one offering He has perfected for all time those who are sanctified. And the Holy Spirit also testifies to us; for after saying, 'This is the covenant that I will make with them after those days,' says the Lord: 'I will put my laws upon their heart, and write them on their mind,' He then says, 'and their sins and their lawless deeds I will no longer remember.'"*

We find that Jesus Himself faced the most difficult of times and He offered Himself up so that we might be victorious in all we do. He redeemed all things and He is worthy! Give Him a thank offering today!

TAMMUZ 14

Tonight there is a full moon in the night sky.

In the tumultuous times we face in Tammuz, we find ourselves growing in our faith. I would like to share with you some points that will encourage you to stand in difficult times. Go back and read yesterday's Scripture in Hebrews 10:11-17.

Let us remember *forgiveness:* When we have complete and total relationship with Christ, the atoning sacrifice and the shed blood of Jesus Christ washes us clean. He writes His laws upon our hearts and will not remember our sins and lawlessness anymore. We will become properly seated with Him in heavenly places.

Let us remember *favor:* Favor is still being poured out over you from Heaven, even during spiritual warfare and tough times. Continue to proclaim, declare, and decree His favor over your life. You are a child of royal inheritance.

Favor was bestowed upon the Israelites as the chosen people, and we who are grafted in have God's favor through the blood of the Lamb, Jesus Christ.

TAMMUZ 15

Some more important points to rest in during the month of Tammuz is your positional authority in Christ, from Hebrews 10:11-17.

Let us remember that our enemies are our *footstools:* In the Scripture, we see that Jesus's enemies were made His footstool. Likewise, our enemies will become our footstool because we have been positioned and seated with Christ at His royal table. You are in complete and total relationship with the Lord. Your enemies will become your footstool, and that footstool will become your launchpad as you step into the greater things of God!

Let us remember it is about our *faith:* Stay seated and stay steadfast. Those who have been sent to buffet your flesh cannot have an effect on you. Instead, they will help keep your mind on the Spirit of the Lord and cause you to see things from Christ's perspective. Some will try to rob you of your favor and steal your joy.

But when we keep our focus on Christ, we will overcome in every area! He is faithful who calls you His own!

TAMMUZ 16

God is moving in a mighty way, and He needs you to release His glory upon your enemies. By allowing God's glory to move through you, you will be able to bless your enemies and declare good things will happen to those who persecute you. This is how the Kingdom of Heaven gets deposited on earth.

I know you've been going through some spiritual warfare. I know things have been coming at you. You feel the buffeting. But don't let that distract you! Your enemies cannot have any effect on you. No matter how hard they try, they cannot deter you from the calling God has for your life. You are an overcomer. You are victorious in every way! No matter what comes, or better said, *tries* to come—you have the victory! Encourage yourself in this; then encourage someone else today to stay the course and overcome.

Romans 8:37-39 (NIV): *"No, in all these things we are more than conquerors through him who loved us. For I am convinced that neither death nor life, neither angels nor demons, neither the present nor the future, nor any powers, neither height nor depth, nor anything else in all creation, will be able to separate us from the love of God that is in Christ Jesus our Lord."*

TAMMUZ 17

Historically this is the day of *Tzom Tammuz*, the Fast Day of Mourning, when the second breaching of Jerusalem's walls by the Roman Empire occured. The fast which continues to *Tisha B'Av* on Av 9. A Roman general burned the Torah and placed an idol in the second Temple. On this day, the Jewish people take these three weeks as a time of mourning until Av 9. This is called *"between the straights"* or *Bein Ha-Metzarim* and represents a time of mourning for Jewish people because of the many calamites in Jewish history that occurred during this time. They remember how the walls of Jerusalem were breached, the second temple was destroyed, and how they let an idol take the place of God in their lives.

Lamentations 1:3 (KJV): *"Judah is gone into captivity because of affliction, and because of great servitude: she dwelleth among the heathen, she findeth no rest: all her persecutors overtook her **between the straits**."*

I challenge you to take time to evaluate your life and see if there are any idols present. Idols are not necessarily golden calves we put on our mantels. They represent things that take our time and attention away from our relationship with God. If you find areas out of focus, retrain yourself to worship the Lord and Him alone.

Maybe you haven't believed God for something, instead you are working extremely hard to obtain it. Why haven't you used your faith in this area? What is holding you back? Are you attached to something that is preventing you from moving forward? Have you allowed fear, sadness, or confusion to rule you? Are you attached to your job or relationships or possessions more than you are to God?

Share this with a friend, and lay hold of your inheritance together today!

TAMMUZ 18

Historically, today is the day Moses burned the golden calf and judged those who made it and worshipped it.

The Lord spoke to me that in this month of Tammuz, He is bringing His people into a time of divine alignments. As the Hebrew new year or Head of the Year is coming when *Rosh Hashanah* begins as the Fall Feast season, we enter a time of double portion! This is amazing news, but this also means that

365 Prophetic Revelations from the Hebrew Calendar

God will be expanding and strengthening our current foundations so we can handle a heavier load on our lives.

When would God do this? About three months before the new year so He can tear down, uproot, and rebuild. One foundation that God is working on this month is relationships. He will shift your relationships to accommodate the weight of double portion. This means you will meet new people who God has fashioned into the plan of your life to be divine connections for this time and season. Whenever double comes, you have to be ready!

He will also release some people from your life who require too much management on your part. You may find that you're not spending as much time with some people as in the past. Instead of coffee every day, it might be coffee once a month. That's okay. Don't be nervous about these changes. God needs you to follow His lead and make new alignments for Kingdom advancement.

TAMMUZ 19

Historically, today Moses reascended Mount Sinai for the third time after judging the people for the golden calf. He then reascended Mount Sinai for 40 more days until Av 29.

These new alignments you are making this month are God's divine connections for His purposes. God is always in the process of advancing His Kingdom. Psalm 121:2-4 (NIV) says, *"My help comes from the Lord, the Maker of heaven and earth. He will not let your foot slip—he who watches over you will not slumber; indeed, he who watches over Israel will neither slumber nor sleep."* Since He never sleeps He is always changing things to move His Kingdom forward.

How will God make these divine alignments for Kingdom advancement? The Lord has been sharing with me that He will go before us as in Isaiah 45:2 (NASB). This month God wants to go before you into the new places He is calling you to advance into the new Hebrew year approaching at Rosh Hashanah. He wants to be "the One who goes before you." That word *before* in the Hebrew is *paniym,* which means "face, countenance, favor."

When He goes before you this month, He is preparing the way for Him to be your very own face, favor, and countenance—going before you in divine alignments. He will put your name on certain people's hearts and mouths so they will contact you. He will put a picture of your face in their minds so they will think of you and reach out to you. The same goes for you—as you see faces of people or hear names in dreams, visions, and prayer, you need to reach out to them because they may be part of the divine alignments God is making for you.

TAMMUZ 20

In Revelation 3:8 (KJV) we read about what the Spirit of the Lord said to the angel of the Church at Philadelphia, *"...I have set before thee an open door, and no man can shut it...."* God has set these doors before you for His purposes and no one can shut them. God will go before you through each door of divine alignment and connection.

What is another reason He would do that this month? Since this is the Hebrew month of Tammuz, historically this is when the Israelites waited at the base of Mount Sinai for Moses to come down with the Law. Exodus 32:1 (NIV) tells us, *"When the people saw that Moses was so long in coming down from the mountain, they gathered around Aaron and said, 'Come, make us **gods who will go before us**. As for this fellow Moses who brought us up out of Egypt, we don't know what has happened to him.'"*

The people were actually thinking of letting an idol or false god be the one that goes before them—thinking that the golden calf would be their face, favor, and countenance. They had forgotten their identity and were looking for something to pave the way ahead so they could follow.

Take a few moments and let God reveal to you what you are putting before Him. What goes before you as you take the land? Is it God, or your achievements and exploits? He wants to be the only true living God and Provider in your life.

TAMMUZ 21

We could misinterpret the past relationships that were designed by God for just one season, or, if those past alignments met our basic needs, then we might want to hold on to them for fear of the unknown. Responding this way means we may miss the new divine alignments God has designated for favor this season.

When we build idols, we build them out of lack. No one builds an idol when they feel they are abundant and without need. The danger this month is that we could choose to allow false idols to go before us. If you know who you are and *whose* you are, you are less likely to put your life efforts into things that are not purposeful and Kingdom focused. The Israelites revealed this; only in their lack did they build a golden calf. Only in their insecurity of who they were as a nation and where God was in all of this identity confusion did they make an idol and actually think it would be the one that had the power to go before them. They elevated a false image to go before them as their very own face or identity.

In Exodus 20:3 (KJV), the Word reads, *"Thou shalt have no other gods before Me."* This commandment means that God is to be the only One we worship. In the period of divine alignments, we must have God go before us in all the relationships we make this month. We must trust in Him to connect us to the right people for His Kingdom advancement and for His building purposes as we approach the new year. We must not hang on to codependent relationships or addictive relationships or even good relationships that take up too much time and distract us from the bigger picture of Kingdom advancement.

Let us remember this month, the same weakness that befell the Israelites could be our weakness if we are not ready to move with God by submitting to Him to be our face, which is His very own favor and countenance that will go before us. We can see amazing things happen if we ask God, in prayer, to take His rightful place in our hearts and go before us so that we can follow Him strongly into the Hebrew new year at *Rosh Hashanah*.

TAMMUZ 22

Over the last few days, we have talked about the time frame known as Between the Straights, and how the Jews use it to remember how they worshipped idols, how the walls of Jerusalem were breached, and how the first and second temples were destroyed. The destruction of the temples meant that no more sacrifices could be made there.

What does all of this mean for you? When Christ's body was broken and His blood was shed, He gave you complete access to the forgiveness of sins. All you have to do is receive Jesus as your Lord and Savior. Then you become a living sanctuary, a temple of the Holy Spirit and a place for Jesus to dwell. He is the *One* true official sacrifice who cleans our hearts and souls.

Give your life to Yeshua today! If you have not already done so, simply ask the Lord Jesus for forgiveness of your sins and He will forgive you and come to live in your heart! Pray: "Lord Jesus, please forgive me of my sins and mistakes. I am sorry that I went my own way. I want to start fresh and new with a personal relationship with You. Please come into my heart as I surrender myself to You, Yeshua, today."

Maybe you have prayed that prayer before, if so, then just pray it again as you recommit your life to Him.

TAMMUZ 23

Take the next couple of days to really look at what you worship. Is there something you are worshipping more than God? Has your temple been breached? Are your borders—the ones that are supposed to protect you from evil—compromised?

The good news is that your temple can be rebuilt. Think about it! Before something can be rebuilt, it first has to be broken down. This is why I encourage you to do a soul detox. A soul detox is when you identify anything unhealthy that is in your mind, will, and emotions and remove it. You are called to keep your temple clean, holy, and righteous. By the power of the Holy Spirit, you serve and enjoy relationship with the living God!

If you have been bound by negative thoughts, fears, anxiety, depression, and worry, if you have allowed the enemy to gain control of your temple, remember Matthew 6:24 (NIV): *"No one can serve two masters. Either you will hate the one and love the other, or you will be devoted to the one and despise the other. You cannot serve both God and money."* The word *master* in our passage is the Greek word *kurios*, which means "supreme authority." Only God should have supreme authority in your life.

When you take time to examine yourself, you may find out that you have been serving things that are not of God. You can do a weekly detox by observing Shabbat (a day of rest) once a week. Take the time to pray, study, and meditate on the Word of God. If the Lord leads you to include fasting, then fast. It will draw you closer to Him.

Share this with a friend who may need you to walk with them through the detox process.

TAMMUZ 24

Just as the Jews take this month to reflect, you also need to evaluate your life and see if you have erected any idols that you need to repent of and tear down. God doesn't want you to dwell in your sin. He wants you to be repentant.

God is preparing your heart. He is allowing this time of pruning and purification to happen. Maybe you feel that things are getting cut out of your life or that the vision you had is changing. Know that the challenge you feel is really God drawing you back to Himself.

Take this time to ask, "What is it, Father, that I need to change in my life? Where have I been unfaithful to You? Where have I been worshipping other idols? Where have I been doing things that I shouldn't be doing?"

God wants to be your Source. He will provide for you, so stop putting emphasis on what doesn't matter. God wants your complete focus to be on Him, not your ministry or job. He wants you to take these summer months and realign your focus. He wants a deeper relationship with you. God is building your character so you can walk successfully under the new mantle assignments He wants to give come September!

Ask Him: "Lord Jesus, my heart is open. Let me receive this revelation. Reveal Yourself to me. Make that deposit. Let me write it down. Give me that new, fresh vision for September and for the new year." As you say those prayers, He will meet you right where you are!

TAMMUZ 25

Psalm 44:3 (NASB) says, *"For by their own sword they did not possess the land, and their own arm did not save them, but Your right hand and Your arm and the light of Your presence, for You favored them."*

There is a favor pouring down from Heaven right now. God is moving and advancing in His Kingdom and He needs you to be part of that. Are you in agreement with God to receive His favor? You must properly position yourself in agreement with Christ to receive the favor on your life. Stop looking at your circumstances and look toward God and what is happening in the heavenly realms—favor is pouring out.

Favor is part of His plan and purpose for your life. He wants to use you in His advancement of the Kingdom. The Light of God's presence and His favor are the tools that help us take territories. Do you want to take these territories? Position yourself in His presence, lift up His name and worship Him. I know you may not feel like it, but I am speaking life to you right now! Get up! Position yourself! Declare and decree His favor over your life. Favor is a shield that encompasses you and protects you from predators that come to harm you. It is a crown you wear.

Say this proclamation with me today, "God has blessed me with favor. I'm going to activate this favor by faith. I will respond to the favor Christ has given me." Now, pray this with me: "Father, thank You that my spiritual eyes and ears are open right now, in the name of Jesus. I will step fully into places of favor that You have given me. I receive Your favor coming upon me by the Word and by the blood of the Lamb, amen."

TAMMUZ 26

First Corinthians 6:19-20 (NIV) says, *"Do you not know that your bodies are temples of the Holy Spirit, who is in you, whom you have received from God? You are not your own; you were bought at a price. Therefore honor God with your bodies."*

The writer of the letters to the church at Corinth called you the "temple of the Holy Spirit." He implored you as a believer to keep your temple strong, healthy, detoxed, and properly positioned so that you can protect the Holy Spirit within you.

The Holy Spirit is the life-giving Source who empowers you to walk in step with the Lord. Remember, Jesus came and died on the cross, shed His blood, was buried, resurrected, overcame sin, death, and the grave, and ascended to Heaven for your victory— all because He loves you!

The Lord has been doing a big work on your heart lately. He has been revealing to you the breaches in your walls—your spirit, soul, and body—that protect His sanctuary because He needs you to have strong boundaries. For more information on soul detoxing and rebuilding your temple, you can get a copy of my Bible study, "Soul Transformation: A Personal Journey" at www.candicesmithyman.com.

TAMMUZ 27

Now, God does not cause breaches or breaks in your walls. He does, however, allow pressure to come, to show you where your breaches and breaks are located. When there are weak spots, you are open to the attack of the enemy. God doesn't want that for you! He doesn't want the enemy to gain entrance to your life.

Weak or breaches places can be rebuilt and strengthened. You may be required to repent or submit to the Lord for the rebuilding to take place. It might feel like large sections of your walls are being completely torn down, but have assurance that God is committed to rebuilding you on His firm foundation.

God's desire is for you to have a capacity for *more* of His Spirit so you can walk in signs, miracles, and wonders and be set up for the brand-new Hebrew year approaching at *Rosh Hashanah* in the month of Tishri.

Let God strengthen you and increase your capacity for new mantle assignments. Share this with a friend!

TAMMUZ 28

The Lord is saying today, "*the blind are seeing, deaf are hearing, lame are walking, leapers are being cleansed, the dead are being raised, and the gospel is being preached to the poor.*" This is from Matthew 11.

When John asked, "Is He here? Is the Christ here?" Jesus said, "Yes, I am here. If these things are seen, then I am here." I really believe right now that God is revealing Himself so strongly from Heaven. The vats are open and grain (revelation) is falling on earth. He is giving a new revelation of Himself that will empower you to step into your destiny.

So clearly He says, "I'm going to open your eyes to see something about Me that you don't already know. It will empower you to step out in destiny. Fast acceleration. Once you grab hold of these truths about Me, they're going to position you to run like a herald with the vision, to get out there and press in to what I have for you."

Give Him praise! When we praise Him with our eyes are open and we see Him, then we know where we are going. We get a glimpse of who He is and He reveals where He is taking us. Let's be willing to follow, willing to go there, willing to step into purpose and destiny. God is moving quickly! It's fast acceleration! Once your eyes are open, you are able to put your foot on the pedal and go quickly! God has great things in store for you!

TAMMUZ 29

This is Jabotinsky Day, an Israeli national holiday to commemorate *Ze'ev Jabotinsky* and his contributions to the modern Jewish state.

There is another dimension of knowing God. I can hear Him say, "I am going to reveal Myself that you might know I Am that I AM." That is how God referred to Himself in Exodus 3 when He called Moses to tell Pharaoh, "Let my people go." Moses said, "Well, who shall I say is sending me?" He said, "Say I AM is sending you."

The Lord is going to reveal the "I AM" part of who He is. This means you're going to feel more inclined to die to self and let God be who He is, in and through you. As He reveals Himself to you, you will discover what you need to get in alignment with Him. You're going to have to let go—even of things you like—in order to step into that place God has for you. God wants to use you and your giftings.

The I AM wants to come on the scene. Every time I AM shows up, it is so we become less and He becomes more. We have to turn it over to Him. God told Moses and He is telling us, *"This isn't about who you are, but who I Am."* (See Exodus 2–3.)

You have to die to self so that I AM can come forward. He is the One who sets the oppressed and the captives free. I encourage you today. Be filled with the faith of God, and let the great I AM do what He wants to do, in and through you. God will reveal Himself to you.

THE MONTH
OF AV

*This is referred to as the month of comfort
during and after a struggle.*

This is the fifth month of the religious calendar and the eleventh month of the civil year.

Av is named after *Menachem Av*, which means Father God, our Comforter.

Isaiah 51:12 (NKJV) reveals, *"I, even I, am He who comforts you."*

Tribe of Israel (Conventional): Simeon

Gemstone in Aaron's breastplate: Peridot

Constellation in Sky/Hebrew name: Leo/Aryeh

AV 1
Rosh Chodesh Av

Tonight there is a new moon in the night sky.

Historically this is the day when the high priest Aaron died at age 123. Historically this is the day when the wall was rebuilt in Israel by Ezra.

In the month of Av there is a struggle with the flesh, warfare, and a stripping phase that we go through to prepare our hearts for promotion that comes as we approach the next month of Elul.

Today, I saw the vats of Heaven open and I saw grain falling. That means revelation. *That means God is revealing Himself to His people.* God is bringing revelation from Heaven that we can write down and begin to develop a strategy for a vision or accomplish a plan that God has for us before the Hebrew new year at Rosh Hashanah, or Feast of Trumpets, in the fall.

Habakkuk 2:2 (NKJV) says, *"Write the vision and make it plain on tablets, that he may run who reads it."* This revelation coming from Heaven—whether you see it in a picture, whether it's from a seer's anointing, whether it is the written Word coming forth, or an impression upon your heart—you are to write down what God is sharing with you right now. Get in alignment with Him. This is the Month of Alignment! This is so He can build a strong enough foundation for you to begin running with His vision in September. This is the will of the Lord for this time.

Ask Him. Say, "Lord Jesus, my heart is open. Let me receive this revelation. Reveal Yourself to me. Make that deposit. Let me write it down. Give me that new, fresh vision for September and for the new year." As you begin to say those prayers, He will meet you right where you are.

AV 2

Revelation 4:1-2 (NIV): *"After this I looked, and there before me was a door standing open in heaven. And the voice I had first heard speaking to me like a trumpet said, 'Come up here, and I will show you what must take place after this.' At once I was in the Spirit, and there before me was a throne in heaven with someone sitting on it."*

The Lord has been speaking to me about us returning our hearts to Him. It doesn't matter where we have been, what we have done, or what we haven't done. God loves us so much. He desires that we turn to Him and ask for forgiveness. Through

Jesus Christ we are placed in a perfect and divine relationship with God. He longs for us to come up to where He is.

When we commit ourselves to Christ, we start a process of surrendering the very things that prevent us from having a deep and abiding relationship with the Lord. We lay down the cares and obsessions of this world and move toward His desire for our lives. His will is to be with each of us all the time, without us being distracted.

Rise up to where He is seated today! It's a glorious place, and He longs for you to sit next to Him there! Stay focused. Right now in the spirit realm I know that many of you are going through rough times. You're experiencing spiritual warfare. You're concerned about finances. God says, "Put your eyes on Me, not your finances, not your circumstances. I will release all that you need."

AV 3

Everything is done by faith. In Hosea 2, we find that the vats of Heaven are available for your release. God wants you to increase your faith; because as you believe His Word, He is freed to release the glory into your atmosphere and bring change! Choose to remain in Him and not allow the things of the world to infiltrate your mind. Take every though captive. Position yourself with Christ and learn to live by the Spirit in a place of peace, life, and fullness.

My prayer for you today is that you will be encouraged in the Lord. I declare that the vats of Heaven are open over you, in the mighty name of Jesus. Gold, silver, grain, oil, and wine are coming to your life. God is giving you strength to rise up, to take your seat. As you continue to follow your calling, all demonic forces, everything the enemy will try or is already trying, is under your feet. As you go where God is, you will find love, joy, peace, and His glory.

Know that God celebrates you. You are exceptionally important to Him and He loves you. You are His favorite.

Hosea 2:21-23 (NIV): *"'In that day I will respond,' declares the Lord—'I will respond to the skies, and they will respond to the earth; and the earth will respond to the grain, the new wine and the olive oil, and they will respond to Jezreel. I will plant her for myself in the land; I will show my love to the one I called "Not my loved one." I will say to those called "Not my people," "You are my people"; and they will say, "You are my God."'"*

AV 4

Take this time to remember and reflect on how the Israelites worshipped the golden calf, how Moses broke the Ten Commandments at the sight of idol worship, the destruction of the Temple (twice), and most importantly, make it a time of repentance.

You need to make sure your life is in alignment with the Lord. Lay down whatever you are worshipping or exalting above the Lord.

But what if you feel oppression? Maybe your own personal temple is being attacked right now? Maybe it's your health, family, job, or parts of your life are being tested? Do you find yourself having to stand firm and stand in faith? Is there an assault against your mind? In these times you have to remember that the Lord is sending you in *His strength* just as He did Gideon!

Judges 6:11-16 (NIV) says: *"The angel of the Lord came and sat down under the oak in Ophrah that belonged to Joash the Abiezrite, where his son Gideon was threshing wheat in a winepress to keep it from the Midianites. When the angel of the Lord appeared to Gideon, he said, '**The Lord is with you, mighty warrior.**' 'Pardon me, my lord,' Gideon replied, 'but if the Lord is with us, why has all this happened to us? Where are all his wonders that our ancestors told us about when they said, 'Did not the Lord bring us up out of Egypt?' But now the Lord* *has abandoned us and put us into the hand of Midian. The Lord turned to him and said, '**Go in the strength you have** and save Israel out of Midian's hand. Am I not sending you?' 'Pardon me, my lord,' Gideon replied, 'buthow can I save Israel? My clan is the weakest in Manasseh, and I am the least in my family.' And the Lord said, 'I will be with you, and you will strike down all the Midianites , leaving none alive.'"*

See yourself as a mighty warrior for Him and keep the faith as you stand firm!

AV 5

Have you ever wondered where God was in your life? I find it interesting that in yesterday's passage from Judges 6 we see there was a time of great sorrow and oppression, BUT GOD! He raised up Gideon. God raised him up even though Gideon saw himself as oppressed and weak. The Lord says, *"My power is made perfect in weakness"* (2 Corinthians 12:9 NIV). Praise the Lord! Do you see that? You just need to confess to the Lord when you are weak and His power will come upon you.

If you're going through a difficulty right now, just say, "Lord, I'm feeling weak. Reveal to me what I need to change, how to put things into alignment with You, and what I need to restructure in my life. Open my eyes to the things that cannot go with me in my time of promotion." When you do this, He will come, show you things, and make you strong!

He is faithful! You will come through this time of testing!

AV 6

This is a time of prayer and fasting in Israel, a time of remem-bering the destruction of the first and second temples and the breaches to the walls of Jerusalem. It is a time of sorrow. It's the culmination of the three weeks of mourning these difficulties and remembering how God is cleansing our very own temple.

I have been walking you through how to detoxify your soul these past weeks. God has been revealing idols to you, things you have placed before Him. He is vying for your attention and focus. He wants your whole heart to be completely His.

I know you might be thinking about the loss, confusion and grief you've experienced. God wants you to leave those things behind and grab ahold of the good you don't even know is coming. The Messiah lives in you. Proverbs 3:5-6 (NKJV): *"Trust in the Lord with all your heart, and lean not on your own understanding; in all your ways acknowledge Him, and He shall direct your paths."*

We must keep our thoughts on Christ and make any shifts necessary in our thinking patterns to fully trust Him. I hope this encourages you today. No matter what you have been going through, your Father in Heaven loves you! He is properly positioning you to take those next steps in your destiny. Acknowledge Him in every area of life and in every situation you face. That's not just arbitrarily saying, "Oh, I trust in the Lord." It's believing in and knowing His goodness wholeheartedly. It's having confidence that He causes things to work together for those who love Him and are called according to His purpose (Romans 8:28).

AV 7

Historically this is the day that King Nebuchadnezzar invaded the first temple. Historically this is the day civil war broke out in Jerusalem. Historically around this date might be *Shabbat Chazon* or the Shabbat of Vision or Prophecy or Black Shabbat, which is prior to the mournful fast of *Tisha B'Av* (Isaiah 1:1-27). The Shabbat dates change based on when the Sabbath is before the major fast day. Shabbat of Vision is also a day the Jews focus on their hopes of a third temple being built since the other two were destroyed. We who believe in Yeshua as Messiah, have a temple already built in our hearts that is constructed when we receive Yeshua as our Lord and Savior and then His Holy Spirit inhabits our temple.

Your promotion means that you will have passed through the mourning phase and are getting ready to step into a rebuilding phase. God wants you to commit to a rebuilding for promotion. It's a time of surrender. Let the Lord build up your spirit, soul, and body and give you a new vision, like the Shabbat of Vision or resting in the vision of a hope and future. The transition that is coming prepares you to stand on a stronger foundation based on your identity in Christ and understanding that you are the head and not the tail, above and not beneath.

"The Lord will open to you His good treasure, the heavens, to give the rain to your land in its season, and to bless all the work of your hand. You shall lend to many nations, but you shall not borrow. And the Lord will make you the head and not the tail; you shall be above only, and not be beneath, if you heed the commandments of the Lord your God, which I command you today, and are careful to observe them" (Deuteronomy 28:12-13 NKJV).

You are called to obey the commandments of the Lord, to live by His Word, and to stand in integrity, authenticity, and morality that is in line with who God is. The stripping is coming to an end for this season. It's time to celebrate that you are beginning a new journey! God is doing a new thing; keep your eyes on a new vision before you! Share this exciting news with a friend.

AV 8

Eight is the number of new beginnings, and today doors of destiny are opening. I can hear in the heavenly realms the clanking of doors and the stomping of angels. Each time the doors begin to close, the angels stomp so the doors will stay open. God is giving you keys to open doors of destiny right now.

Psalm 75:6-7 (KJV) tells us that promotion does not come from the east, west or the south, but God is the Judge and He raises up one and brings down another. Promotion comes from the Lord. This is a very special time: just about seven and a half weeks until *Rosh Hashanah!*

Destiny doors are open before you. You need to step through them. You need to ask God, "Lord, how can I get there? Who do I need to call? What do I need to do? How can I step through these doors of destiny?" You need to be bold. You need to be confident. God has prepared a way for you. He is going before you, shifting, moving, and setting up the doors that you need to walk through.

The angels are helping you by giving insight and revelation. Let's praise the Lord as He shows you how to step through and gain the promises on the other side. When one door opens, other doors will open for you. Go through this door now because *Rosh Hashanah* is coming and God needs to build on what you are stepping through right now. Go through a door of vision and hope and then see what God has in store for you!

Trust Him, believe, acknowledge Him, and stand in faith. It's going to happen!

AV 9

Historically this is *Tisha B'Av,* which culminates the Three Weeks of Mourning or Between the Straights. This is a day of fasting and prayer in Israel for the destruction of the first and second temples, which happened about 655 years apart (586 BC and AD 70, Solomon's Temple), but strangely happened on the same Hebrew calendar date.

Tisha B'Av cannot be observed on a Shabbat; if Av 9 falls on a Saturday, the fast is postponed until Av 10.

The Jewish people recite Lamentations 2:11 (KJV) to remember the sadness of this day. Close to this day is *Shabbat Chazon or Vision* as mentioned earlier (Isaiah 1:1-27).

Historically this is the day when the spies who entered into Canaan, the Promised Land, returned and gave a bad report not in faith and the congregation cried out (Numbers 13:32, 14:1).

The spies saw a vision ahead but they refused to attach their faith to it as they believed the giants were too big in the land and they could not take the land as God promised. Don't be like the spies. Have the vision that God is good and wants you to receive your Promised Land.

I know you have been through a lot lately. I have too! It's been a time of testing and trials during the three Weeks of Sorrow. Av 9 is a very solemn time, also a time to repent and ask the Lord what you may be worshipping instead of Him. It's a time to pray and fast, to reconsecrate yourself to Him and to following His will. A new wine is coming forth in the midst of this! God is bringing forth something new that will carry you into your next level of promotion, coming in Elul, or the month of August!

AV 10

You've endured this time of testing, but I don't want you to be discouraged. *You are called* to wear a mantle of splendor. Your mantle doesn't change in the trial. You are part of the body of Christ. You are the Kingdom of God made manifested on earth.

Keep your eyes on Him, stay steady and remain firm in knowing that HE is going to bring you through! A great glory has come upon you, and you are being filled with new wine, a greater presence of the Lord, and fresh glory.

The following is a Scripture passage that the Lord laid on my heart about staying in proper alignment during this time. You have to keep your focus. The apostle Peter says in 2 Peter 1:3-4 (NIV): *"His divine power has given us everything we need for a godly life through our knowledge of him who called us by his own glory and goodness. Through these he has given us his very great and precious promises, so that through them you may participate in the divine nature, having escaped the corruption in the world caused by evil desires."*

Take time today to set aside all evil desires or anything that could mess up your relationship with the Lord. Stand in the knowledge of His love and beauty. It will be a great place of freedom for you and the foundation you need to stand on His precious promises.

AV 11

Historically this is around the time when the Shabbat happens after *Tisha B'Av,* a Shabbat called *Shabbat Nachamu* or the Sabbath of comforting the Jewish people in their loss and despair (Isaiah 40:1-26).

Let's continue from yesterday in 2 Peter 1:5-9 (NIV): *"For this very reason, make every effort to add to your faith goodness; and to goodness, knowledge; and to knowledge, self-control; and to self-control, perseverance; and to perseverance, godliness; and to godliness, mutual affection; and to mutual affection, love. For if you possess these qualities in increasing measure, they will keep you from being ineffective and unproductive in your knowledge of our Lord Jesus Christ. But whoever does not have them is nearsighted and blind, forgetting that they have been cleansed from their past sins."*

When you truly come alive in Christ, you develop great compassion and remember how the Lord cleansed your heart and life. You know how to stand in the divine promises of the Lord and grow in His virtues. Determine in your heart to grow daily and increase in the attributes of Jesus.

Share this with a friend and encourage them to stand firm in their faith. The Lord will bring them through!

AV 12

Today's word from comes from Isaiah 43:18-19 (NIV): "Forget the former things; do not dwell on the past. See, I am doing a new thing! Now it springs up; do you not perceive it? I am making a way in the desert and streams in the wasteland."

God spoke to me this morning about how He is restarting things in people's lives. This is right in line with the doors of destiny that He declared a few days ago would be opening for us. I see people's lives restarting in so many ways, much like a defibrillator restarts a heart. I see in the spirit a flowing electrical current that is creating restarts in people's lives. God is giving you fresh vision and new eyes to see all the new starts He has given you.

I really believe that it is crucial for you to step through these doors of destiny. God is restarting things for you. You have to have a vision of Heaven and see things as God sees them!

Let me pray with you right now: "Father, I praise You and I thank You right now. We cry out for a restart to our eyes and heart, in the name of Jesus. I thank You that blind eyes will see and hearts will beat in rhythm with Your heartbeat again."

AV 13

Let's join in agreement together. You are going to see rivers spring forth and deserts disappear. You will begin stepping into the places God has for you. Declare that a restart to your life is getting ready to happen! Give the Lord praise!

This month of Av is referred to as *Menachem Av*, which means "the Comforter Father." Our Father is our Comforter, isn't that wonderful?

The last few days have been full of special events that characterize this new month. *Tisha B'Av* (the Day of Mourning) ended, and quickly you stepped into the official month of promotion! You may feel like you had already been promoted, and that's because the month of August is a prophetic month of promotion, but the promotion takes greater effect once you pass *Tisha B'Av* and step into your new role officially.

Have a heart that delights in God, and He will lead you in the right path! *"Take delight in the Lord, and he will give you the desires of your heart"* (Psalm 37:4 NIV).

AV 14

Tonight there is a full moon in the night sky.

During the month of Av, I want you to remember that your heavenly Father is your Comforter.

You may be asking, "How is this relative to the time of promotion?" It is relative because your promotion correlates to your depth and intimacy of relationship with your Father God.

Do you want to understand more and be able to access truth? Do you want your soul—your mind, will, and emotions—to recognize what comes to breach the walls of your temple? Do you want to know what is impeding your process? Do you want to recover from whatever intense trauma or difficulty you survived? Of course you do!

If you don't trust your relationship with the Lord or you aren't sure He is really your Comforter and Healer, let me encourage you today to confess your doubt to the Lord. He says you are seated with Him in heavenly places. He wants you whole so that you can be in an intimate relationship with Him. He will make you aware of the breaches and holes in your life so you can fill them with His Word and with faith.

You are called to have an intimate relationship with your Father, where He comforts you and causes you to step into your destiny: *"'For I know the plans I have for you,' declares the Lord, 'plans to prosper you and not to harm you, plans to give you hope and a future'"* (Jeremiah 29:11 NIV).

AV 15

Historically this is *Tu B'Av (Ḥag HaAhava),* a minor Jewish holiday of celebration of rebirth, redemption, and new beginnings after the destruction of the temple. This a special day of love when young Jerusalem women would dance with special linen in the vineyards to find grooms. Many weddings happen on this day.

During the time of the Holy Temple, this day was called "Breaking of the Ax" when firewood cutting would be completed for burning on the altar, and afterward they would break their axes in celebration and rejoicing.

Just like those dancing in love, you are seated with Christ at the royal banquet table, which is going on now! This is where God has positioned you to be intimate with the Father. Here, you are able to talk with Him. There are no boundaries and no more separation at the table. You are one with Him, so nothing can stop you from being intimate with the Lord.

Let God prepare you for promotion this month. Before you is a new season with new favor, new power, new faith and new destiny. You need to know that your relationship with God is solid and strong. You need to know that you can walk in a new level of authority. You can get new pillars that will hold your house, your temple, in such a way that you will be able to live out the plan, purpose, and destiny God has for you.

God is saying to you today, "Listen, child, I have promoted you." In the spirit realm, you are seated higher than you were last year. You now have access to a higher level of the knowledge of God, His presence, and His glory. The fullness of your promotion will be realized in the brand-new Hebrew year on *Rosh Hashanah*. Get ready to see amazing things happen and your life bring glory and honor to God in a greater way!

AV 16

Be encouraged today—God is restarting your life! We have been speaking about doors of destiny opening and how the restart is beginning right now. I saw in the spirit realm tectonic plates that are moving, geographical plates around the world are shifting. That means God is shaking foundations right now.

Whenever foundations are shaken, we can get fearful and not know which direction to go. Psalm 23:3 (NKJV) says, *"He restores your soul. He leads you in the paths of righteousness for His name's sake."* No matter the warfare that is against your life, it is normal. When there is a restart or new doors open, spirits of deception come and spiritual warfare takes place.

You must stay resolute, remembering the Lord is your Shepherd, you shall not want. He leads you beside still waters. Though you may walk through the valley of the shadow of death, fear no evil, because He is with you.

Rest in His Spirit today. God will guide you step by step. Do not fear if you don't have all the answers right now while your foundation is shifting. God will lift you up higher and place you on a stronger foundation. Read Psalm 23 and be encouraged today.

God is not only restoring you, He is restarting you!

AV 17

Today, the Lord shared with me that divine relationships and alliances are being created right now for Kingdom purposes. He is preparing you for divine connections that will take place during *Rosh Hashanah*. God wants you to be prepared. He will connect you with people you don't even know yet, and there is a great purpose in your connecting! Now is the time to start answering texts, emails, and phone calls. Favor is coming to you from Heaven!

God wants to take you to the Promised Land, but you can't get there by yourself. You need comrades! Ecclesiastes 4:12 (NASB) says, *"a cord of three strands is not quickly torn apart."* We as the body of Christ, are being positioned alongside people who will help us cross the finish line. Stand strong. Continue to press toward what God has for you. He has great things ahead and is ready to connect you with some new opportunities that involve these divine relationships.

I challenge you to get in the game and trust God!

Pray this with me: "Father, I thank You that You will open my spiritual eyes and ears. Enhance my spiritual senses so I know where You are working and I can join the divine relationships that You have set up. Thank You for bringing people who can communicate, encourage, sharpen, and move me forward. Thank You in advance for financial blessings and all kinds of great things that will come from these divine relationships. Lord, I praise and thank You for them right now in Jesus's name, amen."

It's going to be a great day! God has some great people for you to meet.

AV 18

A transition time is here. You may have continued to feel a crushing, pulverization, or even a heaviness. Or you may still be going through a difficult time. It's okay if you're feeling this way. A transition can also be difficult or feel like a crushing time.

After the transition, trial or crushing comes, so you now have to rethink how you are going to make changes, live your life, and determine what God is calling you to do. There can be many questions, but one thing is certain—you must abide in Him.

John 15:1-5 (NKJV) says, *"I am the true vine, and My Father is the vinedresser. Every branch in Me that does not bear fruit He takes away; and every branch that bears fruit He prunes, that it may bear more fruit. You are already clean because of the word which I have spoken to you. Abide in Me, and I in you. As the branch cannot bear fruit of itself, unless it abides in the vine, neither can you, unless you abide in Me. I am the vine, you are the branches. He who abides in Me, and I in him, bears much fruit; for without Me you can do nothing."*

When we abide in Him in that love relationship, He bears fruit through us! Yield yourself to Him today!

AV 19

Abiding in Him is a very important truth that you need to grasp from the passage in John 15. Abiding in the vine, the Lord, is necessary if you want to see amazing results happen during this transition time. Just like physical branches get purged, you may be experiencing a time when things have been cut back and purged. It hurts. But no matter what emotional battle you are fighting, whether it was anger, frustration, discouragement, depression, or oppression, you cannot disconnect yourself from the Lord.

Instead, allow this to be a time of repentance and ask the Lord to reinstate His divine nature in you. Staying connected allows you to receive nutrients from the true vine, Jesus. Tell Him, "Lord, I've been through this crushing, but I want to abide in You. I want to get closer to You. I want to hear Your voice. Give me the knowledge I need for this time of transition. Amen."

This is so vitally important because intimacy and a relationship with the Lord is the only thing that will help you walk through this transition time.

Stay encouraged! A new wine and a new birth are breaking through and coming forth! This will take place during the promotional time on or around August 1-15; and into the month of Elul, you are going to experience it! Seasons are shifting and you are properly being positioned to step into your new season!

Share this exciting revelation with a friend who needs to stay connected with the Lord.

AV 20

Today there is a newness upon us. It is a time of celebration.

The Bible tells us in 2 Corinthians 5:17 (NASB), *"Therefore if anyone is in Christ, this person is a new creation; the old things passed away; behold, new things have come."* In six weeks on *Rosh Hashanah,* the calendar turns over to the Head of the Year. God is beginning to build new foundations and start new things.

I challenge you to take time today to celebrate your life in Jesus. Thank Him and rejoice! The old things are in the past and you are a new creation in Christ. You don't have to live in the past—you can advance to the future. Prepare yourself. Build a strong foundation on Him because things are doubling—double portion comes at the Head of the Year!

Let's celebrate our newness in Christ and that He is doing new things in and through us!

AV 21

There is a real enemy roaming around who wants to stop your advancement into the Promised Land. Don't worry! God is preparing you with His strategy on how to resist the devil and stand up to the evil one!

Joshua 1:7-9 (NIV) says, *"Be strong and very courageous. Be careful to obey all the law my servant Moses gave you; do not turn from it to the right or to the left, that you may be successful wherever you go. Keep this Book of the Law always on your lips; meditate on it day and night, so that you may be careful to do everything written in it. Then you will be prosperous and successful. Have I not commanded you? Be strong and courageous. Do not be afraid; do not be discouraged, for the Lord your God will be with you wherever you go."*

The Word of God (the Bible) is one of the five pillars of our temple. The other four are the faith of God, spirit power, the love of God, and the gospel of salvation. The Word of God is what your foundation must be built upon.

Get in His Word today and begin to murmur or meditate on these truths so you can be a tree planted by streams of living water.

AV 22

Joshua is a great example of an obedient servant of the Lord. He took the Israelites into the Promised Land that the Lord gave them. He was convinced that God would make a way even though there were giants in the land.

God is taking you now into a very special place. He is strengthening you. You will be able to carry out the things that are coming in the new Hebrew year because of this time. He is getting you ready to use you in ways that He has not used you before. Praise Him!

God wants you to be strong and courageous and to meditate daily on His Word. That word *mediate* means *murmur,* meaning to say it over and over again. You have to wash your soul in the Word of God on a consistent basis. That's why meditation on the Word is so vital. Your soul needs to be positioned in alignment with God, and the way you do that is by heeding the Word of God. You must stay focused on what His Word says and what He is telling you to do!

Psalm 1:1-3 (NIV) reads, "**Blessed is the one** *who does not walk in step with the wicked or stand in the way that sinners take or sit in the company of mockers, but whose delight is in the law of the Lord, and* **who meditates on his law day and night***. That person is like a tree planted by streams of water, which yields its fruit in season and whose leaf does not wither—whatever they do prospers.*"

Share this with a friend who needs to strengthen their temple for the days of promotion ahead.

AV 23

God is repositioning His people right now, in this very moment. I can feel in the spirit realm that He is at work! He has made you alive with Christ to bear fruit and gain a new position. Remember, Ephesians 2:6 says we are seated with Him in heavenly places. As the Hebrew calendar turns to the Head of the Year at *Rosh Hashanah,* you will be repositioned to rule and reign. You need to be!

God is building your foundation right now. He is straightening things and placing you where you need to be so that you will be able to hold the double portion that is on its way to you. Double portion is coming!

If you've been experiencing spiritual warfare, if you've been drowning in fear or discouragement, take heart! All this has come because you've entered through the gate and God is repositioning you. *All* repositioning is done by *faith,* which means that you stand in faith for all Christ has already done for you. Your seat is bought by Him. You are now found in Him.

Hold on to your seat in heavenly places, stay positioned, open your arms to Him. Reposition! God is getting ready to build double on top of you!

AV 24

The time of promotion is here!

Psalm 75:6-7 (KJV) tells us, *"For promotion cometh neither from the east, nor from the west, nor from the south. But God is the judge: He putteth down one, and setteth up another."* You have already been promoted in the spiritual realm. Have you been answering your text, phone calls, emails, and letters? Have you been doing what's necessary to receive your message of promotion?

God is giving you this divine setup, and He needs you to do your part. Today, start walking in the favor of God. See those doors of opportunity open and step out in faith!

You might be asking, "Why would God do that now?" *Rosh Hashanah* is the celebration of the Hebrew new year, like our January 1 is on the Gregorian calendar. It is about to be a new Hebrew year. God is using this time to build foundations, to set you up for success, to launch you forward, and to prepare you for the new things He has for you. It's beautiful and it's amazing!

AV 25

What if you have been dealing with an attack recently? That's normal! It's normal to experience warfare in the days before and after promotion occurs. Warfare is evidence that you have received your promotion. Don't get weary. Stand in faith and stay properly positioned. God wants you to benefit from all the great things He has for you in the new year.

Let me pray for you: "Lord, I thank You for my friend who is reading this. I thank You that You have indeed promoted them already on the calendar. They are beginning to walk in new mantel assignments, new anointing, increase and multiplication. Thank You, Father, that You are holding my friend near and dear during this time of promotion. You, Lord, are preparing the way and helping us follow You into the destiny that You have for us in the new year. Lord, we give You glory, honor, praise, thanksgiving, and we worship You and You alone, amen."

Declare this with me: "I am promoted. I have received new mantle assignments, and I am ready for the great things God has for me!"

AV 26

I have a powerful word for you today. August is the eighth month on the Gregorian calendar, and the number "eight" means *new beginnings*. On the Hebrew calendar, this period covers anywhere from the last week of Av to the first few weeks of Elul. It is also the beginning of the rebuilding time in the Season of *Teshuvah* or repentance, which culminates at *Yom Kippur,* the Day of Atonement for the Jewish people, which is the highest holy day of the year.

In the month of Av, during the Three Weeks of Sorrow many were crushed and pulverized in hearts and bodies. This is just like when the temple of the Lord had been destroyed in history by the Romans and King Nebuchadnezzar.

If you felt crushed and pulverized in your body, which is the temple of the Lord, you are now coming out into your time of promotion and God is cleansing your temple and rebuilding it in the month of Elul so you can carry double glory at Rosh Hashanah, the new Hebrew year.

Gideon found himself in this very situation (see Judges 6:11-12). The Lord sent an angel to Gideon even though his identity at the moment was not one of power and might. Gideon was feeling depressed. The Israelites were under oppression. Then God came! Even though Gideon was questioning the Lord after all the amazing things He had done, in God's love and mercy He sent the message through an angel to call Gideon, *"thou mighty man of valor."* God gave Him a new identity!

God specifically spoke about how Gideon's identity had to change. He had to stop identifying with loss, tragedy, and oppression and begin to see himself as the mighty man of valor he was called to be! If he was going to come out in victory, he was going to have to renew his mind and thoughts to align with God's declaration. The same is true for you.

AV 27

Now is the time of change! If you're going to transition into God's strategies of promotion, you have to start seeing yourself as God sees you. Your identity is in Him and Him alone! You have to start seeing things as God sees them. He is rebuilding you now for double glory!

The angel called Gideon a mighty man of valor. The word *valor* in Hebrew is the word *khalil,* and it means the glory of the Lord, the wealth and resources of God. So basically, the angel was saying to Gideon, "Hey, mighty man of valor. Hey, man with great resources who carries the Lord's glory." Praise the Lord!

If you're feeling like you aren't carrying the glory of the Lord right now, all you have to do is allow your identity to begin to shift and transition for this promotion time. You are going to carry more of the glory of the Lord when you find yourself in Him! Your new identity in Christ as a person of "valor in Him" is your new foundation for your temple for the new Hebrew year!

I'm telling you right now, when the calendar turns over on *Rosh Hashanah,* the brand-new Hebrew year, you're going to walk in double glory! Yes! Double glory! There is going to be a double explosion coming. Prepare yourself! And share this with a friend who needs to be empowered to change their way of thinking.

AV 28

Do you feel like everything in your life is being uprooted, torn down or removed? I want you to be encouraged today. Right now God is doing a major restarting of people's lives in the spirit realm. A restart can be very radical. Sometimes a huge shift takes place. It can feel like you left one life behind and took on a new life. During a shift like this, our mind, will, and emotions—our soul—can't always catch up with what the Spirit is doing. This is why it is so important to lean into the Scriptures for wisdom and guidance.

Matthew 5:20 (NASB) says, *"For I say to you that unless your righteousness far surpasses that of the scribes and Pharisees, you will not enter the kingdom of heaven."* The scribes and Pharisees were avid followers of the Law, which was a set of rules, regulations, and standard expectations for serving God. But Christ came to fulfill the Law and give us a new standard! He rebuilt on something fresh: His righteousness.

It is time for a shift. I am seeing in the spirit realm great acceleration and great movement. God is putting things in order and alignment! He is calling you to step out and to let things go. Position yourself for change, because change is coming! The Lord says, "I am shifting you, moving you into the next dimension of what I have called you to do. It is time to start moving right now. Get ready."

The promises of God are "yes" and "amen." He has given you many promises, and He is going to do great things in your life! He is going to make these promises come to pass! Do not waver from what His Word says. Instead, meditate on His Word and commandments day and night. As you do, your foundation will strengthen and your anointing will increase.

Today is the day to accelerate by faith into the plan, purpose, and destiny that God has for you! Whatever was holding you back has been broken in the spirit realm, allowing you to fly like an eagle and move quickly in every way!

Share this with a friend who needs help launching into what the Lord has for them.

AV 29

Historically this is the day Moses descended Mount Sinai only to reascend again next month on Elul 1 for 40 more days until *Yom Kippur,* the highest holy day of year.

God has been speaking to me about open-heaven encounters. One of the key aspects of open-heaven encounters is righteousness. Christ's righteousness becomes your righteousness.

Matthew 6:33 (NKJV) says, *"Seek first the kingdom of God, and His righteousness, and all these things shall be added to you."* We often spend so much time seeking for and praying about our needs or the things we want to add to our lives. Our focus is on what we're going to wear, eat or drink, where our resources are going to come from, who will accept us, who will provide for us. So many questions! It's a sign of our humanity and how we feel disconnected from God in a fallen world. But, listen, the good news is that Christ gave you His righteousness. He says, "Seek Me first, My kingdom and My righteousness. I'll add all the other things to you."

Righteousness is spiritually discerned. You need to memorize all the Scriptures on righteousness that you can find. You need to focus on His righteousness in your life. But what does that look like?

When we stop defending ourselves, we begin to wear His righteousness. Christ didn't defend Himself. He remained silent even when He was accused. If you keep rising up to try to gain things in your life, then it's questionable as to where you stand in righteousness. If you can't get rid of fear, shame, and anxiety, it's questionable where you stand in righteousness. It's a sign that you feel you're not meeting laws or expectations that you have for yourself or for other people. Once you get a handle on that, you position yourself to walk in His righteousness.

AV 30

Historically this day begins *Teshuvah* or the 40 days of repentance; it begins at sundown and continues until *Yom Kippur* or the Day of Atonement, which is the highest holy day on the

Hebrew calendar, when sacrificial offerings were made in the temple by the high priest for the sins of the people.

You have been promoted and are being set up for a rebuild! Now we are getting ready to step into the month of Elul, which is a rebuilding time. We see in the book of Haggai that God spoke to Zerubbabel saying, "Now is the time to start building the second temple. The Lord needs a house where He can reside." Having a house where the glory of the Lord resides is so important.

God wants to rebuild a strong structure in you, starting with your soul, which is your mind, will, and emotions. He wants to fortify your strength, your faith in Him and His glory in you. God wants to build your temple strong!

Let us begin the journey in the month of Elul.

THE MONTH
OF ELUL

Elul is referred to as the month of promotion and soul searching.

This is the sixth month of the religious calendar and the twelfth month of the civil calendar.

Elul is named after the Akkadian word *harvest*. Elul is said to be the acronym *Ani L'Dodi V'Dodi Li*, which means *"I am my beloved's and my beloved is mine"* (Song of Solomon 6:3).

Haggai 1:1-2 (NKJV): *"In the second year of King Darius, in the sixth month, on the first day of the month, the word of the Lord came by Haggai the prophet to Zerubbabel the son of Shealtiel, governor of Judah, and to Joshua the son of Jehozadak, the high priest, saying, 'Thus speaks the Lord of hosts, saying: "This people says, 'The time has not come, the time that the Lord's house should be built.'"'"*

Tribe of Israel (Conventional): Gad

Gemstone in Aaron's breastplate: Jacinth/Yellow

Constellation in Sky/Hebrew name: Virgo/Betulah

ELUL 1
Rosh Chodesh Elul

Tonight there is a new moon in the night sky.

Historically this is the day Moses ascended Mount Sinai for the third time. Historically this is the day that Haggai received a word to build the second temple. Historically this is Rosh Hashana LaBehemot, the new year for tithing animals, one of the new year festivals according to Mishnah. During the temple times the mature animals would be tithed. This is one month before Rosh Hashanah.

Welcome to the month of soul searching and ultimately pro-motion to a new year. This soul searching, or *cheshbon hanefesh,* and repentance is when we seek God for what is next in the civil new year which will begin in month of Tishri in 29 days. It is equivalent to the Gentiles' month of December on the Gregorian calendar when we get ready for a new year.

We have entered into the very important time of the 40-days of *Teshuvah. Teshuvah* means repentance and a time when we come into the presence of the Lord, a time when we intensely look at what has been happening in our lives. We purposely go into a place of prayer, fasting, worship, and repentance, which helps us prepare our hearts for the upcoming year, which takes place at *Rosh Hashanah* or Feast of Trumpets, the beginning of the Hebrew Head of the Year.

I ask the Lord to speak life into you right now. Every part of your body is full of life. There is a strengthening taking place in your bones and soul. I believe God is rebuilding you into a house that can host His glory. He is taking you into great places and giv-ing you boldness to accept new opportunities. Creative miracles, thoughts, ideas, visions, and dreams will take place in your life. The windows of Heaven are opening for you. You will begin to see the plan that God has for you, and you will encounter His glory in a supernatural way. Your relationship with God will deepen. Your spiritual eyes and ears will be opened and your senses awakened to spiritual things.

Whenever you are promoted, there is a chance that warfare will take place, but God is moving on your behalf! Don't doubt it for one second! He has great plans for you and He will see them to completion as you continue to walk in step with Him.

ELUL 2

If you have been experiencing incredible spiritual warfare, it's because you have been promoted! The enemy brings warfare to test your promotion. He comes to challenge what the Lord has already done. God can use the warfare that the enemy brings to strengthen and reveal things to you for the journey ahead.

You may have been through tremendous pressures, trials, temptations, difficult circumstances, and economic struggles the past month. But as you've been stepping more into your Christ-identity over this past season, the Lord has been preparing you for the release of double glory!

The Bible says in 2 Kings 2:9-10 (KJV), *"And it came to pass, when they were gone over, that Elijah said unto Elisha, Ask what I shall do for thee, before I be taken away from thee. And Elisha said, I pray thee **let a double portion of thy spirit be upon me**. And he said, Thou hast asked a hard thing: nevertheless, if thou see me when I am taken from thee, it shall be so unto thee; but if not, it shall not be so."*

Here we read that Elisha asked the prophet Elijah for a double portion of the Spirit, in reference to his mantle. In 2 Kings 2:11-13, the Lord opened Elisha's eyes and he witnessed Elijah go up to Heaven. The word *see* is the word for vision. Elisha saw visions, chariots, horsemen. He watched the mantle fall. As soon as it fell, a double portion of that mantle glory fell upon Elisha. Powerful!

Ask God for a double portion of His Spirit in your life for where He is taking you!

ELUL 3

Double is coming! This is a prophetic word for you right now. God is positioning you in relation to your promotion. You need to take this time to seek God and ask Him to show you things in the supernatural realm. When you ask for the glory of the Lord to be released and for amazing things to happen, you must have eyes to see into the supernatural and have these visions released to you! That only happens by preparing your heart, understanding, and keeping your identity in Him and seeking His face.

Since we are in the season of *Teshuvah,* this is a time of repentance with prayer, fasting, and preparing our hearts for the Hebrew new year. Remember, whenever there has been a crushing or pulverization, His glory comes in! Praise God! He is doing a work to raise you up and promote you. God is getting ready to move in a mighty way and bring His double glory!

At *Rosh Hashanah,* or the Hebrew new year, you will be stepping into the tremendous things God has for you. I'm so excited! God is properly positioning you with a new mantle and has a big year in store for you!

ELUL 4

There is a lot of spiritual warfare going on in the heavenlies right now. The enemy has come to sift some as wheat. You may ask, "What does that mean?" It means that you must be ready to step into a new aspect of your destiny because you've caught the enemy's attention! There are doors opening in your life that no one can shut!

Through the enemy's attack, God will reveal those open doors. In 2 Chronicles 20:17 (NKJV) we read, *"You will not need to fight in this battle. **Position yourselves, stand still** and see the salvation of the Lord, who is with you, O Judah and Jerusalem! Do not fear or be dismayed; tomorrow go out against them, for **the Lord is with you**."* You don't need to fight this battle. God will fight it for you while you stand in faith.

I know sometimes it's difficult to stand in faith when you're being sifted as wheat. Remember what the Lord told Peter, "I will pray that your faith will not fail you." I'm telling you, if you'll just stand, some miraculous things will start happening. You must stand in faith, praise Him in faith, and lift up His name in faith. Getting into a place of faith will bring increase, in the mighty name of Jesus.

You don't need to fight this battle physically, mentally or emotionally because faith is going to carry you through. I believe that in about two days you're going to see the end of all this. You will see some great things start to happen. A double portion is coming at the end of the month when *Rosh Hashanah* arrives! God is making you aware of open doors and showing you where you need to step out in faith.

So be encouraged. Don't worry about what the enemy is doing. Stand in faith and see the deliverance of the Lord!

ELUL 5

Historically today is the day Ezekiel received a prophecy of the destruction of Solomon's Temple.

As you stepped into this month of Elul, there has been a great acceleration and shifting. You are in a phase of completion and finalization, the result of the past few months in which God has anointed, appointed, consecrated you, and set you apart.

Psalm 127:1 (NKJV) says, *"Unless the Lord builds the house, they labor in vain who build it; unless the Lord guards the city, the watchman stays awake in vain."*

God is solidifying your temple, its foundations, walls, and roof. Remember, your body is the temple of the Holy Spirit. Your family home, your church building, and your business are also temples that God will solidify for you. He is reestablishing you. Why? Because the greater glory is coming to you. This month you are going to feel more connected to God and intimate with Him.

In Haggai 1:8 (NKJV) the Lord spoke through the prophet Haggai to Zerubbabel, the son of the governor of Judah. He said to him, *"'Go up to the mountains and bring wood and build the temple, that I may take pleasure in it and be glorified,' says the Lord."* God not only wants your temple rebuilt; He wants you to step into new portals and a revelation of His greater glory flowing through you.

ELUL 6

The Lord has been challenging me in certain areas. Every person can make decisions that are going to help open these portals. I made some decisions recently, and God opened a portal just this week for me! Praise the Lord! I am stepping into promotion right along with you!

Be aware that distractions could come against you. Nehemiah faced evil forces as he diligently worked to finish the walls of Jerusalem, but he stayed steadfast and rebuilt the walls. You too have the ability to stay focused, strong, and rebuild your walls.

God wants to bless you. Be sure to take time preparing your temple for the upcoming Hebrew new year.

Reach out to a friend today who needs encouragement to prepare for the good things that are ahead in Christ.

ELUL 7

God is rebuilding and strengthening you just like He did in Haggai 1, when the prophet Haggai spoke to Zerubbabel about rebuilding the second temple in this sixth month of Elul. You may be wondering, *What would God be strengthening and rebuilding this year in me?* Every year at this time it is your temple! He wants your spirit, soul, and body prepared for the days to come.

The apostle Paul tells us in 1 Corinthians 6:19-20 (NIV), *"Do you not know that your bodies are temples of the Holy Spirit, who is in you, whom you have received from God? You are not your own; you were bought at a price. Therefore honor God with your bodies."*

"Now" is a new season! God is taking this time to rebuild in our lives. He is preparing us for the mantles that we received at promotion. Yes, a new mantle and assignment was given to you upon promotion at the beginning of this month. It is your job to carry out that assignment. Your temple of the Holy Spirit needs to be a fortified container that is conditioned for carrying this God-given assignment into the new year. Humble yourself today as He begins the rebuild on your temple.

ELUL 8

Praise the Lord for your new mantle and new assignment! He is helping you take this time to examine your temple, private home, family life, workplace, church, neighborhood, and living environments. God is lining up every area to His Word. Your temple has to be rebuilt in order for you to be strong enough to carry forth this Kingdom assignment that He has for you.

Read Haggai chapters 1 and 2. Let me tell you: this is the best part ever! After the time of *Teshuvah,* His great glory comes! In Haggai 2, it is revealed to us that once the temple was rebuilt, God promises a greater glory would come. There is a former glory and a greater glory. Keep your temple strong for the greater glory of the Lord to be revealed in and through you! You are a glory portal and a carrier of His glory. God is setting you up to shine super bright in this new year! He has given you a divine setup and He needs you to be on board with His plan.

Pray this with me and receive your new mantle assignment: "Father, I agree with You that I was promoted at the beginning of Elul. I am going to go through the next 40-day process of prayer, worship, communion, fasting, and whatever is necessary to get my temple in order and prepare myself for what is going to take place at *Rosh Hashanah*. You are taking me into greater glory and greater opportunities to share the gospel and to be moved in my Kingdom assignment. Lord, I thank You that You have a call, plan, purpose, and destiny on my life. In Jesus's name, amen."

ELUL 9

I'm here to tell you today that God has heard your prayers. I know you've had a rough couple of days of spiritual warfare, but be encouraged—miraculous provision is coming!

Psalm 91:11 tells us that He will give His angels charge concerning you to guard you in all your ways. This provision can come in a variety of different ways. Yes, financially, but also by connections and relationships. These last two may require you to pick up the phone and call whoever the Lord asks you to call or answer the phone and talk with that person. Be obedient either way, because there is a provisional aspect that is happening when you connect with God's will.

God wants you to begin to move toward His promises by faith. The angels are assisting you!

ELUL 10

Historically, this is the day Noah sent out a raven to check if there was dry land after the flood. Genesis 8:7 (KJV): *"And he sent forth a raven, which went forth to and fro, until the waters were dried up from off the earth."*

I saw a treasure box being opened in the spirit realm. Each one of us was opening a treasure box. God is positioning you for that double portion right now! Miraculous provision is coming from Heaven and angels are being dispatched to bring you what you need. They will care for you. They harken to the voice of the Lord concerning you.

Remember, provision can come through a variety of different sources. It may not be exactly what you think, but it is coming to you. It's more than just financial. It's wholeness, fullness, abundance. It's many things! It is new relationships and divine opportunities.

Praise God for His provision! Stay in an attitude of prayer. You can have confidence to enter His throne room because of the grace of Jesus and the blood He shed. Come boldly and give Him praise today!

ELUL 11

Exciting times! As we approach the new Hebrew new year and *Rosh Hashanah*, be sure to take these next few weeks to reflect on the following:

Repentance. This is a season of repentance. You need to sit down and spend time with the Lord in worship, prayer, fasting, and studying the Word of God. Now is the time for cleansing and purification. Being in His presence will properly position and align you to be a glory carrier of the Lord.

Remembrance. You might remember being crushed in the month of Av, but in Elul you've stepped into a time of promotion! God will give you strategies that are uniquely and perfectly filled with insight on how He can rebuild your personal temple.

Rebuilding. The glory of the latter house is greater than the glory of the former house! (See Haggai 1 and 2.) You're stepping into a new place. Your temple—spirit, soul, body, mind, and emotions—are being transformed. Your old self is gone, and this new you is being rebuilt! You are not lacking anything. You have prosperity of mind. You are ready for this brand-new year carrying double glory!

Decree and declare today these new things happening for you!

ELUL 12

Proverbs 3:9-10 (NKJV) says, "**Honor** *the Lord with your possessions, and with the firstfruits of all your increase; then your barns will be filled with plenty, and your vats will overflow with new wine."*

That word *honor* in this verse from Proverbs is actually the same word for "glory." Let's read that verse again, "**Glory** *the Lord with your possessions, and with the firstfruits of all of your increase; then your barns will be filled with plenty, and your vats will overflow with new wine."*

Your possessions is your substance and is compiled from your past and present. God is looking for you to give Him glory and honor now. You must keep your mindset prosperity focused because you are seated with Christ in heavenly places and have a new identity in Christ.

Renew. As this powerful new year approaches, renewing your commitment to give God your firstfruits will give Him praise and honor and glory. The firstfruits of your increase and substance are very important to the Lord, and open ways for Him to bless you. So give Him the firstfruits of all your increase today and always!

ELUL 13

Song of Songs 6:3 (NKJV): *"I am my beloved's, and my beloved is mine. He feeds his flock among the lilies."* Be encouraged: the King is in the field. In the month of Elul, the king was known to leave the royal palace and go into the field to commune with his laborers and servants.

In conjunction with the Jewish calendar, I believe that our King is going to meet you in your current place this season. I see in the heavenly realms that He has been releasing and dispatching angels with little blessings and gifts for His people. They are the extension of His presence, sent to meet you in the field. Be prepared to receive from the King! He has much in store for you!

Provision can come in many different forms; it's not just a matter of finances. God is releasing revelation, pouring out His anointing oil on you, and restoring relationships in your life. Psalm 68:17 (KJV) says, *"The chariots of God are twenty thousand, even thousands of angels: the Lord is among them, as in Sinai, in the holy place."*

When He comes down to be with us, His angels are dispatched alongside Him. I feel this so strongly on my heart. I keep seeing angels everywhere, and they are bringing gifts to people! Open your heart and hands to this revelation today by faith and watch what Yeshua does!

ELUL 14

Tonight there is a full moon in the night sky.

Song of Songs 2:16 (NIV), *"My beloved is mine and I am his; he browses among the lilies."*

Again your relationship with Lord is blossoming this month. You may be in a battle, but you are going to see the victory!

The month of Elul is a big month. God has promoted you. The enemy has pushed back, but you can rest confident that you have been promoted. You are in a deeper relationship with Him.

How do you know you are promoted? The fact you are in a battle is your sign! The enemy will push back right before a promotion and then again afterward.

I don't mean to ignore or disregard the fact that the battle is real and is really tough to go through, but it's good to know that the battle is a sign of promotion and that the battle is the Lord's. You are His precious possession. Everything He blesses you with He will fight for you to keep.

Open your heart to receive. Ask God to give you the faith to see an angel. There are angels assigned to you to bring you into the new season God is calling you to. The Bible tells us we need to have childlike faith to engage the spiritual (see Matthew 18:3). He is faithful.

Let's give Him glory, praise, honor, and thanksgiving. The Lord cares so much for us and will meet all of our needs. He is in the field and is connecting with you!

ELUL 15

Today a word of encouragement as you are pressing into your promise!

"You will not have to fight this battle. Take up your positions; stand firm and see the deliverance the Lord will give you, Judah and Jerusalem. Do not be afraid; do not be discouraged. Go out to face them tomorrow, and the Lord will be with you" (2 Chronicles 20:17 NIV).

God had given the land of Judah to His people, the Israelites. The enemy came up against Judah and King Jehoshaphat. It was a difficult time, but King Jehoshaphat went into prayer and sought the Lord. Then he called for a fast. That's when the revelation in this passage of Scripture came forth from one of the prophets.

Right now you are in a battle, but you are pressing hard into the brand-new Hebrew year and the glory of the Lord is going to be greater than it has been.

ELUL 16

Song of Songs 7:10 (NIV), "I belong to my beloved, and his desire is for me."

There is going to be a greater revelation of who God is in your life and the power you carry by faith with your new mantle. Keep your eyes and ears open to receive!

What an amazing time! You are pressing into your promise. As the brand-new year is approaching, your temple has been challenged. You are being rebuilt, stretched, and promoted so that you can boldly step into your new season with a new mantle.

I want to encourage you right now to keep going! Keep praying, studying, fasting, and seeking after the Lord. Keep that attitude of repentance in Teshuvah. God is cleansing you for more to come. Receive all He has for you!

Connect with a friend who can study with you, who will press into God's Word with you. It will be a time of faith-building for you both!

ELUL 17

Historically today is the day Noah dispatched a dove to see if there was dry land but dove returned.

Genesis 8:8-9 (KJV), *"Also he sent forth a dove from him, to see if the waters were abated from off the face of the ground. But the dove found no rest for the sole of her foot, and she returned unto him into the ark, for the waters were on the face of the whole earth: then he put forth his hand, and took her, and pulled her in unto him into the ark."*

Friend, a tipping point is taking place! God spoke to me today, "Hezekiah warning." In 2 Kings 19, King Hezekiah was being pursued by the King of Assyria. Hezekiah was scared and went to the Lord saying, "I need Your help here. What are You going to do?" God said, "Listen, I'm going to take care of this for My name's sake and the sake of My servant David." Then God dispatched His angels and they took out the whole Assyrian army—185,000 enemies! God is dispatching angels on your behalf today.

I also saw a bowl with oil pouring down from Heaven on all God's people. This oil, a consecration oil, is setting you apart for a time of consecration. God is getting you ready for next-level assignments! He will meet your needs, handle your problems, and resolve your issues. God showed me that you may be trying to hold on to things that you need to turn over to Him. Give everything over to the Lord. Place it in His hands. Stop trying to fix things yourself. He does a much better job of fixing than we can do on our own. Release it to Him!

ELUL 18

Once you give things over to the Lord today, leave them with Him and watch Him do double. God hears your prayers! Your prayers have gone up to Heaven as incense and are now being lit with His holy fire.

Revelation 8:3-5 (KJV): *"And another angel came and stood at the altar, having a golden censer; and there was given unto him much incense, that he should offer it with the prayers of all saints upon the golden altar which was before the throne. And the smoke of the incense, which came with the prayers of the saints, ascended up before God out of the angel's hand. And the angel took the censer, and filled it with fire of the altar, and cast it into the earth: and there were voices, and thunderings, and lightnings, and an earthquake."*

So we see these prayers are hurled back down to the earth for change to take place. Your change is coming. Set apart some time for consecration. Consecrate your life! You are moving into your destiny. God has great things in store for you...and it begins today!

The Lord told me today that He wants to see His people start to move quickly! He is beginning to make some fast shifts in your life. He actually showed me a picture symbolizing you holding up your staff. God is doing a new thing and causing newness to spring up in the desert for you. Great moves are happening in His Kingdom!

In Exodus 12:11, God told the people to put on their shoes, hold up their staffs and begin marching forward. The Lord is with us now. As God begins to shift things, you need to be willing to let things go. Let go of what has been holding you down, oppressing you, heavy weights that you have been carrying, disappointments and losses. None of these can go with you into the new year. You must release them now. Grab hold of Jesus Christ, the Cornerstone, and allow Him to prepare you.

ELUL 19

The Lord may even ask you to let go of some good things, even important things. He spoke that to me. He had me let go of good things for better things. I tell you, sometimes there is nothing harder than letting go of a good thing and trusting Him for a better thing. You have to have faith that the better thing God revealed to you is really going to happen.

Normally we say, "Let's get rid of things that are bad and not good." But God is saying, "Get rid of the good for something better!" Prepare yourself and be obedient to get rid of anything He tells you to. You can't carry them into the new Hebrew year anyway.

Let me pray over you: "Father, You are making us shift swiftly and quickly. Help my friend to hold up their staff, Lord Jesus, and to march forward into the plans and purposes You have for their life. Cause this person to step into the great things you have prepared in this new season. I thank You for this new day and all that's new springing up in the desert. We are going to experience a shift! Father, You just said, 'A swing shift, a swift shift is coming, and they need to be on board with Me.' Help my friend get into Your Word. Keep their mind, heart, and focus on You, that their eyes will be on the Author and Finisher of their faith. Thank You for taking my friend into greater things and leaving the past behind. Lord, we declare that the gospel shoes of peace will be on their feet, and these shoes and staff will equip them to run into the new year. In Jesus's name, amen."

ELUL 20

This is around the dates of Leil Selichot when special prayers are leading up to the high holy days in the next month, Tishri. They are said the Saturday night before the high holy days.

Tishri, Rosh Hashanah, or also known as the Feast of Trumpet, is a month of revival and excitement. God is preparing our hearts to honor the Lord at this time, therefore let us learn some principles for end-time revival.

Revival first starts with prayer: *"If My people who are called by My name will humble themselves, and pray and seek My face, and turn from their wicked ways, then will I hear from heaven, and will forgive their sin and heal their land. Now My eyes will be open and My ears attentive to prayer made in this place"* (2 Chronicles 7:14-15 NKJV).

Angels respond to the prayers of the Ekklesia, the Church of God that has governmental authority from God on earth. When we pray, Heaven moves and angels of fire are dispatched from the throne room of God. The angels receive the prayers of the people and help to distribute the answers from Heaven back to earth in the form of fire. The angels are helping to bring the revival fire on earth, and our prayers are the catalyst.

Keep praying!

ELUL 21

Revival comes when the fire of God comes to purify His people, who are ready to live as God has always desired them to live. He comes to bring purity and holiness to earth. He comes to clean it up. We first cry out in repentance and humility asking God to deal with us. The Word says in 1 Peter 4:16-19 (NIV), *"However, if you suffer as a Christian, do not be ashamed, but praise God that you bear that name. For it is time for judgment to begin with God's household; and if it begins with us, what will the outcome be for those who do not obey the Gospel of God? And, 'If it is hard for the righteous to be saved, what will become of the ungodly and the sinner?' So then, those who suffer according to God's will should commit themselves to their faithful Creator and continue to do good."*

We must be willing to let God deal with us. Purity, holiness, and righteousness are character traits of God, and the seraphim and cherubim carry these attributes from His throne to purify His world as He sees fit. In all miracles and healings there is an element of fire that comes forth through His Word. The angels are present when these things happen. Where He is, angels are. They reside with Him. They carry His fire, glory, love, justice, peace, protection, provision, restoration, purification, holiness, and righteousness. They are an extension of Him. Angels help bring the purification for the end-time revival. For more on this topic, get a copy of my book, *Angels of Fire: The Ministry of Angels in the End Time Revival.*

ELUL 22

Yesterday, I felt a shaking in the spirit world. Warfare is taking place. Foundations are shaking. It's been tough! You may feel like you're losing things—even good things! Listen, God is doing some pruning. He's cutting off what needs to be removed so that you can produce double the harvest. In John 15:2 (NKJV), Jesus says, *"Every branch in Me that does not bear fruit, He takes away; and every branch that bears fruit, He prunes it so that it may bear more fruit."* This process can be painful, but it is necessary.

It may be hard to see in the midst of your pain that God's pruning is leading to a better harvest for you. Just like a vine-dresser goes through and prunes his vines, God is pruning your life. The vine feels the pain, and so will you, but the pain is always worth the gain when it comes at the hands of the Vinedresser. He is setting you up to produce an abundance of fruit. I believe the fruit will begin to show as we enter into *Rosh Hashanah*. God is preparing to give us double as we enter into the Hebrew new year.

ELUL 23

Historically today is day when the dove Noah sent out returned with an olive branch, confirming it found dry land. *"And he waited yet another seven days, and again he sent the dove out from the ark. Then the dove came to him in the evening, and behold, a freshly plucked olive leaf was in her mouth; and Noah knew that the waters had receded from the earth"* (Genesis 8:10-11 NKJV).

Right now, we are in Teshuvah, a season of repentance. I know that you have gone through some intense warfare. You have been standing and waiting. You have seen the deliverance of the Lord and are resting in Him. While it has been an intense time, it's also been a time of purging, purification, and promotion.

The Lord wants you to remember to abide in Him. Allow Him to work on your temple. Pray and fast, listen in new and fresh ways, read the Word and seek His heart.

Jesus tells us in John 15:1-4 (NKJV), *"I am the true vine, and My Father is the vinedresser. Every branch in Me that does not bear fruit He takes away; and every branch that bears fruit He prunes, that it may bear more fruit. You are already clean because of the word which I have spoken to you. Abide in Me, and I in you. As the branch cannot bear fruit of itself, unless it abides in the vine, neither can you, unless you abide in Me."*

The new year is about to begin—allow the purification and holiness to come forth in Teshuvah.

ELUL 24

God hasn't brought the difficulties you face, but He will use them to get your attention and reveal to you what needs to be removed from your life. He prunes back and purges what doesn't belong in your life. That's His role as the Vinedresser.

When something is pruned, it will begin to bear greater fruit. God wants to bring you into a fruit-bearing season. Will you let Him? Will you keep your heart open to the Lord and ask Him to reveal His will to you? He wants to teach and train you, to draw you into a deeper relationship with Him so you can abide in Him at all times.

God wants you to be in complete and total submission to Him as you step into the new year. I encourage you to surrender your will to His will. True freedom only comes when you have completely surrendered to the Lord. As you do, you will celebrate the new year as a completely whole, clean, purified, and righteous believer.

"*In the four and twentieth day of the sixth month,*" we also find Zerubbabel and the people gathering to work to build the new temple (Haggai 1:14 KJV). As God purifies you and prunes you, He wants you to join Him in being a new temple for His glory.

Share this with a friend today. Encourage someone that they will see great increase in their divine relationship and in every area of their lives!

Since we are approaching *Rosh Hashanah,* it is a time to bless the Lord with a Feast of Tabernacles offering, according to Deuteronomy 16:16-17 (KJV): "*Three times in a year shall all thy males appear before the Lord thy God in the place which he shall choose; in the feast of unleavened bread, and in the feast of weeks, and in the feast of tabernacles: and they shall not appear before the Lord empty: Every man shall give as he is able, according to the blessing of the Lord thy God which he hath given thee.*"

Consider blessing the Lord today and giving a Feast of Tabernacles offering for the new year to the Lord.

ELUL 25

I see in the heavenly realm that God is pruning things very intently. He is cutting back the vine. He is accelerating your destiny quickly, and there are doors opening right before you. In activities or relationships that have come to a stop, God is calling you to step into something new. A quickening is taking place. Rapid thoughts, ideas, relationships, and connections are a sign that God is properly positioning you for the new year.

We all have a promise from God that we hold dear to us. What's yours? Have you been waiting for it to manifest for a long time? I believe the new Hebrew year is going to be an awesome year for you. God has some great things planned. Begin now to take steps toward the completion of that promise and the establishment of His covenant with you. Covenants last for many generations. A covenant is a promise that God makes with us, but it is also something that we must agree to and make the changes necessary to receive in both obedience and faith. It is truly important for us to cooperate with God in faith for the covenant promise to come to pass. What's your promise from God?

There may have been things that held you back from your promise until now. Start the new year by repenting of any sin, anger, unforgiveness, disobedience—anything that hinders you from His presence. God wants to restructure you. He is going to start restructuring things by giving you a strategy for all aspects of your life. These things need to be in place so that your work, home, finances, and relationships can be ready for the establishment of the covenant. God may even ask you to restart something you have given up on.

In this season, consecrate yourself, put God first in all things, and remember Him in every process you navigate through. God is calling you to make this commitment spiritually, mentally, physically, emotionally, and financially. Keep your eyes open. He intends to do something great and mighty—and you are right in the middle of it! Acceleration time is here!

ELUL 26

The Lord has been speaking to me about rebuilding the temple. Let me teach you what that means and how we should operate. In John 20:17 (NKJV), Jesus appeared to Mary Magdalene and said, *"Do not cling to Me, for I have not yet ascended to My Father."* Even though Jesus was filled with the Spirit, He didn't want anyone to touch Him until He ascended. He was Kingdom-focused.

When God is rebuilding your temple, He will do it from a spiritual perspective, not soulish. Things exist in part or completely in the soulish realm that you need to let go, respond to God on this. Your temple is to be filled with the Holy Spirit.

It is important for you to *let go*. Let go of what is not right, demonic. Don't allow evil to cling to you. Say, "NO." That may be relationships, business contacts, and/or other forces that continue to knock at your door. I know that may be hard, especially if you are already in relationship. But you cannot allow it to continue, to come in and invade the territory (your temple) that the Lord has called you to steward. You need wisdom on how to handle each situation. If something demonic begins to arise, ask God how to deal with it so you can strategically move without harming yourself or another.

Next you need to *recognize*. Recognize that God wants you to live a life of ascension. God wants you to be in a place where your temple can contain the greater glory. Once you get rid of what is defiled, impure, and demonic, you can operate in a higher place. Even though Jesus operated in the earthly realm, He always did it from a spiritual perspective. You can too!

ELUL 27

When you are associated with people and situations that are demonic or difficult—do not leave your position. Do not leave the Holy of Holies in order to deal with them. Instead, release glory into those things and *hold your position*. Remember, you are seated with Christ in heavenly places. Let God deal with all that tries to touch your temple and wreak havoc.

Finally, *keep yourself holy*. When you do this, it helps prevent you from getting into messes and traps that are set up by the enemy. Some things are really just trying to get you to come out of your private place with the Lord. Stay! Hold on to your place. Pray, intercede, stay strong. Allow God to deal with them and do what only He can do. He will release His angels and Holy Spirit. God is going to also release the glory, and then you're going to see things change.

Bonds are broken when Jesus enters your situation. The minute He comes, the evil forces can no longer stay. So stop engaging with the enemy. If you start messing around in a pit of the demonic and expect to survive, trust me—it's not going to happen. Stop allowing the enemy to mess with your compassion—he wants to entrap you in your naivety and innocence and steal from you. Yes, God wants you to be compassionate, but He wants you to operate in it from your seat next to Him in heavenly places, then you will be giving to others from God's perspective. When you follow His example, glory will be released.

Stay vigilant and don't allow yourself to get caught off guard with things that are vying for your time and your attention. They are detours. Understand that Jesus had boundaries. He was single-minded and single-focused. We have to stop living in the earthly realm from a soulish perspective. Instead live in this earthly realm from a spiritual perspective. Use the compassion that God has given you and release the glory!

ELUL 28

As we come into this brand-new year and the last few days of the month of Elul, the time of repentance, let's ask the Lord what else needs to be taken care of in our lives before we step into this next season. I know this month may have been rough and there has probably been a lot of spiritual warfare, but God has also used this time to reveal many ways He is rebuilding your temple.

Proverbs 20:27 talks about the lamp burning like a candle in our bellies. This is replicated when we light candles in our homes on *Rosh Hashanah*. Candles are lit in remembrance and as a sign that we are the light in the temples.

I saw the Lord lighting people on fire. He said, "I'm restarting fires. I'm restarting things. I'm getting people ready as we move into the new year." I want you to know that you're going to have a fresh anointing on your life. You're going to have fresh fire, fresh power. God is causing people to step into the destinies that He has for them. We need to allow God to light that fire.

Let me speak over your spirit right now: "Come alive, in the mighty name of Jesus. I declare that God will touch you with the fire of Heaven right now and you will start feeling your spirit burning. You will start to feel the overflow of joy. You are coming into the new year with new promises, new hope, a new temple being rebuilt on the cornerstone of Jesus Christ. A lamp is shining in the Holy of Holies—the lamp that emits light into the darkness. Though things have been dark, light is coming!"

ELUL 29

You are getting ready to step into all that God has for you in the new Hebrew year. This will be a year of the revelation of the resurrection power of Jesus Christ. What does that mean exactly? It means that the Lord is calling you as a member of the body of Christ to revel, rejoice, take great pleasure and delight in the resurrection event.

The resurrection event is fundamental to Christianity. Christ's death, burial, and resurrection ended the rule of sin, death, and the grave. Now His Church can walk in *exousia* power!

Exousia power is the authority of God administered, and comes from *kratos* power, God's sovereign rule.

With all that's happening on earth and our culture today, God's people are being required by their King to step up to the plate and declare and decree His majesty, His resurrection power. We are overcomers by the blood of the Lamb and His resurrection and ascension to Heaven!

If you want to see the greater glory of the Lord released upon the earth, you as the Church must declare and decree, speak up, and have *exousia* power and *dunamis* power present in your life. *Dunamis* power is the miracle power of God. It also comes from *kratos* power.

The earth needs to know that Jesus has overcome. Remember that every demonic force has been bound. "No weapon formed against you shall prosper." God has anointed you to speak about His resurrection and His power. You have nothing to fear! You will be blessed wherever you go, and the increase of God upon your life will be evident to all. Declare and decree the majesty of the Lord!

God says, "I have called *you* to be My voice on earth today!"

Will you respond to His call?

THE MONTH
OF TISHRI

This is referred to as the month of beginning.

This is the first month on the civil calendar and the seventh month on the religious calendar. This is the second major new year on the Hebrew calendar, and starts the civil calendar.

Tishri or *Tishrei* is a Babylonian name. In the Hebrew Bible it is called *Ethanim* or the seventh month from Nisan.

Joel 2:15 (NIV): *"Blow the trumpet in Zion, declare a holy fast, call a sacred assembly."*

Tishri is a new start and a time when we prepare our hearts for the promotion we just stepped into. It is a time of repentance but also acceleration in our destinies and double portion.

Tribe of Israel (Conventional): Ephraim

Note: As Joseph's tribe was split between Manasseh and Ephraim, that is Joseph's inheritance (Joshua 16:4).

Gemstone in Aaron's breastplate for Levi: Emerald Green

Note: Levi was of the original 12 tribes, but the Lord told them they had to share in the inheritance (Deuteronomy 18:1); so when we look at what month is pertinent to each gemstone, we give Levi a gemstone but not a month.

Constellation in Sky/Hebrew name: Libra/Moznayim

TISHRI 1

Rosh Hashanah or L'Shana Tova, the beginning of the Hebrew Civil Calendar.

Tonight there is a new moon in the night sky.

Today is *Shana Tova!* Happy *Rosh Hashanah!* It's a wonderful time to celebrate.

Historically this means the number of years since creation of Adam and Eve. When you come into the new Hebrew new year, it is categorized by four numbers. When this book was published, we are in the Hebrew age 5000 years plus. This means it has been roughly 5,000 years since Adam and Eve or humanity as a whole was created.

Historically this day is prophesized to be the day Yeshua Messiah will be coronated as the King.

According to Jewish tradition, this is also the day that God will write into His Book of Life the destiny of each person for one year. Then on *Yom Kippur* or Day of Atonement, the book is sealed with the verdict, but it is not final until after *Sukkot* or Feast of Tabernacles is complete on Tishri 21.

This day is called the Feast of Trumpets and also begins *Yamim Noraim* or the Days of Awe in which ten days of prayers, fasting, and repentance begin to prepare one's heart for *Yom Kippur* or Day of Atonement, the highest holy day of year to receive forgiveness on the Hebrew calendar. *Yom Kippur* is significant because on this day the High Priest would go into the Temple and sprinkle blood on the Mercy Seat.

But our Highest Priest is Jesus Christ. His shed blood for the forgiveness of our sins is why we celebrate. In Hebrew the word for feast or festival is *moed*. It is an appointed time, a season to which God says, "Come together, celebrate, and bring Me a blessing." So celebrate! Don't hold back! God loves to see His children overflowing with joy, recognizing His goodness.

Historically this is the day Noah opened the ark's covering to see if land was dry. We do not know if he sent the dove and then this happened all in same day, but it is seven days from the last dove to now and corresponds with the first day of *Tishri* for both.

This is an exciting month! Let us blow the trumpet in Zion!

TISHRI 2

Rosh Hashanah is celebrated for two days. Consecrate yourself and get ready for this new season. Remember you are a glory carrier!

Habakkuk 2:14 (NIV) says, *"The earth will be filled with the knowledge of the glory of the Lord as the waters cover the sea."* That word *knowledge* is broken down to the Hebrew word *yada*, which actually means "detection, recognition and observation." You can see, recognize, and observe through a variety of senses.

When the earth is filled, it's going to be filled with fullness and knowledge of the glory of the Lord. The knowledge, as in *perceiving with our senses* the glory, is also known as the *kabowd*, which is the weighty and powerful presence of God. This powerful presence is a result of Him being our Kinsman Redeemer.

You are a glory carrier—Christ in you is the hope of glory. God is setting you up. In 2 Kings chapter 2, we find that Elisha received the double portion of the Spirit of the Lord. He received it when he could see what was happening to Elijah in the spirit realm, when he saw the chariot taking Elijah to Heaven. Spiritual discernment is when you tap into the realms of the supernatural and have the ability to understand it. It is a special sight that will open our senses to the glory of the Lord. Ask the Lord to open your spiritual senses today!

TISHRI 3

This day is around the date of *Tzom Gedaliah* or the Fast of the Seventh month which is for the assassination of the righteous governor Judah, called Gedaliah, that ended Jewish rule following the destruction of the temple.

I hear the Lord saying, "This is a time of acceleration. Windows of opportunity are opening. Things are moving fast in the heavenly realms. New grain, new wine, and new oil is coming from Heaven."

All of this is begins to come to pass during the Days of Awe because it fulfills the requirement found in Joel 2:15 (NIV) to *"Blow the trumpet in Zion, declare a holy fast, call a sacred assembly."* We blew the trumpet and declared a holy fast. And we are returning to God in repentance and humility.

God is preparing to answer according to His promise in Joel 2:19. God is revealing our hearts and uncovering what needs to be changed. We must be still and listen for His voice, come into agreement with Him, and obey direction. Joel 2:18 (NIV) shows us that God *"was jealous and took pity on His people."* That word *jealous* is not the sinful attitude that comes to mind. It represents God's desires to spend time with us because of His deep love toward His creation.

The prophetic realms are open during this time and God is speaking. Lend your ear to Him and He will reveal many truths to you!

TISHRI 4

I encourage you to take time today to remember what Jesus Christ has done for you! Share this message with a friend and celebrate together!

Every year my husband and I practice the Feasts of the Lord, His appointed times and season, and we always respond to God's mandate in Deuteronomy 16:16-17 (KJV) which reads:

"Three times in a year shall all thy males appear before the Lord thy God in the place which he shall choose; in the feast of unleavened bread, and in the feast of weeks, and in the feast of tabernacles: and they shall not appear before the Lord empty: Every man shall give as he is able, according to the blessing of the Lord thy God which he hath given thee."

When we bless the Lord in faithfulness by following His commands, He gives to us so much more than we can ever imagine. He doubles our sowing into blessings for the Kingdom!

Consider not only blessing God by bringing yourself as a sacrifice unto Him in prayer and fasting, but also in your giving. A threefold cord cannot be easily broken.

TISHRI 5

Historically this day is around the time of *Shabbat Shuvah* or also called White Sabbath or Sabbath of Return. This Shabbat occurs during the Ten Days of Awe or Repentance between *Rosh Hashanah* and *Yom Kippur*. Only one Shabbat can occur between these dates. The reference is to Hosea 14:1-2 (KJV), *"O Israel, return unto the Lord thy God; for thou hast fallen by thine iniquity. Take with you words, and turn to the Lord: say unto him, Take away all iniquity, and receive us graciously: so will we render the calves of our lips."*

God is preparing the people of God to walk in His glory. We need the purification and glory to come and break every demonic stronghold in our lives. We have also just stepped into the Days of Awe, a time of fasting, prayer, repentance, and cleansing. This period goes from *Rosh Hashanah* through ten days to *Yom Kippur. Yom Kippur* is the highest holy day of the year. It's the Day of Atonement during which we remember that Jesus went and sprinkled His blood on the heavenly mercy seat inside the Tabernacle.

Jesus's sacrificial act of love made you holy and righteous before Him. I hope you will take time to celebrate the Jewish feasts over the next three weeks. The Feast of Trumpets *(Rosh Hashanah)* is happening right now. The Day of Atonement *(Yom Kippur)* and The Feast of Tabernacles *(Sukkot)* will happen before the end of this month. During this time there is great rejoicing, fasting, prayer, and giving. It's also a time of celebration as we come into a deeper knowledge that God is taking care of us in all things.

TISHRI 6

Take time out for four more days, until *Yom Kippur,* to continue to prepare your heart. Bless the Lord in praying, fasting, and giving. *Yom Kippur,* the Day of Atonement, is when we remember that Jesus shed His blood as our High Priest and sprinkled it on the mercy seat. This is a time of reflection. It is a time of thinking about what needs to be changed in your life. What kind of strength do you need to have? What kind of belief in the Word do you need to develop in order to really step into the fullness of the assignment God has for you?

God wants you on His team. He is increasing your faith right now so you can take more territory for Him and advance the Kingdom. Give Him glory, honor, praise, and thanksgiving! God is doing great and mighty things.

It's a new and fresh time in the spirit! We just celebrated *Rosh Hashanah* and have now stepped into our new year. Things are brand-new! The Lord spoke to me from John 14:12 (NIV), *"Very truly I tell you, whoever believes in me will do the works I have been doing, and they will do even greater things than these, because I am going to the Father."*

TISHRI 7

God is giving you a new assignment and a new mantle for the new year! He is asking you to step out and walk into the places He is calling you. You need to remember that Jesus has ascended; and because of His resurrection and ascension, you will do even greater works than He did! Take time to develop and stretch your personal relationship with Him today. Ask the Lord to increase your faith. Allow Him to position you to see Him work miracles, signs, and wonders around you.

When we stay seated with Christ in heavenly places and speak the Word out loud, the glory of the Lord will come to perform His Word. Do you know that the angels come to perform His Word too?

Understand that you need to get beyond the resurrected life. Yes, it's an important truth, and sin, death and the grave have been overcome, but we need to expand our thinking. Now is the time to live in His ascension and be seated with Christ in heavenly places. Purpose in your heart to walk totally in faith. If you want more understanding on ascension realms, pick up a copy of my book, *Heavenly Portals: How Eternity Impacts Your Past Present and Future.*

TISHRI 8

Historically today is the fourteenth day of dedication of Solomon's temple.

It is very important to stay in the Word and get strengthened. This year, if you will let Him, God will position you to rule in more areas and give you dominion. Remember, dominion is taken by faith. God is going to stretch you. He is going to ask you to do some things you have not yet done.

I feel the fire burning under my feet. God is saying, "I'm causing My people to step into destiny, step into revival fire. I need them to get out there and really step into those places of faith because I'm going to join them in the work I've called them to."

God has called you to a work, but He's not going to leave you to it alone; He's going to join you! He is standing behind you as your rear guard. He is pushing you into the places He wants to invade. You are His hands and feet. You are a holy temple and a royal priesthood He wants to use! Consecrate yourself as we get closer to *Yom Kippur.*

TISHRI 9

Nine days ago we celebrated *Rosh Hashanah* and the Feast of Trumpets. Blow those trumpets in Zion! Today we are finishing up the Ten Days of Awe, a time of cleansing and purification.

Tomorrow is *Yom Kippur* in its fullest, though it begins tonight at sundown. *Yom Kippur,* the Day of Atonement, is the highest holy day of the Hebrew year and begins at sundown on Tishri 9.

I think it's beautiful that the Lord positioned this day directly in between the Feast of Trumpets and Feast of Tabernacles. On this day, the priests would take an unblemished lamb and place its blood inside the Tabernacle for forgiveness of the sins of the people. Thankfully, in the book of Hebrews, it tells us that Jesus took

His own blood and sprinkled it on the mercy seat in the heavenly tabernacle. This heavenly tabernacle, built by the hands of God, exists today. It is eternal.

Hebrews 9:11-12 (NIV), *"But when Christ came as high priest of the good things that are now already here, he went through the greater and more perfect tabernacle that is not made with human hands, that is to say, is not a part of this creation. He did not enter by means of the blood of goats and calves; but he entered the Most Holy Place once for all by his own blood, thus obtaining eternal redemption."*

Jesus became our ultimate Sacrifice and shed His blood for you. He went to the Holy of Holies to make a way for us to be reconciled with God. Therefore, we no longer have to physically sacrifice an animal to cover our sins. He is the Lamb of God that takes away the sins of the world (John 1:29). Now we can just ask for forgiveness and receive it knowing that Jesus's sacrifice was enough to please God.

Stay intentional and focused as you finish up the final day in this period of cleansing and purification. Step into the Day of Atonement with a right heart. Allow God to come in and heal you. Let Him reveal things and renew your spirit. God wants you to be excited about who He is and how He created you—special and unique.

TISHRI 10

Historically this is *Yom Kippur* or the Day of Atonement—the highest holy day of the year to the Jewish people. They fast for 24 hours to seek God for forgiveness of their sins for an entire year. Because there is no constructed temple in Jerusalem, there is no animal sacrifice given by the high priest for forgiveness of sins, so fasting is their only way to be cleansed and purified.

Messianic believers and Gentile Christians believe Yeshua Messiah is their sacrifice for sin, so this day is a day of repentance but also remembrance of how Yeshua sprinkled His blood on the mercy seat of in the heavenly tabernacle.

Historically this is also the day that Moses returned from Mount Sinai and brought the second set of tablets and a message from God concerning the sinful worship of the golden calf.

Leviticus 23:26-29 (NIV), *"The Lord said to Moses, 'The **tenth day of this seventh month** is the Day of Atonement. Hold a sacred assembly and deny yourselves, and present a food offering to the Lord. Do not do any work on that day, because it is the Day of Atonement, when atonement is made for you before the Lord your God. Those who do not deny themselves on that day must be cut off from their people."*

The call of repentance is going forth. We are in the Days of Awe, the time from *Rosh Hashanah* until *Yom Kippur*. This is the time to come before God with a repentant heart. The apostle Paul, in Romans 12:1 (NKJV), urges us to *"present your bodies a living sacrifice, holy, acceptable to God, which is your reasonable service."* A reasonable act of service is worship unto God. Jesus shed His blood on the cross for the forgiveness of our sins. When we come to Him with a repentant heart, we just have to ask for forgiveness and He is quick to grant it.

Previously I shared that Joel 2:15 tells us to declare a holy fast. Today is a day to fast, pray, and give yourself unto the Lord. God is calling us to live holy lives. To do this, we must position ourselves before God and allow Him to come in and cleanse us. See also Hebrews 10:19-22 and Matthew 27:50-51.

TISHRI 11

Historically today is *B'shem Hashem*, which means Name of God, and is another holiday.

Did you know that God set this special time for you to remember that Jesus Christ shed His blood so you could be forgiven, saved, and redeemed? It's true! By the end of the month, you are going to be experiencing great joy! The Feast of the Tabernacles is coming. During the Feast, joy comes in abundance. Bless the Lord for all He has done and bring Him an offering!

What you're going through is a process. It's His plan and it's necessary. You are going to be walking in this joy as you have been cleansed, purified, and you take the time to remember what Jesus has done for you.

As you're faithful and do what God is telling you to do, He will divinely set you up and properly position you. God has double glory and amazing things ready to enter your life.

These Jewish feasts should remind us of our Savior and how much He loves us. The enemy comes to steal, kill, and destroy; but our God comes to bring us abundant life! He overcame sin and death, and He defeated the grave. The dominion of life is no longer the enemy's; it is yours! The enemy has been defeated.

TISHRI 12

Today, the Lord has a special word for you: God is releasing increase into the earth. Joel 2:23-32 has seven blessings of the Day of Atonement that are yours for this season. A season is separated into two six-month periods. The first season is Passover to Feast of Trumpets, called the Spring Rains of each year. The second season is from Feast of Trumpets or Rosh Hashanah, the Hebrew New Year to Passover, called the Fall Rains or double portion season. So anything we are blessed with in the Spring Rains season will double itself in the Fall Rains season.

I see this increase happening now. God is releasing the vats of Heaven upon you—new wine, new grain, and new oil are coming forth. He is releasing a double-portion blessing and financial abundance on you as you lend your heart to Him, repent, pray, seek His face, and allow Him to cleanse you. Even more blessings are available to you this season when you remember the Lord, bring Him an offering, and position yourself before Him.

I encourage you to read and study Joel 2. There you will also see that the Lord will bring salvation to those who call His name, restoration, miracles, deliverance, a blessing on your sons and daughters and His divine presence. Over the next few days we will discuss the seven blessings of the Fall Rains. Let us begin with the first two blessings.

Blessings 1 and 2 of the Fall Rains season:

Joel 2:23-24 (NIV): *"Be glad, O people of Zion, rejoice in the Lord your God, for he has given you the autumn rains in righteousness. He sends you abundant showers, both autumn and spring rains, as before* [double portion]. *The threshing floors will be filled with grain* [what has been purged]; *the vats will overflow with new wine* [seize and occupy] *and oil* [anointing, financial abundance].

Blessing 1: The double portion leads to financial abundance.

Blessing 2: Double portion leads to what is purged out to overflowing—seizing and occupying—and anointing lead to financial abundance.

TISHRI 13

Blessings 3 and 4 of the Fall Rains season:

Joel 2:25-26 (NIV): *"I will repay you for the years the locusts have eaten—the great locust and the young locust, the other locusts and the locust swarm—my great army that I sent among you* [restoration]. *You will have plenty to eat, until you are full, and you will **praise** the name of the Lord your God, who* has worked **wonders** for you; never again will my people be **shamed**" [miracles].

Blessing 3: The anointing and overflow lead to restoration.

Blessing 4: Miracles during this season.

In this passage these special words can be highlighted: *Praise* means to make a boast, to be clamorously foolish, celebrate, give glory to His name, His character and authority. *Wonder* means marvelously things have worked out, miracles performed. *Shamed* means disappointed or delayed, confounded, or become dry. *Restoration* leads to miracles; what is restored opens our hearts to the miraculous in our life; we come out of that into praise; no more disappointment or shame—walking in victory.

Receive these blessings as they are yours by faith in this new season!

TISHRI 14

Tonight there is a full moon in the night sky.

Blessings 5, 6, and 7 of the Fall Rains season:

Joel 2:27-32 (NIV): *Then you will know that I am in Israel, that I am the Lord your God, and that there is no other; never again will my people be shamed* [God's divine presence]. *And afterward, I will pour out my Spirit on all people. Your sons and daughters will prophesy, your old men will dream dreams, your young men will see visions. Even on my servants, both men and women, I will pour out my Spirit in those days* [blessings on sons and daughters]. *I will show wonders in the heavens and on the earth, blood and fire and billows of smoke. The sun will be turned to darkness and the moon to blood before the coming of the great and dreadful day of the Lord. And everyone who calls on the name of the Lord will be saved; for on Mount Zion* and in Jerusalem there will be deliverance, as the Lord has said, among the survivors whom the Lord calls [deliverance]."

Blessing 5: Seeing the *miracle* leads to the pouring out of the Spirit. People get excited from the miracle and are open to the Spirit's move.

Blessing 6: Pouring out of His Spirit on sons and daughters.

Blessing 7: This then leads to deliverance and spiritual awakening for those who come to the Lord! They who see the Spirit in action.

Take time to pray and ask God to show you the depths of each of these blessings and how He wants to make them manifest in your life today.

TISHRI 15

This day starts the Feast of Tabernacles or *Sukkot,* the third of the Fall Feasts. *Sukkot* is a seven-day celebration when the Jewish people remember they lived in tabernacles or booths called *sukkah* in the wilderness when God was making all provision for them. During this time in the wilderness crossing into the Promised Land, they lived in these booths that were so fragile and not strong enough to protect them. They had to rely on the protection of the Lord.

Nehemiah 8:17 (KJV): *"And all the congregation of them that were come again out of the captivity made booths, and sat under the booths: for since the days of Jeshua the son of Nun unto that day had not the children of Israel done so. And there was very great gladness."*

As Messianic believers or Christians, we remember that Jesus tabernacled among us.

This time for the Jews is also remembered by the four letter name for God, YHWH, which is a sequence of four consonants

Yod, Heh, Waw, and *Heh.* Each symbol is not an exact letter but a representation. God is seen through four symbols of plants or trees. The first one to mention is through the *lulav* which is a closed frond of the date palm and represents the W or V as *vuv,* as in Psalm 92:13, and this represents God's presence. The second symbol is the etrog and is called the fruit of the goodly tree in Leviticus 23:40 in which God is clothed in splendor and majesty in Psalm 104:1. Then the willow in Psalm 68:5 which means He rode on the clouds. Lastly the myrtle in Zechariah 1:8, as in He stood among the myrtles. You can read more on this at: https://www.myjewishlearning.com/article/lulav-and-etrog-symbolism/.

John 1:14 (KJV): *"And the Word was made flesh, and dwelt among us, (and we beheld his glory, the glory as of the only begotten of the Father,) full of grace and truth."*

TISHRI 16

We have now begun the Feast of Tabernacles. It comes in the autumn after the start of the Hebrew new year, Rosh Hashanah, and the Day of Atonement. It's also known as the Feast of Booths, the Feast of Sukkot, and the Feast of Ingathering.

The Feast of Tabernacles is a very special celebration. In Exodus 34:22-24 (NIV) we read, *"Celebrate the Festival of Weeks with the firstfruits of the wheat harvest, and the Festival of Ingathering at the turn of the year. Three times a year all your men are to appear before the Sovereign Lord, the God of Israel. I will drive out nations before you and enlarge your territory, and no one will covet your land when you go up three times each year to appear before the Lord your God."*

In this passage from Exodus 34, we see the Lord's specific instructions on how the Israelites are to celebrate the Feast of Weeks and Feast of Tabernacles and how three times a year their men were to appear before the Lord God of Israel not empty-handed but with an offering. Read again Chapter 2, "Sowing in the Right Season for Blessing."

TISHRI 17

Again, Joel 2 shares the seven blessings that come upon your life when you stand before the Lord with thanksgiving, praise, and gratefulness for what He has done. The third fall feast, *Sukkot,* is a celebration of joy!

This season is not about giving an offering just to get something, but to bless and honor the Lord. God says, "I am already going to give these blessings to you because of your repentant heart and your desire to honor Me." Every year my husband and I practice the Feasts of the Lord, His appointed times and season, and we always respond to God's mandate in Deuteronomy 16:16 (NIV): *"Three times a year all your men must appear before the Lord your God at the place He will choose: at the Festival of Unleavened Bread, the Festival of Weeks and the Festival of Tabernacles. No one should appear before the Lord empty-handed: Each of you must bring a gift in proportion to the way the Lord your God has blessed you."*

The Feasts of Tabernacles is coming up on October 2-9. It's the last fall feast. I want you to remember to bless the Lord during this time with an offering. An offering is above your tithe. Bless your church with an offering or bless a ministry that has made a deposit into your life. For years, I have seen great financial increase and a double-portion blessing on my life as I have continued to bless the Lord with an offering.

I encourage you, if God lays an offering on your heart with which to bless a ministry, go and do it. It is an act of obedience in accordance with Deuteronomy 16:16-17. This is a special time of the year that we can honor Him. Through your giving, you are lifting your voice to Him. You are praising His name! God is bringing you a double portion, a financial blessing, along with all the other blessings of this season. He's doing great and amazing things in your new year. Give Him honor today!

TISHRI 18

For you, it is also very important to the Lord that you come to Him during this time. It is important that you present an offering to Him and bring Him a blessing. Most of all, He wants you to give your heart and recognize that He is Jehovah Jireh, your Provider. In this way you will give Him honor, glory, and praise.

This feast is also a joyful time of celebration. It's a time to have a festival in your heart as much as physically around you. Let's read Deuteronomy 16:13-15 (NIV): *"Celebrate the Festival of Tabernacles for seven days after you have gathered the produce of your threshing floor and your winepress. Be joyful at your festival—you, your sons and daughters, your male and female servants, and the Levites, the foreigners, the fatherless and the widows who live in your towns. For seven days celebrate the festival to the Lord your God at the place the Lord will choose. For the Lord your God will bless you in all your harvest and in all the work of your hands, and your joy will be complete."*

Praise the Lord for how you can celebrate Him not only this week but every week as He continues to tabernacle among you in the Person of the Holy Spirit indwelling your temple daily!

TISHRI 19

Jesus Christ makes your joy complete! When you confess Him as Lord and Savior, you know that the One who sprinkled His blood on the mercy seat provides for you. It is then when your joy is complete!

I want you to know this and to be encouraged during this season. The Lord is properly positioning you to step into this season full of joy. It truly is an exciting time!

The Jewish people make a "sukkot" as a way of remembering their history during the Feast of Tabernacles. It is a structure that has at least three walls and is framed with wood and canvas. The roof is made of cut branches and leaves for a roof they could see through to the sky. This sukkot, or booth, helps them remember their ancestors' 40 years in the wilderness of Sinai and how isolated they were from the rest of the world. It also reminds them how the presence of God dwelt in their midst, how He covered them daily with His cloud, and how at night He warmed them with His fiery presence. Wow! Amazing! God is so good! Their clothes didn't even wear out, and no matter what they faced or if they felt vulnerable, they were covered!

Even in times when you feel vulnerable or weak, know that the Lord will come and bless you with His overwhelming presence. He tabernacles among you. Jesus is the Word; and in John 1:14 (NIV) we read, *"The Word became flesh and made his dwelling among us. We have seen his glory, the glory of the one and only Son, who came from the Father, full of grace and truth."*

TISHRI 20

Your heavenly Father loves you greatly! He wants you to recognize this is your season of joy and blessing. When you believe Him to be your Provider in all things, He is able to come in and properly position you and enlarge your territory! As He stretches and advances you, know that He is your Provider. The joy of the Lord is your strength!

Purpose in your heart to bless the Lord by giving an offering to your favorite ministry, your church, or whatever you feel called to do in honor of the Lord.

Share this with a friend today. Remind them that the Lord is their Provider in all things!

TISHRI 21

Historically today is the day called *Hashanah Rabbah,* where according to the Jews there is a verdict written in the Book of Life, which seals their fate for the upcoming year. On this day a Aramaic blessing is cited called a *Pitka Tava or* in Yiddish it is called *A guten kvitel,* which means "A good note." They are hoping the verdict will be positive, so they speak this blessing.

This is also a time when the prophet Haggai got a word about the *"glory of the latter house shall be greater than the former,"* to arise in the second temple, *"in seventh month in the one and twentieth day of the month"* (Haggai 2:9,1 KJV).

I am believing a special blessing for you because of the shed blood of Yeshua Messiah and your new heavenly ascended position in Him. It will indeed be a good year and your name is written in the Book of Life because of our Passover Lamb, Jesus Christ's great sacrifice for your sin.

God spoke to me saying, "I am increasing people from a positional standpoint." God is releasing new grain, new wine, and new oil from Heaven. This is a result of the Feast of Tabernacles. You turned your heart to the Lord and repented. You have positioned yourself to celebrate, and Jesus is tabernacling, dwelling, with you!

You will begin to see financial abundance in double portion because of positional increase. "Positional increase" means that you will experience promotion from a new place in your life and receive a new assignment. God has equipped and positioned you already. He's causing you to step into that place of ascension.

TISHRI 22

Historically this is *Shemini Atzeret* or Eighth Day of Assembly and is its own holiday. It is a day of tarrying one day longer in the presence of God. On this day one does not have to sleep in the Sukkah. It is also Simchat Torah or a celebration of the Torah which culminates the end of the annual cycle and beginning of a new cycle.

Leviticus 23:36 (NKJV) says, *"For seven days you shall offer an offering made by fire to the Lord. On the eighth day you shall have a holy convocation, and you shall offer an offering made by fire to the Lord. It is a sacred assembly, and you shall do no customary work on it."*

During this positional increase you will experience great peace and rest. You will also see financial blessings. Whenever new grain, wine, and oil are released, revelation from Heaven is coming too! You will learn and grow from wisdom that is being deposited into your spirit straight from Heaven.

Let me pray for you: "Father, thank You for releasing angels to help raise my friend up and give them new revelation and understanding of the ascension realms. Help them know that they are being seated with You in heavenly places and learning how to operate from this place of positional increase. Lord, I thank You for new opportunities, for the anointing, the special oil that is pouring down upon this reader. This is the way to start a new season! Give them the strength to move forward so they will be able to accomplish all that you have for them. Father, thank You for all that You're doing in and through this person with this new seat of positional authority. In Jesus's name, amen."

TISHRI 23

The Hebrew word *atzeres* means restraint. We are called to continue to restrain ourselves now that our festivities are over and the Feast of Tabernacles has ended. Let us remember to enter *His* rest. Hebrews 4:8-11 (NASB) says, *"For if Joshua had given them rest, He would not have spoken of another day after that. Consequently, there remains a Sabbath rest for the people of God. For the one who has entered His rest has himself also rested from his works, as God did from His. Therefore, let's make every effort to enter that rest, so that no one will fall by following the same example of disobedience."*

The Jews practice *Shabbat* (Sabbath), which starts at sundown every Friday night and goes until nightfall on Saturday. It's a special day of the week during which the Jews recognize that they are entering into God's rest. They remember that God rested from His work after seven days of creation, and God wants that same rest for them. Sabbath rest distinguishes them and distinguishes believers as those who belong to God.

God also wants this practice for you! Nowadays, many Christians practice their Sabbath rest on Sundays. However, in our busy world, there are some Christians not practicing a Sabbath rest at all. Practice one day of rest unto the King so He knows that *you* know He is your Provider and you trust Him!

TISHRI 24

The author of Hebrews shared that you can enter Sabbath rest *every day*. God is inviting us to be at rest with Him. There is a day, a moment, and a time when you can enter into this state of rest. It's when you remember the fact that Jesus died, was buried, resurrected, and ascended. And even though we live in a world full of toil, He is our complete peace.

Hebrews 4:9-11 (KJV): *"There remaineth therefore a rest to the people of God. For he that is entered into his rest, he also hath ceased from his own works, as God did from his. Let us labour therefore to enter into that rest, lest any man fall after the same example of unbelief."*

God wants you to get to a place where you stop trying to always toil and get things, but instead to come to a place of proper positioning in which you recognize you are in full alignment with His inheritance. God's rest is where He abides. It's a place of relationship with Him—a secret place, a deep place. "Rest" in the Hebrew is *katapausis,* which means reposing down or abode. This abode is resting in the dwelling of God Himself.

TISHRI 25

As we have just finished Feast of Tabernacles a few days ago, this is a time when God does not want you to just rush forward and begin working hard again; instead, change your habits to a life of rest in Him.

So why do you toil? What are you working for? Most people toil all the time. Our world works to gain, works to get, and is focused on having more, more, and more. It's a "get" mentality in our natural mind from the fall of man. However, when you enter into a state of rest, you find that nothing is missing, nothing is broken. It's a supernatural place. It's *shalom,* peace—a *Shabbat Shalom!* It's a Sabbath rest for the people of God, an abode in God.

We are called to be givers, not getters. It's hard to be a giver if we are always trying to get and fulfill our needs. Jesus is enough. The work is finished. You don't have to toil or be constantly thinking about getting. You need to shut off that way of thinking sometimes so you can rest.

How do you do that? You shut down those thoughts by meditation, prayer, and the Word of God washing your soul. Then fear flees and you can experience His Sabbath rest by faith!

Today, believe that God is Jehovah Jireh, your Provider. Remember that even when the Israelites were in a vulnerable state in the desert, the Lord provided for them. God will provide for you, child of His inheritance! Enter His rest today!

If you would like to know more, I encourage you to check out my *Soul Transformation* class or any course in my *School of the Supernatural* on my website at www.candicesmithyman.com. Share this with a friend who needs to learn to rest in Jesus and be blessed!

TISHRI 26

The Lord has been speaking to me about how you can abide in Christ and remain in His love. In John 15, we learn why abiding is so important, and how you can bear fruit because of how much the Father loves you. It's critical that we position ourselves to abide in Him, in a state of love. When we do this, we remain seated in heavenly places.

Think about when Jesus died and resurrected. He defeated sin, death, and the grave! When He ascended, He took His permanent seat in Heaven. You are now able to abide with Him. He bought it for you; you didn't earn it. All you have to do is receive Jesus as your Lord and Savior.

John 15:4-5 (KJV): *"Abide in me, and I in you. As the branch cannot bear fruit of itself, except it abide in the vine; no more can ye, except ye abide in me. I am the vine, ye are the branches: He that abideth in me, and I in him, the same bringeth forth much fruit: for without me ye can do nothing."*

Continue in your time of rest! Rest is a state of mind and being in Him!

TISHRI 27

If you've been going through intense struggles, if you feel like you are toiling, if you're being crushed by all the pressure—stop! Picture yourself seated with Christ at the royal table, spending time with Him and resting in His love. I have a vision of that daily from my encounter with the Lord that I speak about in my book, *Releasing Heaven: Creating Supernatural Environments through Heavenly Encounters.*

God is love, and that love exudes from Him. It flows from Him to your spirit, into your soul, then into your body. I encourage you today to take some time and tarry in His presence. That word *abide* means "to tarry, to wait, to continue in, to remain" in His love. It is important for you to take a few moments and rest in Him each and every day. When you rest in His love, all the work you are doing will become inconsequential and your love for Him will become premiere. Then will you begin to bear fruit that will not only be a blessing to Him, but to the world!

God wants your work to be Kingdom work rooted and grounded in His love. If you are having trouble grabbing hold of His love, just tell Him. Say, "Lord, I'm having trouble grasping Your love for me and how I'm seated with You in heavenly places." He will surround you with His angels and minister His love to you. No matter what has happened in your life, God loves you. He truly does!

TISHRI 28

If you ever start to question His love, just look at the cross! The cross is a symbol of how Jesus was perfect and sinless, yet He still died for you. He shed His blood that you may be saved, redeemed, and healed. That is pure love! His unconditional love allows you to have a relationship with Him and gives you the power of the Holy Spirit.

You can now continually be in a love relationship with the Lord and receive from Him as He receives from us! It's mutual and a blessing that goes back and forth.

Study John 15. Make it part of your mental thinking. Ruminate on how much He loves you and you will begin to pour out love in everything and to everyone around you! Rest in Him. It's the fuel you need to finish the year strong. God will develop beautiful fruit in and through the time you spend together, and this feeds the world. Now when the world sees you, they will know you've been in the presence of the Lord!

Galatians 5:22-23 (KJV): *"But the fruit of the Spirit is love, joy, peace, longsuffering, gentleness, goodness, faith, meekness, temperance: against such there is no law."*

TISHRI 30

You have come through the Head of the Year or the first month of the beginning of the Hebrew calendar. You are ready now to experience the Seven Blessings of the Atonement and the Fall Rains. This will continue to accelerate you into your destiny and the prosperous blessings that follow for you to carry forth God's plan for the next six months.

Continue in an attitude of peace and rest. During this month of Tishri you have grown closer to God and in your relationship with Him; now is the time to put all your spiritual growth into work for His kingdom. Remain in Him and He will do the rest.

Psalm 37:1-6 (NIV): *"Do not fret because of those who are evil or be envious of those who do wrong; for like the grass they will* soon wither, like green plants they will soon die away. Trust in the Lord and do good; dwell in the land and enjoy safe pasture. Take delight in the Lord, and he will give you the desires of your heart. Commit your way to the Lord; trust in him and he will do this: He will make your righteous reward shine like the dawn, your vindication like the noonday sun."

Prepare your hearts now to step into double-portion time, the fall rains, and our next month, which is *Heshvan*. There is lots of rain coming in that month!

THE MONTH
OF HESHVAN

Marcheshvan, which means mar, bitter, or droplet.

Heshvan (Cheshvan) is the second month of the civil year and the eighth month on the religious calendar from Nisan. The Babylonia name is Bul. It is referred to as bitter because there are no feasts or fasts.

1 Kings 6:38 (NIV): *"In the eleventh year in the month of Bul, the eighth month, the temple was finished in all its details according to its specifications. He had spent seven years building it."*

Tribe of Israel (Conventional): Manasseh

Note: As Joseph's tribe was split between with Manasseh and Ephraim, that is Joseph's inheritance (Joshua 16:4).

Gemstone in Aaron's breastplate for Joseph: Onyx

Note: Joseph was of the original 12 tribes but the Lord split his inheritance between Ephraim and Manasseh (Joshua 16:4); so when we look at what month is pertinent to each gemstone, we give Joseph a gemstone but not a month.

Constellation in Sky/Hebrew name: Scorpio/Akrab

HESHVAN 1
Rosh Chodesh Heshvan

Tonight there is a new moon in the night sky.

Historically this is also the month that according to the Jews the Third Temple would be finished. Messianic Believers and Christians do not hold to this because Yeshua our Messiah has already come. It also what the Jews focus on in the Shabbat Chazon or Shabbat of Vision, which you read about on Av 7.

It's now acceleration time. The month of Heshvan is a time to remember the cleansing rains of the Lord. In Israel, it is literally the rainy season, but this is also meant in a spiritual perspective. Joel 2:23 (KJV) says, *"Be glad then, ye children of Zion, and rejoice in the Lord your God: for he hath given you the former rain moderately, and he will cause to come down for you the rain, the former rain, and the latter rain in the first month."*

The former rains technically refer to the spring rains. Spring rains take place from Passover all the way to the Day of Atonement. Anything that you have received in this time frame will double now in the latter.

There is an intense acceleration and a great move of the Spirit happening right now! Things are moving rapidly, but you have to keep your focus on the Lord. God is opening all kinds of doors of opportunity for you. His vats are overflowing, and the storehouses are being filled right now, in His mighty name. God has also been showing me about divine alignments. He is positioning you in amazing ways to bring you new grain, wine, oil, abundance, and a fresh word from Heaven.

This is such an important time for you to keep your focus on the Lord. Oftentimes, as things began to accelerate you felt as if life was spinning out of control. Now, though, just get into the Word of God, take time in His presence, and meditate on Him.

Being God-centered will keep you in alignment with Him as you walk out His strategy for your life.

HESHVAN 2

The Lord showed me a picture of what *Heshvan* is going to bring forth on earth this year. It will be a month of multiplication!

I saw God fishing. He had bait on His fishing rod, and He was casting it out. He was releasing it to catch many fish. Then the Lord spoke to me, "I am going fishing, and I am going to be casting My fishing rod and hook. I am putting it out there just as I am sending you, My people." God is releasing you, sending you out as bait to bring great amounts of people (fish) into His Kingdom. He wants to see a great multiplication happen this month.

God gave me a Scripture to share with you. Hebrews 6:13-14 (NASB), *"For when God made the promise to Abraham, since He could swear an oath by no one greater, He swore by Himself, saying, 'Indeed I will greatly bless you and I will greatly multiply you.'"*

God's promise to Abraham was to make His descendants many on the earth. Just the same is His promise for the Church today. God is getting ready to bring increase! Remember, He is using you to go out and bring a lot of people back to the Lord. *You* are part of His bait for this multiplication.

Take time today to look at your life and do an assessment. What is God restarting in your life?

HESHVAN 3

Yes, you may have gone through a time of crushing, but now God is going to restart some of what He gave you before the crushing took place. It's a restart and a release. God is going to birth new things in dead places.

God is repositioning you to go out and expand and gather fish! I hear Him saying, "I'm going to restart some things. I'm going to start sending people out. I'm going to send them forth. I'm going to use them to pull in a great supply of fish, a great supply of movement, a great supply of multiplication. Be fruitful and multiply!"

The Lord is bringing cleansing rains, multiplication, and increase during this month of Heshvan. The Lord is saying, "I'm cleansing and I'm bringing forth increase in the earth. I want you to participate with Me for increase."

We hear God say something similar to Adam and Eve in Genesis 1:28 (NASB), *"God blessed them, and God said to them, 'Be fruitful and multiply, and fill the earth, and subdue it; and rule over the fish of the sea and over the birds of the sky and over every living thing that moves on the earth.'"* This verse applies to you too. This is exactly what God wants you to do! He wants you to begin to step out and start ruling over the earth. He wants you to be fruitful, multiply, and fill the earth with His Kingdom! He gave you *kratos* power—dominion power and rulership. You are called to bring forth life!

HESHVAN 4

Those who are life-givers *will* produce fruit. God is the One bringing the fruit. New doors of opportunity are going to open for you because this is harvest time. New things are about to multiply! They're going to break forth, but expect that you may be asked to jump through some hoops first. You may be called to step out into unknown areas in faith.

God wants you to be ready. You have everything inside you to complete the tasks at hand. We need to ask God, "What is the strategy? How do I rule over this thing? How do I do this so I can bring about the increase and multiplication?"

Right now, you are seeing a double portion take place. God is saying, "Begin now to strategize with Me." Abundance is taking place right now in finances, restoration, His presence, miracles, deliverance, and your family. Write down your revelations and make them plain so you can refer to them again.

HESHVAN 5

God loves relationship. He loves to be in relationship with you. You will see yourself sowing and reaping in the same season, and autumn and spring rains will both fall! Yes! God is doing something really mighty in the month of October!

Let me pray for you: "Lord, I just praise You and thank You for my friend. Thank You for showing, revealing, and opening up this reader's spiritual eyes, ears, smell, taste, and touch to the new opportunities that are coming. Lord, help bring the strategy of how to subdue, rule over, and multiply as You told Adam and Eve to do. Show this person Your blessings and how to be a leader. I thank You that my friend is part of the dominion of life, causing life to flow through their veins, knowing they have the power to step out and begin to subdue the earth in their home environment and in the nations. Hallelujah! In Jesus's name, amen."

This is such a blessed time. Today, purpose to step out, use your faith, move forward, walk in dominion, and be a blessing to those around you. Share this with a friend who needs to know that they are in a double-portion time!

HESHVAN 6

I have a special word for you this week—the sound of abundant rain is here.

Can you hear the sound of abundance coming from Heaven? Have you ever heard rain on a rooftop? It can come down so hard that you think you shouldn't even go outside because of so much rain. God is sending that kind of rain to you today.

In 1 Kings 18:41 (NIV), Elijah spoke to his servant, Ahab, *"Go, eat and drink; for there is the sound of a heavy* [abundance of] *rain."*

After this, the servant ran back and forth, checking the skies, until he finally saw a small cloud the size of a man's hand. That little cloud was getting ready to bring the abundance of rain.

Today, the Lord would say to you, "There is a sound that is here, and it is the abundance of rain that is coming to you—the abundance of blessings and overflow."

HESHVAN 7

During this month of Heshvan, cleansing and abundant rains will take place. You have been through a process. Now, God is giving you strategies for how you are to receive all of the blessing that He wants to give you.

Receive the rain. Listen to the Lord for His strategies. Divine appointments, alignments, and opportunities lie ahead. Grain, wine, oil, wool, flax, silver, gold, fire, and all the resources of Heaven are being released into your life. Praise God! The vats of Heaven are pouring forth into your life this month.

Be sure that you are listening and being obedient to your heavenly Father. He wants to bless you so much, but you must listen to His voice. When He tells you what to do with the resources He's giving you, do it in obedience. Let the Lord begin to advance your vision. Don't let anything hinder or hold back the abundance of rain in your life.

Deuteronomy 27:9-10 (NKJV): *"Then Moses and the priests, the Levites, spoke to all Israel, saying, '**Take heed and listen**, O Israel: This day you have become the people of the Lord your God. Therefore you shall **obey the voice of the Lord your God**, and observe His commandments and His statutes which I command you today.'"*

This is a very special time and season. Share this with a friend who needs to know that abundance can come to their life too!

HESHVAN 8

This month of Heshvan is a time of restoring! I hear words for the month—*restoration and rain.* Take a moment to remember how God cleansed, restored and saved humankind through Noah during this month. Noah was recognized by God as a righteous man in Genesis 7:1 (NIV): *"The Lord then said to Noah, 'Go into the ark, you and your whole family, because I have found you righteous in this generation.'"*

When you know Jesus as your Lord and Savior, you are called the righteous of God. This means you're now considered to be a man or a woman whom God stands beside. His righteousness not only brings protection but also identifies you in the spirit realm. You have been given Christ's robe, breastplate, and crown of righteousness as gifts! Because of Yeshua and His distribution of gifts, the angels are with you and God will carry you into the land He called you to inhabit. Just as He did Noah!

HESHVAN 9

Rain. God is bringing rain. During this month, the floods came and cleansed the earth. God only saved the righteous, Noah's family. You may be going through a difficult time right now. Situations are arising in your family. Your marriage may be on the rocks. You may be having problems with friends and division is present. But there's good news! God is sending rain to cleanse you and make you whole. Anything that is broken, God is drawing to Himself and making it like new. It doesn't matter what kind of brokenness you are experiencing; God is cleansing you and will restore you!

We read in 1 Corinthians 6:19-20 (NKJV), *"Do you not know that your body is the temple of the Holy Spirit who is in you, whom you have from God, and you are not your own? For you were bought at a price; therefore glorify God in your body and in your spirit, which are God's."*

Rest in the Lord and have Him take you through that cleansing and purification process today so you can bear more fruit in Him!

HESHVAN 10

Restoration. One of the blessings during this month is restoration! God will restore things in your life and your family! Whatever the locust has stolen, God is going to return it. Get ready! God is going to do some rebuilding. Keep in mind that God is also going to close some doors. You may see something leave that you considered to have value, but God will take the broken and fragmented part and rebuild something new. God is getting ready to build new generations, new things in your life that will last for generations to come. You will leave a legacy of righteousness on this earth!

Psalm 23:3 (KJV): *"He restoreth my soul: he leadeth me in the paths of righteousness for his name's sake."*

Be encouraged. God is working. He's moving in your heart. Read Genesis 7, the account of Noah, with the perspective that you are righteous in Christ and God has given you access to all you need through His Son, Jesus Christ. God *will* protect, provide, bless, and give you increase and prosperity as He did Noah. He is going to rebuild, reestablish, reposition, and restore you, in the mighty name of Jesus!

Now your job is to stand firm—even if things don't seem to be working out. Hold on tight to Him. He is your Anchor and your root system. God is restoring even our nation. He is doing what only He can do. We must submit to Him and stay encouraged. Share this with a friend!

HESHVAN 11

Historically this is the day when Methuselah passed away at age 969. Genesis 5:27 (KJV) tells us, *"And all the days of Methuselah were nine hundred sixty and nine years: and he died."*

Historically this is the day that Rachel died while giving birth to Benjamin (son of the right hand).

As we continue in this wonderful month of Heshvan—a time of being fruitful, multiplying and of cleansing rains—I have a prophetic word for you. God is coming for His harvest! Rachel's harvest was her children. One being Joseph, another being Benjamin. Both having had significant influence on earth.

God made a deposit inside you, and He is expecting you to step out and start moving! Just as God expected Noah to get in the ark—no matter how difficult it was going to be, he didn't know where he was going or if he would survive, Noah obeyed.

God says let Me carry you into a new season with a sphere of influence. Take a risk today and trust the Lord as He carries you into a new season of giving of yourself.

HESHVAN 12

This day is around Yitzhak Rabin Memorial Day, celebrated in Israel in memory of the late Prime Minister of Israel and Defense Minister.

When Jesus came, died, was buried, resurrected, and ascended, He then made a seat for you with Him in heavenly places. God has given you a sphere of influence. He properly positioned you to *give!* Now, He is asking you to *act* on it!

Luke 6:38 (NIV) says, *"Give, and it will be given to you. A good measure, pressed down, shaken together and running over, will be poured into your lap. For with the measure you use, it will be measured to you."*

What does that mean? It means that God wants you to learn to live in the capacity of the Kingdom, which is prosperous. Luke 6:38 shows that He called you to be a giver and He prospered you enough to give. "Give" in Greek is *didómi,* which means to "bring forth." God is saying to "bring forth," as in "give and it shall be given to you." When you do, you end up having what is brought forth brought back to you!

Didómi also means "adventure." Can you imagine that?! Bringing forth giving, is an adventure! It's entering into an endless, limitless, forever and heavenly realm. That's where you're called to give from! You give based on the measure, or the capacity, that you have. You can't give something to the Kingdom or anyone else unless you have something to give. But there is no deficiency in the Kingdom of God. There's no lack or poverty. You have something to give because you are prosperous in Him!

HESHVAN 13

When God is asking you to give, He isn't asking you to give from a place of deficiency but from a place of prosperity. He says, "Enter into those realms by faith, where you know you have all that you need."

See, all your needs have been met. You are now living like you are in the Garden of Eden. All you need has been provided, and it's in this capacity that God wants you to minister to others, to give and bless others.

You must know that the only thing restricting or limiting you right now is your unbelief. Don't fall for the whispers, the lies of the enemy saying you're not as prosperous as you really are. You are prosperous, in Jesus's name!

Even your soul is prospering! *"Beloved, I pray that you may prosper in all things and be in health, just as your soul prospers"* (3 John 2 NKJV). Believe it and receive it today! Ask the Lord to help you with your unbelief. Ask Him to show you the prosperity He has given you so that you can give to others.

Share this with friends who need to know the Lord has made them prosperous too!

HESHVAN 14

Tonight there is a full moon in the night sky.

You are quickly approaching Heshvan 17, the month of abundant and cleansing rains! Yes! This is the time when God instructed Noah to get into the ark. He remained inside with his family for a year.

What happens when there is an abundance of something? The enemy likes to push back. But also, if you have been in spiritual warfare, it could be because God is advancing you. He is moving you quickly and rapidly. He is positioning you for the new.

I hear the Lord saying new assignments and new angels are being assigned to you. There are new assignments coming to you just as this time of year brought a new assignment to Noah. He was instructed to build the ark, and then at the right moment, he was told to get on it with the animals and his family.

Now is your moment! If you have been feeling pushback from the enemy, know that promotion is proved by enemy interference. Don't let the enemy run you over. You need to say, "No! I cancel your demonic plans on my life, in the mighty name of Jesus."

Right now, the political arena is shifting! There are lots of shifts taking place. People are being sent to new positions. This is an exciting time! New angels are being released for new assignments.

HESHVAN 15

Historically this was the day King Jeroboam called for an alternative feast of Tabernacles or Sukkot for those in the Northern Kingdom according to 1 Kings 12:32-33 (KJV): *"And Jeroboam ordained a feast in the eighth month* [on religious calendar since Nisan], *on the fifteenth day of the month, like unto the feast that is in Judah, and he offered upon the altar. So did he in Bethel, sacrificing unto the calves that he had made: and he placed in Bethel the priests of the high places which he had made. So he offered upon the altar which he had made in Bethel the fifteenth day of the eighth month, even in the month which he had devised of his own heart; and ordained a feast unto the children of Israel: and he offered upon the altar, and burnt incense."*

The Feast of Tabernacles was celebrated by King Jeroboam; it was a time of celebration when the people remembered how God had protected them in the wilderness. God is protecting you today!

Listen, you have been faithfully standing. Glory! I can hear the Lord say that He is releasing fire from the vats of Heaven. He is releasing gold and silver even though they are His! I can feel it right now in the spirit. You are receiving provision for the vision, in the mighty name of Jesus!

Keep standing strong and tall. All provision has been made for you in every area, not just financially. I see great resources coming to you. The vats are open—wool, flax, fire, water, the wine of opportunity, fresh oil coming forth, and the grain of fresh revelation. I'm believing for new angels for you. Hallelujah! They are going to help combat the demonic forces that may be trying to push back the great destiny God has for you.

Persevere in the faith, and do not shrink back. God is with you! I pray for you today to see increase and multiplication as you step into your new assignment with new angels.

HESHVAN 16

God is doing mighty things! During this current Hebrew month of Heshvan, rain and restoration are coming upon you, child of God. God is pouring down blessings upon your life! Last month and this month God said you will receive excessive rain and excessive blessings (Joel 2:23)!

But take heed: this is also a time of testing. Just like Noah was tested when God told him to build the ark and to take aboard his family and two of every kind of animal, you will endure some tests. Rain came upon him for 40 days and 40 nights and flooded everything. He had to put his complete trust in God for every moment of the journey. Yes, rains of blessing are coming upon you, but also a time of testing.

God doesn't want you to hold on to what you are receiving this month. He will send the rain and then ask you to release the blessing to someone else. He doesn't want you to be attached to it. It is so important that you trust God enough to release it as He tells you to. When you do, you show Him that you believe He is your Provider and Healer, that He is perfect love, life, joy, peace, and all you need. In a sense, your actions tell God, "Lord, I really trust You for who You are!"

Give away what God has given you!

> *Each of you should give what you have decided in your heart to give, not reluctantly or under compulsion, for God loves a cheerful giver* (**2 Corinthians 9:7 NIV**).

HESHVAN 17

Historically this is the day that King Solomon completed the first temple. "*And it came to pass, when Solomon had finished the building of the house of the Lord, and the king's house, and all Solomon's desire which he was pleased to do, that the Lord appeared to Solomon the second time, as he had appeared unto him at Gibeon. And the Lord said unto him, I have heard thy prayer and thy supplication, that thou hast made before me: I have hallowed this house, which thou hast built, to put my name there for ever; and mine eyes and mine heart shall be there perpetually*" (1 Kings 9:1-3 KJV).

Historically this is the day Noah got in the ark. Genesis 7:11-12 (NIV), "*In the six hundredth year of Noah's life, on the seventeenth day of the second month—on that day all the springs of the great deep burst forth, and the floodgates of the heavens were opened. And rain fell on the earth forty days and forty nights.*"

Problems come when you try to grab hold of the rain (blessings, provision). The more you hold on to it, the harder it will be to release it when the Lord tells you to. You must hold it loosely! God is sending blessings to you, but He could ask you to give them up as quickly as they come.

Imagine Noah in the ark with every kind of animal and his family, trusting God to provide for their needs and safely carry them to dry land. Awesome faith! After the rain ended, the blessings came. They began to rebuild.

Be encouraged that this test of yours isn't going to last much longer. You may be feeling like you are giving things away at a rapid pace, but God is testing your heart. God wants to make sure you don't love the rain (blessings) and forget about Him.

HESHVAN 18

Do you know that God your Provider is all you need? You have access to all you need from your ascension seat in Him. The only thing that causes a blessing delay is *fear*. Fear is an element of separation that began in the Garden of Eden. But good news! Jesus defeated death, sin, and the grave! When He ascended into Heaven, you were seated with Him in heavenly places and given access to His storehouse.

I hear the Lord saying, "Do not be concerned about your health issues. I have your health in My hands. I am releasing what is necessary to bring healing to your body, mind, and soul." Hold on to this word. Do not give place to fear. Hold on to the Word and release your faith. In other words, you may need to take an action step: take communion, proclaim, declare and decree over your body the healing power of Jesus: "By His stripes I have been healed. I'm ascended with the Lord and seated with Him. I have no pain in this area." Then maintain your healing by standing on the Word in faith and staying focused on Christ.

Who his own self bare our sins in his own body on the tree, that we, being dead to sins, should live unto righteousness: by whose stripes ye were healed (1 Peter 2:24 KJV).

HESHVAN 19

With rain, the water flows. Get excited! God is doing great things. Thank Him for it and watch it come to pass!

Let me pray for you today: "Father, remove any fear, worry, or anxiety that pertains to my friend's health, finances, family, or relationships. Jesus, release the rain from Heaven upon this person. Give them peace and let them know You have taken care of every need. Help them to release Your blessing instead of clutching it tightly in fear. Restore them, Lord, in Jesus's name, amen."

I want you to declare this over your life: "I am permanent portal. I will do whatever God asks me to do. I will thank the Lord in all things. I will honor and respect God, my Provider. I am a releaser. I will release the rain that is coming to me; I will not be attached to it!

HESHVAN 20

God wants you to learn how to expand your thinking. He wants you to know that you can live without limits, a limitless life.

Adam and Eve were given specific instructions and boundaries by the Lord (Genesis 1:28).

The Garden of Eden was self-sustaining, lush, and they had everything they needed. They were all set up for increase. There was just one boundary. They were told not to touch the tree of the knowledge of good and evil. It was a healthy boundary that

God set in place. However, the enemy confused them and they chose to disobey God's instructions and touch the forbidden fruit. Adam and Eve were kicked out of the Garden, and they entered a realm of limitations.

Through a relationship with Jesus and confession of sin, time is redeemed. You can now live a life of redemption, a life of limitlessness. It's like being placed back into the Garden of Eden! Heaven is limitless, you are seated in Heaven, and you are limitless by faith.

Hebrews 11:1 (KJV), *"Now faith is the substance of things hoped for, the evidence of things not seen."*

HESHVAN 21

We gain back dominion through what Jesus has done for us. He has redeemed the time, and it has now been lengthened and expanded. The dominion that the Lord gave to Adam and Eve, He has now given to you! It's time to step into this dominion and walk in His authority.

Determine to take time in this month of Heshvan to make sure you are being fruitful, multiplying, increasing. Examine yourself. Are you fulfilling God's plan for you? Or do you find that you are full of anxiety, confusion, and constantly under attack? If you're not aligned with God's command to be fruitful and multiply, simply ask the Lord to forgive you and to reposition you with Him.

Rise up! Begin to take dominion! God is saying to you today, "It's time to take dominion again so you can live without limits!" When you take dominion, you will put a protective boundary around yourself. The enemy will be restricted in your life, and your fruit will grow quickly!

Share this with a friend. Choose to live with the confidence that you are seated with Christ in heavenly places! Here, there is rest, peace, and authority.

HESHVAN 22

"For I know the plans I have for you," declares the Lord, "plans to prosper you and not to harm you, plans to give you hope and a future" **(Jeremiah 29:11 NIV).**

After years of building the ark and coming under incredible scrutiny from those who watched, the Lord told Noah to enter the ark. I'm sure it was a time of mourning because he had to say goodbye to the people who did not believe and would die. However, he went in with his family and remained there for an entire year.

In a split second, things rapidly shifted for Noah. Can you imagine? All of a sudden, your environment rapidly changing like that? God is saying, "Your environments are going to change rapidly over the next couple of months. As they do, I want to reveal some things to you about yourself."

You have been prepared until now, but things are getting ready to come, some good and some challenging. Either way, they will reveal your heart toward God. Your environment is getting ready to change and God is getting ready to give you some new ground to build upon.

Isaiah 28:16 (NIV), *"So this is what the Sovereign Lord says: 'See, I lay a stone in Zion, a tested stone, a precious cornerstone for a sure foundation; the one who relies on it will never be stricken with panic.'"*

HESHVAN 23

So many times, you try to make your own plans. You try to establish yourself and figure out how you will be noticed so you can move ahead. You consider all the opportunities that could come available to you. God says He will deal with you on the many aspects of your life. Just remember He loves you.

Expect that from the middle of November through the middle of January things are going to shift. It will be a time of great joy! There will be a lot of celebration and changing of environments as God works on your heart.

Hear me again: The Lord is saying to you, "I *know*. I know the plans that I have for *you*. Calm down and rest!" Stay responsive to God. His plans for you are one of a kind. No one else has them. Stay in faith and trust Him every step of the way!

Share this with a friend who needs to know what to do when the environment shifts happen. Help him or her learn how to rest in the season and trust God with the future.

Hebrews 11:6-7 (NKJV), *"But without faith it is impossible to please Him, for he who comes to God must believe that He is, and that He is a rewarder of those who diligently seek Him. By faith Noah, being divinely warned of things not yet seen, moved with godly fear, prepared an ark for the saving of his household, by which he condemned the world and became heir of the righteousness which is according to faith."*

HESHVAN 24

Today is a beautiful day that the Lord has made! Hebrews 11:1-3 (NKJV) says, *"Now faith is the substance of things hoped for, the evidence of things not seen. For by it the elders obtained a good testimony. By faith we understand that the worlds were framed by the word of God, so that the things which are seen were not made of things which are visible."*

It is vitally important for us to understand that God is eternal. You need to wrap your mind around that truth and know that God has also called you to be an eternal being like Him. What does that mean? You have eternity in your heart and should be expressing eternity all the time. Eternity is limitless and boundless. It's a place of peace, joy, and hope. Do you carry these attributes every day? If you've been having a lot of negative thoughts, take them captive and reposition yourself today by reading His Word and obeying His word.

HESHVAN 25

God, the King of the universe, has control of all things. There isn't one thing that gets by Him, but He is relying on you to live *by faith.* Grab hold of faith as though it was reality.

God says in Psalm 50:9-12 (NIV), *"I have no need of a bull from your stall or of goats from your pens, for every animal of the forest is mine, and the cattle on a thousand hills. I know every bird in the mountains, and the insects in the fields are mine. If I were hungry, I would not tell you, for the world is mine, and all that is in it."*

Now listen, that Scripture passage ought to be encouraging to you! God has His hand on the earth. You are an heir of salvation and seated with Him in heavenly places. Praise Him! He has everything in His hands. Remember, even before Christ was crucified, He told His disciples that He would die, be buried and resurrect. When Jesus died, the disciples became fearful and doubted. They questioned if the promise had been false. No matter if something in your life looks dead, multiplies fear, or feels too difficult, God is still in control and He will do what He promised!

You need to stop thinking with a temporal mindset and start responding to every situation in faith. The resurrection happened even though there were three days of stress and difficulty among His people. The Lord is fully aware of our humanity. Yet, He still died for us—frail, feeble, weak, and gullible as we are. Now because of Christ's death, burial, resurrection, and ascension, we *have been already* seated with Him in heavenly places. There is nothing for you to be concerned about. Your Father owns cattle on a thousand hills. He has a perfect plan. He is causing matters on earth to come into alignment with Him.

HESHVAN 26

Praise Him! Jesus has not left His throne. He is seated at the right hand of the Father and you are seated on His lap. Stay in this place of joy, peace, and faith. It is where you need to be and where you are called to rule from. In Genesis 1:28 (KJV) He says, *"Be fruitful and multiply, and replenish the earth, subdue it; and have dominion over it."* You don't do that from an earthly seat—but from a heavenly one!

You have been made an heir to the throne. You have the authority to come into earthly realms and speak the light and truth. Declare it! Decree it! You will positively conquer your mind, will, emotions, and the environment around you.

I declare peace, calmness, boldness, and faith over you. You will not fret or be discouraged. You will rest in the fact that God is in control and knows everything. He has assigned you to be fruitful, to multiply, replenish, subdue, and have dominion. I speak that dominion life over you right now. You will rise up from the grave and have an eternal mindset. Peace will overwhelm you when you properly position yourself, in Jesus's name.

HESHVAN 27

Historically today is day Noah left the ark. By the twenty-seventh day of the second month, the earth was completely dry. Genesis 8:14-16 (KJV), *"And in the second month, on the seven and twentieth day of the month, was the earth dried. And God spake unto Noah, saying, Go forth of the ark, thou, and thy wife, and thy sons, and thy sons' wives with thee."*

It is said that Noah spent 365 days in the ark, on the solar calendar—one year and 11 days on the lunar calendar.

Praise the Lord! *"Let the redeemed of the Lord say so!"* (Psalm 107:2). The power of redemption is upon your life!

Do you know you have been redeemed? Do you know that the Lord has a seat of habitation for you? Do you know that Jesus is your next of kin? That He is your Brother who ransomed you, and brought you back from death, hell, and the grave? That you ascended with Him and are seated with Him in heavenly places?

Psalm 107:1-9 (KJV) says, *"O give thanks unto the Lord, for he is good: for his mercy endureth for ever. Let the redeemed of the Lord say so, whom he hath redeemed from the hand of the enemy; And gathered them out of the lands, from the east, and from the west, from the north, and from the south. They wandered in the wilderness in a solitary way; they found no city to dwell in. Hungry and thirsty, their soul fainted in them. Then they cried unto the Lord in their trouble, and he delivered them out of their distresses. And he led them forth by the right way, that they might go to a city of habitation. Oh that men would praise the Lord for his goodness, and for his wonderful works to the children of men! For he satisfieth the longing soul, and filleth the hungry soul with goodness."*

HESHVAN 28

Take note: *The redeemed of the Lord say so!* That is so important. Jesus is taking you to a city of habitation. That word *habitation* is the Hebrew word *moshab*, which means "a seat or sight in a place of dwelling." The word *redeemed* is the Hebrew word *gawal*, which means "to redeem as in kinship, a next of kin who bought back a relative's property, an avenger."

The Lord is our Avenger. He shed His blood on Calvary that you might be saved, healed, and redeemed! Redemption means that everything has been bought back—even right now! You may be thinking, *Nothing looks right in my life, neighborhood, or nation.*

But *be encouraged!* It doesn't matter if it looks right, God said, "It has been redeemed!" He has taken you out from the toiling and wandering. He has properly positioned you in a seat of habitation and satisfied your soul and filled you with goodness. The word *goodness* is the Hebrew is *tob*, and means "prosperity, wealth, and favor."

Through the shed blood of Jesus Christ, He has brought us back to a place of goodness, prosperity, wealth, and favor! Yes, I'm speaking to you right now, in the mighty name of Jesus!

HESHVAN 29

Historically this is considered to be the day when God revealed Himself to Moses. This day is also called *Sigd*, a day recognized by Ethiopian Jews as a day of prostration or worship.

Enter into His joy today because you are favored by God. It doesn't matter what your checkbook says. *All* things have been redeemed, and that's the truth!

Declare and decree in the name of Jesus that what He has done for you has already taken place, that everything you owed has been resolved, every need you have has been provided for, and all provision, protection, acceptance is yours! You can be a game changer by faith and turn things around in your life. Lack and poverty can be turned into prosperity, wealth, and favor.

Stop seeing things from your current circumstances. See everything from the view that the Lord has given you from your seat of habitation.

Ephesians 2:20-22 (NKJV): *"having been built on the foundation of the apostles and prophets, Jesus Christ Himself being the chief cornerstone, in whom the whole building, being fitted together, grows into a holy temple in the Lord, in whom you also are being built together for a dwelling place of God in the Spirit."*

HESHVAN 30

Sometimes Heshvan will be 30 days depending on the year; it is not this way with all the Hebrew months, but Heshvan and Kislev share this same trait. If this happens and you are on a year when there are 30 days, here is an extra prophetic revelation for you! You have sustained this month and now God wants to take you to a new fresh revelation of what is ahead. Much joy is to come!

Every day we need to remember that the joy of the Lord is your strength. Nehemiah 8:10 (KJV) reads, *"Then he said unto them, Go your way, eat the fat, and drink the sweet, and send portions unto them for whom nothing is prepared: for this day is holy unto our Lord: neither be ye sorry; for the joy of the Lord is your strength."*

Let God's joy fill you today so that you will be strong and ready for what lies ahead in the next month. Remember this is a time of acceleration on the Hebrew calendar, and we need His rest and joy to continue to move forward. The rains have come in Heshvan, but the month of Kislev is a month of miracles!

THE MONTH
OF KISLEV

*Kislev means trust or hope and it is also
referred to as the month of dreams.*

This is the third month on the civil calendar and the ninth month on the religious calendar. The Babylonian name is *Araḫ Kislimu*.

Psalm 78:7 (KJV): *"That they might set their hope in God, and not forget the works of God, but keep his commandments."* The word *hope* in Psalm 78:7 is the same Hebrew root word for *kesel* which is in *kislev*.

Tribe of Israel (Conventional): Binyamin/Benjamin

Gemstone in Aaron's breastplate: Plasma/Green Translucent

Constellation in Sky/Hebrew name: Sagittarius/Keshet

KISLEV 1
Rosh Chodesh Kislev

Tonight there is a new moon in the night sky.

Kislev is also another promotion month like Adar before Nisan or Elul before Tishri.

Genesis 37:5-7 (NIV): *"Joseph had a dream, and when he told it to his brothers, they hated him all the more. He said to* them, 'Listen to this dream I had: We were binding sheaves of grain out in the field when suddenly my sheaf rose and stood upright, while your sheaves gathered around mine and bowed down to it.'"

Prophetically the story of Joseph represents Yeshua who was handed over by His brothers to slavery and rejected, only then to become their Savior by being master of all of Pharaoh's estate.

Some scholars believe since Yeshua was born around the time of the Feast of Tabernacles that His conception would be in the darkest month of the year, around winter solstice.

Kislev is most thought of as the month of miracles. It starts Hanukkah or the Festival of Dedication on Kislev 25 and goes for eighty days. This special feast represents the rededication of the second temple after the Maccabean revolt.

Sometimes the Christian holiday of Christmas on the solar Gregorian calendar and the Festival of Dedication or Hanukkah may overlap. Since Hanukkah is always Kislev 25, it could occur in the Gregorian month of November around the US holiday of Thanksgiving or the month of December. You will find some devotionals pertaining to Christmas to encourage you simply because your heart will be yearning for Christmas as we near Kislev 25.

I am so excited! You are about to step into the month of Kislev—the month of miracles! *Yes, the miraculous is coming to you!* I hear the Lord saying that He is going to sow grain, wine, and oil into your life. Abundant blessings are coming.

KISLEV 2

This is a powerful time to learn the giving heart of God. His heart releases special blessings into the earth for you to receive. These wonderful resources are grain (greater revelation), wine (new opportunities), and oil (His anointing). There are also silver, gold, fire, water, wool, and flax that are available to you as a child of the Most High King. You are royalty!

God wants us to seek, knock, and ask in faith. *He is a good Father who desires for you, His child, to prosper. He longs to give good gifts!*

Be grateful! Your Heavenly Father is the great Giver of life and all things! He did not spare His Son Jesus Christ for you. And He gladly gives to you each day. Thank Him today for who He is!

James 1:17 (KJV): "**Every good gift and every perfect gift is from above**, *and cometh down **from the Father** of lights, with whom is no variableness, neither shadow of turning."*

KISLEV 3

The Lord spoke to me two words for today: "shift" and "restart." He showed me that He is going to remove the veil from people's eyes. This removal of the veil is going to create a major shift. New mantle assignments will come down from Heaven that will be life-altering! New businesses, ministries, and leaders are being raised up even as you read this!

In your life there are people groups I call community mountains. These mountains can be made of religion, education, government, business, or any sphere of influence or ministry. As the Lord removes the veil from people's eyes, they are going to start recognizing you. Yes, I said *you!*

God is getting ready to position you and make room for you at the table. People will notice what you're doing, the Word inside you, and the special giftings God has given you. He is shifting and starting and restarting things in your life!

KISLEV 4

God is going to expose agendas that have been created to stop you. He is also going to reveal blockades and obstacles that you have been struggling with in the spirit realms. This month of Kislev is a normal time for people to slow down, so make sure you slow down and listen to the Lord. Then God will accelerate you after the new year.

Make sure you are in a place of prayer. Rest and focus on the Lord. As you position yourself with Him, commune with and love Him, you will be in that exact place you need to be for Him to reveal things to you.

You are going to start receiving revelation on your new assignment this season. God is adjusting and changing things and people to ensure that your assignments can be advanced on earth. This doesn't just benefit you, but God too! He gets the glory and His plan is completed. You don't have to hold back about how you feel about Jesus during this time! You can be bold and forthright. New spheres of influence and favor are upon your life. Take a Shabbat and rest.

Genesis 2:3 (KJV) says, *"And God blessed the seventh day, and sanctified it: because that in it he had rested from all his work which God created and made."*

KISLEV 5

I see seven mountains coming together in unity. God is positioning leaders in unity who will believe the same, see the same, know the love of God, seek His face and stand on the foundation of Jesus Christ. These leaders are getting ready to be raised up, and *you* are one of them! Praise the Lord for choosing you! Take this time in consecration and communion with the Lord. He wants to connect with you on a daily basis.

The Christian holiday of Christmas is coming soon. Allow yourself to be open to receive the spirit of Christmas. Angelic hosts are drawn to the light. They are being dispatched! Place lights and candles in your home and welcome them in as they come to minister joy and peace to you. God is giving you His Spirit, wisdom, knowledge, understanding, counsel, might, and reverence as the seven spirits of the Lord. What a wonderful time to commune with the Father!

This time on our Gregorian calendar is similar to the time of Rosh Hashanah on the Hebrew calendar. We will be stepping into a brand-new year on January 1! Take your time with Him and don't let the devil distract you. Laugh at the devil and keep going! God wants you to rest so He can bring order to your life.

I declare and decree right now, in the name of Jesus, that you are coming into a new season—personally and in the nation where you live. God is revealing Himself to you. He is giving you love, peace, and incredible joy! You will abide with Him, hear His voice, and the joy of the Lord will strengthen you. As you experience this joy, you will start to see yourself in new places and positions, working with new people. This is truly going to be a blessed season as He shows you amazing things. I decree that this will come to pass, and your life is getting ready to be dramatically changed. Amen!

Share this with someone who needs joy and encouragement today. God is saying good things and people need to hear it. Hallelujah!

KISLEV 6

Today is Ben Gurion Day, an Israeli and national holiday to celebrate Israel's first prime minister.

Abide in the joy of the Lord! God is stepping things up and calling forth things that are not, as though they were!

It's a time of joy! Do you know that joy flows when you truly realize you have been redeemed? Jesus bought this redemption when He died, was buried, and resurrected to save you from sin.

Nehemiah 12:43 (KJV) says, *"Also that day they offered great sacrifices, and rejoiced: for God had made them rejoice with great **joy**: the wives also and the children rejoiced: so that the **joy** of Jerusalem was heard even afar off."*

Praise the Lord! Joy is going to start flowing at an unbelievable pace in your life! Now is the time to step into this joy. Make it a point to remember where your strength comes from every day. Push past the grieving, destruction, sickness, difficulty, or trial you may be facing. Purposefully declare that you have been redeemed and are sitting with Christ in heavenly places!

KISLEV 7

When the second temple was destroyed in the Maccabean revolt on Kislev 25, they found only one bottle of oil. However, that one bottle lit the menorah for eight days! It was a miraculous oil that showed the light of the Lord in the temple.

John 8:12 (NIV): *"When **Jesus spoke** again to the people, he said, '**I am the light** of the world. **Whoever follows me will never walk in darkness**, but will have the light of life.'"* He also said this during Feast of Tabernacles when He was declaring He was Messiah to the people.

Yeshua is the light of the world. And when we believe in Him and receive Him as our Lord and Savior, we become the light of the world too as His light lives within us. You have been given joy as part of the oil of gladness. The joy of the Lord fills you so that His light can burst forth from you.

Be encouraged! It is your season for the miraculous! Believe that you will begin to see the glory of the Lord. Double portion and double glory is here. It's coming upon you, and miracles are beginning to flow in your life!

KISLEV 8

This overflow in your spirit is the miracle oil, the anointing oil from Heaven. It's the oil that burns in the menorah, the temple lamps, that brings forth the overwhelmingly beautiful light we see in the earth today. I declare the oil of Heaven is coming upon you.

God is calling you to rejoice, to worship and serve Him only. He longs for you to come closer to His heart. He wants you to abide in Him. When you abide in Him, you will bear much fruit (John 15).

God is also calling you to obey His commandments. When you do this, you show Him that you are joining with Him. Now the joy of the Lord is complete in you. You will walk in a greater level of joy!

Come on, warrior! By faith enter into the season of miracles! God is calling you to bring a fire and a voice to those who are still in darkness. Set them free with your joy!

Share this with a friend who needs to rekindle their joy.

KISLEV 9

This truly is the month of miracles! You have stepped into the open vats of Heaven! God is speaking to you, even now, about purging some things out of your life. You see, the Lord needs to prune. We know this from John 15:2 (NKJV), *"Every branch in Me that does not bear fruit He takes away; and **every branch that bears fruit He prunes, that it may bear more fruit**."*

Remember last week I shared with you that God is opening new doors of opportunities for you? I'm so excited! Eyes are being opened and you are getting ready to walk in the favor of both God and people!

This month of Kislev is also recognized as a time to remember that Jesus is the Light of the world. When we walk in Him, we walk in the light and darkness is expelled. When there is darkness all around, we can enter into Him and the light shines.

Stay alert this month. Just like with Noah, the rain came for 40 days and 40 nights. He did not lose faith during that time—and he saw victory in the end. Stay with your light burning brightly, as God wants to use you in this season!

KISLEV 10

In the Hebrew scrolls we can read about the Maccabees. The Maccabees were the family of Mattathias who protected the temple when it was being attacked by the Greeks. During this time, the menorah (lamp) and the lights were removed from the temple, and the men found only one small bottle of oil. It was miracle oil, as the oil placed in the menorah stayed lit for eight days. Imagine that! One vial of oil burned for eight days straight. The number 8 means new beginnings. We are entering a birthing time, a time of new beginnings—and the miracle oil is present today!

Exodus 25:6 (KJV), *"Oil for the light, spices for anointing oil, and for sweet incense."* This is the oil the Lord wanted in His temple.

I want to pray for you: "Father, thank You so much for my friend. Thank You for the miraculous things coming upon their life, that they will birth new things and carry forth Your oil. As they walk, their light shines so brightly, darkness is expelled. Father, I thank You that my friend is going to overcome in every area today and walk in that overcoming anointing, in Jesus's name, amen."

Share this with someone who needs to know God wants them walking in the light today!

KISLEV 11

Kislev is a time of resting in the Lord, a time for re-evaluation and a restart. God will reveal things to you about yourself, environments you're in, and new doors of opportunity that He is opening for you. God is preparing hearts right now and opening people's eyes to your gifts, talents, and the things you bring to the table. In January you will begin to walk in a newness, a freshness, and something completely different from last year.

Overflow is coming. Continue to cleanse yourself daily and be purified by the Lord. Remain seated with Him and stay in His presence. He is changing things in a mighty way!

Let me speak this over you: May the miracle oil of God be released upon your life. May you see and walk in signs, miracles, and wonders. During this time of rest, may you enter into a place where miracles begin to flow through you. There is an overflow anointing coming into your life and it's filled with the oil of Heaven. As the oil begins to saturate you, may you begin to know God in a deeper and more intimate way. You will take your eyes off yourself. Self-consciousness is bound and God-consciousness is released. You will be a vial of miracle oil that burns and shines brightly for Jesus!

KISLEV 12

Praise the Lord! God is doing amazing things during this month of miracles. He wants you to prosper, increase, and have multiplication in your life.

At this time many years ago, the Maccabees defeated the Syrian-Greek army after they destroyed the temple. After the fight, the Maccabees found a small vial of oil. Typically, an oil vial would contain only enough oil for one day's burn, but this oil burned in the temple for eight days! It was a miracle!

The Lord has been speaking to me that not only will this be a season of miracles for you, but it will be a time for you to begin to flourish and prosper.

I used to pray, "Father, just give me increase. How can I be more of a blessing to the body of Christ? How do I step into that place of really bringing forth fruit?" Then the Lord always took me back to Psalm 1:1-3 (NASB): *"Blessed is the person who does not walk in the counsel of the wicked, nor stand in the path of sinners, nor sit in the seat of scoffers! But his delight is in the Law of the Lord, and on His Law he meditates day and night. He will be like a tree planted by streams of water, which yields its fruit in its season, and its leaf does not wither; and in whatever he does, he prospers."*

Why is this so important? Because the only way to increase and prosper every day is to position yourself to know more of the Word of God. Take time to memorize the Word of God, speak the Word of God, and work the Word of God in your life.

KISLEV 13

Did you know that Jesus is the Word made flesh? John 1:14 (NKJV) it says, "**And the Word became flesh and dwelt among us**, and we beheld His glory, the glory as of the only begotten of the Father, full of grace and truth."

If you want to be a person who brings forth the blessings and fruit, you have to know Him more. You have to know His Word more. You are a blessing when you delight yourselves in Jesus, the Word of God.

When you are growing in your relationship with Christ and meditating, constantly repeating His Word, then your faith increases and turns into action. Action produces more fruit and grows your spirit.

Maybe you have trouble studying or reading the Word, or you're not able to position yourself to receive from the Word. I break that off your life right now, in the mighty name of Jesus! I decree that you will begin to read the Word, be able to meditate on it, understand it, and live by it—starting today.

KISLEV 14

Tonight there is a full moon in the night sky.

Historically, Reuben, the son of Jacob, was born on Kislev 14 and died on Kislev 14 about 125 years later.

Purpose today to put behind you the ways of the flesh and live a healthy and prosperous life! Before you know it, you will actually be bringing forth fruit from the Word. You will be like an oak of righteousness planted by the rivers of living waters, producing much fruit!

In Habakkuk 2:1-3 (KJV), the prophet says, *"I will stand upon my watch, and set me upon the tower, and will watch to see what he will say unto me, and what I shall answer when I am reproved. And the Lord answered me, and said, Write the vision, and make it plain upon tables, that he may run that readeth it. For the vision is yet for an appointed time, but at the end it shall speak, and not lie: though it tarry, wait for it; because it will surely come, it will not tarry."*

Habakkuk was waiting and watching to see how the Lord would answer when he was reproved. The word *reproved* actually means to be corrected, chastened, to come to a place of reason.

God is setting you up for the new Gregorian calendar year before you! Watch, wait, and listen as God is bringing forth something new!

KISLEV 15

Historically this is the day when the Greeks set up the "Abomination of the Desolation," which was marked by the second-century Greek King Antioches VI Epiphanes who left pagan sacrifices on the Jewish altar in the temple.

This day is prophesied by Daniel as a time of fulfillment on the altar in the temple, but later by Jesus as a time that is coming. (See Daniel 12:11 and Matthew 24:14-18.)

If you are feeling any chastening right now or if you know God is taking you to the next level or a shift is taking place and something major is about to happen, it's because God wants you to come into a place of submission. Being reproved and corrected causes you to open your heart and mind to Him. It allows you to be attentive to what He wants to say to you.

In Habakkuk 2 God says, *"Now let me give you a vision. It's a vision that I want you to write down and make plain so that anyone can run with it."* In other words, "Make it so others can participate and can go to their next levels as well." It will come to pass, this vision, but there is a process.

I know that enemy forces have come against you and pressure has been applied to you. Take what has happened and use it as a source of seeking after God even during this time. He is going to show you that even in your weak places and weak moments, a new vision is about to be birthed.

KISLEV 16

Wow, I feel in my spirit that a new vision is being birthed right now, in the mighty name of Jesus! Take time to receive that! There is a revelation from Heaven coming to you right now. I declare over you that the grain of Heaven is opened to you. A new vision is released! It is something big. It is full of legacy. It is a vision that will bless you and others.

Creative ideas are coming to you. God is ministering to you. He is revealing things to you. I see dreams coming from Heaven upon you. You will see dreams and visions and will experience things in the spirit. Increase and multiplication are upon your life!

Grab hold of this and run to where God wants you to be! You *have* to write the vision down and make it plan like Habakkuk 2:2 talks about. When it's written, you can keep going over it again and again. This allows the Lord to deposit more inside you for a fresh vision for the new Gregorian calendar year.

Today, expect to see into the spirit realm! Expect dreams and visions. Let me pray for you:

"Father, I thank and praise You right now for my friend. I speak a new vision, new life, new hope, new direction, a new way over this reader. Lord, help this person write the vision down plainly so that others can follow it too. Amen."

Share this with a friend who needs to know the importance of writing down the vision from the Lord.

KISLEV 17

Proverbs 3:9-10 (KJV) says, "*Honour the Lord with thy substance, and with the firstfruits of all thine increase: So shall thy barns be filled with plenty, and thy presses shall burst out with new wine.*" Today I want to talk with you about substance. What is it and why is it so important?

"Substance" is what's inside you, what you're allowing to pour into your life. I want you to imagine yourself seated on Christ's lap at the right hand of the Father in the throne room of God. There you have all fullness and everything you need. If you stay seated with Christ in heavenly places, if you continue to honor God with your substance, vats will flow into and pour out of your life.

Position yourself to receive the internal overflow of the Holy Spirit. You can in turn pass this substance to others. You may be going through a difficult time right now. Things are happening around you that are frustrating and creating anger. Be encouraged! Know that you can respond with the overflow. You can respond just as though the miracle oil is flowing—because it is!

KISLEV 18

Even in the midst of the temple being destroyed by the Greeks, the vial of miracle oil was found! They placed the oil in the menorah (lamp) and it burned for eight days straight. The number eight means new beginnings. God took a little bottle of oil and performed a miracle. Just like that, He will take your seemingly little substance and turn it into something combustible! A continual overflow is coming into your life. There is more than enough inside you, because *He is more than enough!*

Allow His overflow anointing to come upon you. Get in a place of prayer, sit with Him and soak in His Spirit. When you are filled up, you become a vessel overflowing with miracle oil that won't stop. If you don't get into a place to receive from the Lord, you won't be able to give anything away. We are told to *"Honor the Lord with your substance."* Your substance has a maximum level, a place it can go and no farther. But when the Holy Spirit is deposited in you, an overflow is added, making whatever you have more than enough!

Step out in faith. Live in it. God is taking you to great places. Use your spiritual giftings today. Call someone today and tell them how special they are to you and God. As you reach out to others, they will feel it. Heavenly vats will open upon them too.

This is why we light candles. One life lights up another with the miracle oil of God...and then another and another and so on.

Stand firm. Stand tough. Worship, praise, and thank the Lord! It's a great day to be a believer in Christ Jesus!

KISLEV 19

You are bringing forth blessing! Praise God!

The Lord spoke to me about Revelation 4:1 (KJV): *"After this I looked, and, behold, a door was opened in heaven: and the first voice which I heard was as it were of a trumpet talking with me; which said, Come up hither, and I will shew thee things which must be hereafter."*

In this verse we read that the Lord was inviting the apostle John to come up into the heavenly realm through a door. The word *door* in this passage means portal. John saw a portal opened in the heavenly realm, and he was able to step through it. God is opening heavenly portals for you, and He wants you to step through them as well!

Blessings come from the heavenly realm into the earthly realm. You may be thinking, *How do I have access to them?* You have access because Jesus shed His blood for the redemption of your sins. When you receive Him as your Lord and Savior, you are now redeemed, have a relationship with the Father, and gain full access to heavenly things.

KISLEV 20

Revelation 4:2-3 (KJV) says, *"And immediately I was in the spirit; and behold, a throne was set in heaven, and one sat on the throne. And he that sat was to look upon like a jasper and a sardine stone: and there was a rainbow round about the throne, in sight like unto an emerald."*

The rainbow in this passage was one of many colors with the strength of an emerald. It surrounded the throne of Heaven with purified fire. You have unlimited access to this throne every day because you are seated with Christ in heavenly places.

The Lord wants to bless you greatly. I know that He desires His words to shake your soul so that you will speak what God says into your earthly realms. He wants to change the environments around you on a daily basis. God wants to use you, but you must listen for the sound of His voice. His sound will shake you in such a way that you will feel motivated, encouraged, uplifted, and ready to step into heavenly places.

KISLEV 21

You are called to be a voice in His Kingdom. I see that God is speaking to you, shaking you right now. He is saying, *"I need you to believe **by faith** that you are seated with Me in heavenly places, that I am on the throne, and that you have an open portal to access Me at any time. When you believe, you release the blessings of Heaven into the earth."*

Today, my friend, I declare that your ears will be opened to hear His voice and the sound of the trumpet. You will hear what the Lord is saying to you, and you will be one who brings forth blessings from Heaven to earth. I declare your eyes will be opened to see in the spirit, to see the open portals. You will pass through the door, or portal, into Heaven.

Share this with ones who need to know that they have access to the Father and heavenly things at any time.

KISLEV 22

Exodus 13:21 (KJV), *"And the Lord went before them by day in a pillar of a cloud, to lead them the way; and by night in a pillar of fire, to give them **light**; to go by day and night."*

Just as God led the Israelites in the desert by light at night, He is leading you into a new destiny for the new year before you! All you must do is have the faith to follow His light day and night, and you will come to the place of destiny where He is calling you to live.

Keep seeking Him and He will provide all you need for the vision to be fulfilled. The enemy wants you to lose faith, but you are at the cusp of seeing a breakthrough. Stand firm and watch the enemy be defeated. Just as the Jews had to stand against the Greeks in the Maccabean revolt, your light will shine in the darkness and all will see Him through you!

KISLEV 23

Psalm 119:105 (KJV), *"**Thy word is a lamp** unto my feet, and a **light** unto my path."*

The Word has become flesh and dwelt among us in the person of Jesus Christ. When God is speaking, He will give you a word that will cause you to know that it is Him and where to follow Him. God is speaking now that more words will come as you put one foot in front of the other and follow Him and His Word. Seek after the Word of God and keep His commandments and the portals of Heaven and miracle oil will flow unto you.

Let me pray for you: "Lord, be with my friend today as there have been issues taking place that are hard to work through. I ask You today to help this reader remember that You are for them, not against them and that You will bless them beyond measure if they sow to Your Word in their mind and heart. Lord, give them the blessed assurance of knowing You in Your Word so they can be stable every day in their minds and in decision making. We give You glory and praise, Lord, for You are the Word and You will bring all goodness to light!"

KISLEV 24

Historically today is the remembrance of the laying of the first temple foundation.

Haggai 2:18 (NIV): *"From this day on, from this **twenty-fourth day of the ninth month**, give careful thought to the day when the foundation of the Lord's temple was laid. Give careful thought."*

Through the prophet Haggai, God also said, *"I will shake the heavens and the earth; and I will overthrow the throne of kingdoms, and I will destroy the strength of the kingdoms of the heathen"* (Haggai 2:21-22 KJV).

I feel in the spirit realm that the enemy has been pushing you hard—but there is good news! He has been pushing because He knows that God has great things in store for you. Knowing this truth, what are you going to do when the enemy attacks? What are you going to do when he begins to lie, manipulate, control, and push you backward?

God says, "Press on and press forward. Get up! I want you to fight for it!" He is birthing forth destiny inside you. The only way for you to really know what you are made of is to enter the war. Come on! Get out your sword! You are going to fight forward into the new year!

Read this carefully: God does not want you to be held captive in any area. If you are beginning to feel annoyances and difficulties around you, examine what's in your mind. Get some cognitive awareness of what you are thinking about, what is your focus. God wants you to be aware of what the enemy could use to take you out in this next year.

KISLEV 25

Historically this is the day the Greeks made pagan sacrifices in the temple. Historically this is the day the miracle of the oil for Hanukkah began flowing.

Hanukkah or the Festival of Dedication begins today! This was the day the Jewish priest Mattathias, who was the father of Judas Maccabeus, and his family overcame the Greeks and the miracle oil was found so the menorah could be relit. Donuts are a special custom and gifts are given during these eight days; eight represents new beginnings.

Now is the time for you to press onward and move forward. Press toward the prize of the high calling of God in Christ Jesus: *"Not that I have already attained, or am already perfected; but I press on, that I may lay hold of that for which Christ Jesus has also laid hold of me. Brethren, I do not count myself to have apprehended; but one thing I do, forgetting those things which are behind and reaching forward to those things which are ahead, I press toward the goal for the prize of the upward call of God in Christ Jesus"* (Philippians 3:12-14 NKJV).

When you get pressed, you have a couple of choices. You can fight or you can flee. If you flee and become apathetic, you will become lazy. I'm praying for you right now, for the Lord to quicken your soul—your mind, will, and emotions. I'm calling out to somebody right now in the name of Jesus. You are oppressed and depressed. Come out of that cell of hell right now, in the name of Jesus—get up and start fighting! When you fight back, God will create a miracle to get you through.

Share this with a friend. Don't let the enemy win in your life. You are birthing destiny right now, in the name of Jesus!

KISLEV 26

Christmastime is right around this time! *"A merry heart does good, like medicine, but a broken spirit dries the bones,"* Proverbs 17:22 (NKJV) says. And Proverbs 3:8 from The Message Bible says, *"Your body will glow with health; your very bones will vibrate with life!"* I don't know about you, but I want to glow with health and be strong. We need to be temples of the Holy Spirit, ready to experience all of God!

Remember, Kislev is usually the eleventh or twelfth month on the Gregorian calendar; it falls on or near Thanksgiving or in the month of December. The number 12 represents government. I want to prophesy right now: "You are going to begin to see some great governmental shifts. I'm speaking to apostles, prophets, pastors, teachers, and evangelists—God is going to start infusing you with unbelievable power. You need to be bold and courageous!

"This month, more than any other time, God is going to cause His Kingdom government to rule and reign—and that means you! You are going to start working in the Kingdom, the United States and internationally. Miracles are happening—and you are stepping into Kingdom rulership!"

KISLEV 27

New apostles, prophets, evangelists, pastors, and teachers are rising. Have you felt like you have a prophetic gift? Do you want to go to the next level and operate there? That is exactly where God wants you to be. He is opening doors of Kingdom influence for you. He is shifting hearts for you to step into those roles. Maybe you have operated in the prophetic before. God is getting ready to shift you into an apostolic role. If you would like more teaching in the prophetic, consider my monthly prophetic mentoring; just reach out to me at www.candicesmithyman.com.

Even this week the Lord was speaking to me personally about Kingdom government. "Kingdom government" means that the Kingdom of Heaven is near, the Kingdom of Heaven has arrived! The Kingdom of the Light of the World is here! When Jesus came to the earth, He told the people that the Kingdom of Heaven is at hand (Mark 1:15). God also said to me, "Everywhere I send you, the work is already accomplished."

In other words, when He sends you to nations, the work there is already done. What He wants accomplished has already been accomplished in the heavenly realm. Anywhere He sends you, be sure to walk in that confidence. God delegated authority, instruction, and success to *you*. He sent *you*, and *you* will see healings and the miraculous! Oil is flowing!

KISLEV 28

Be joyful! You are living in Kingdom times! No matter what comes your way, God is doing something great in and through you. The enemy wants to come in like a storm, but he can only attack in the earthly realm. God is calling you up to the plate to be a Kingdom hitter. Hit the ball for the Kingdom! Walk in confident assurance and the knowledge that you are seated with Christ. Raise yourself to the heavenly places so you can rule and reign in the earthly realm. That's how you will bring the overflow of Heaven and the heavenly vats to earth and step into the roles God has called you to.

Get ready! Christmas is a time of celebrating the birth of Christ. It's also a time of celebrating the end of one year and the start of a new one. You are stepping into a new Kingdom assignment with this new year!

The miracle oil is all around!

Celebrate!

KISLEV 29

We experience *Hanukkah,* or the Festival of Dedication, and Christmas in the same month!

This is the time we remember the birth of our Savior, Jesus Christ. He is the best Christmas present we could ever receive. Jesus came to save, heal, and redeem you. He died and overcame death and the grave to remove your sins. When He ascended, He took you and me (the Church) with Him, and seated us in heavenly places.

What God really wants you to be aware of this week is found in Ephesians 4:7-8 (NIV): *"But to each one of us grace has been given as Christ apportioned it. This is why it says: 'When he ascended on high, he took many captives and gave gifts to his people.'"*

You were held captive by the enemy and eternal spiritual death; but because of Jesus's death, burial, and resurrection, you have been set free. Now you are a captive of God Himself, one with Him and seated in heavenly places.

You need to realize that Jesus descended before He ascended. What does that mean? Those who were held captive are now released, in the mighty name of Jesus. He went to Hades and got the keys to set you free. Not only are you released from eternal death, but you have been given the gift of the Holy Spirit inside you. The gifts of God flow in and through you now, special gifts just for you! Miracles are yours!

KISLEV 30

Historically this is a minor holiday that falls around this time called *Chag HaBanot* or Hanukkah Festival for Daughters. It is referred to in Arabic as *Eid al-Banat.*

Sometimes Kislev will be 30 days depending on the year, it is not this way with all the Hebrew months but Heshvan and Kislev share this same trait. If this happens and you are on a year when there are 30 days, here is an extra prophetic revelation for you!

Ephesians 4:10-13 (NKJV) says, *"(He who descended is also the One who ascended far above all the heavens, that He might fill all things.) And He Himself gave some to be apostles, some prophets, some evangelists, and some pastors and teachers, for the equipping of the saints for the work of ministry, for the edifying of the body of Christ, till we all come to the unity of the faith and of the knowledge of the Son of God, to a perfect man, to the measure of the stature of the fullness of Christ."*

Why is this important? Because not only have you been released from captivity but your Releasor went into the depths of hell and released anything that would continue to bind you. You are completely free! No matter how you feel today—even if you feel oppressed, depressed, or broken—He set you fully free from all of that! Take a moment to thank the Lord for saving you today.

Get ready for the new month of *Tevet* and the promotion before you, as well as the power of the new Gregorian year! The miracle is flowing a few more days, even into the month of Tevet.

THE MONTH
OF TEVET

Tevet comes from the root Tov, which means good.

This is the fourth month of the civil year and the tenth month of the religious calendar year. Tevet is unique in that it begins with the Festival of Dedication called *Hanukkah*.

Tevet is also a month when we begin to walk out our promotion, just like month of Adar and Elul.

Esther 2:16 (NASB): *"So Esther was taken to King Ahasuerus in his royal palace in the tenth month, which is the month Tebeth* [Tevet], *in the seventh year of his reign."*

Tribe of Israel (Conventional): Dan

Gemstone in Aaron's breastplate: Lapis Lazuli

Constellation in Sky/Hebrew name: Capricornus/Gedi

TEVET 1
Rosh Chodesh Tevet

Tonight there is a new moon in the night sky.

During the month of Tevet, Hanukkah, or the Festival of Dedication usually continues for a few days.

Historically this is said to be the month when Esther was brought into the king's palace. There, she had to go through a purification process for a year before becoming queen. Both purification and entering the palace were a year apart and started in the same month.

Promotion and miracles came to us all in November during the month of Kislev, but in the month of Tevet you begin to carry it out as the Gregorian new year begins in January. It is also proved by your adversaries in that they confirm the promotion by either speaking poorly of you or attacking you in some way. You will leave behind certain structures this month and take on new ones so you can carry out ruling and reigning well in the new year, just as Esther did.

May God lift up your spirits this holiday season. I want you to laugh a little! Hanukkah continues for a few more days. The miracle oil is flowing. Lift your hands toward Heaven and say, "Lord, bring that miracle oil over me. Do miracles on earth and bring forth light where things appear to be dark." If life looks bleak, start singing a worship song and have a merry heart, everything will change before you.

Share this with a friend who needs to be encouraged. We are in the end times, but it's not the end of the world! God wants us to declare, decree, proclaim, and stand fast in the faith.

TEVET 2

After the fight with the Syrian Greek army over the defilement of the temple, the Maccabees found a small vial of oil. Typically, an oil vial would contain only enough oil for one day's burn, but this oil burned in the temple for eight days! It was a miracle!

Since this is a season of miracles, why not rest in the miracle worker Himself, Jesus Christ and the Holy Spirit!

I used to pray, "Father, just give me increase. How can I be more of a blessing to the body of Christ? How do I step into that place of really bringing forth fruit and blessing?" Then He would tell me to abide in Him and to remain in Him. So how do we do that?

In John 15:5 (NKJV) Yeshua says, *"I am the vine, you are the branches. He who abides in Me, and I in him, bears much fruit; for without Me you can do nothing."*

The only way to increase and prosper every day is to position yourself to rest in God, stay abiding in Him. We can abide in God when we abide in the Word of God and in His Spirit presence. Take time to memorize the Word of God, speak the Word of God, and work the Word of God in your life. If you work the Word of God, in due time it will work for you!

TEVET 3

Today is the eighth day of the last day of Hanukkah, or the Festival of Dedication, but it is not the last day of miracle oil flowing for you! Keep the faith!

I'm so excited for this time of year because you are in a time of promotion! Psalm 75:6-7 (KJV) says, *"For promotion cometh neither from the east, nor from the west, nor from the south. But God is the judge: he putteth down one, and setteth up another."* Have you noticed from the prophetic revelations over the year that there are many times of promotion? Yes, there are about four promotion times each year; again, this is one of them!

Do you know that God has great things in store for you, just as He did for Esther? He is using you in a mighty way to bless and save others. What you are being promoted to do is going to make a difference for the Kingdom of God.

"Father, I praise and thank You for my friend today. You are raising them to the levels You are setting before them. They are seated with You in heavenly places. They have been properly positioned for the new year. Thank You, Lord, for fully equipping them with Your Word, with Your voice today. They will go forth and minister and stand fast in the confessions of their faith. They will move forward in the plan, purpose, and destiny that You have called them to. I know that their destiny will bring salvation to many. May they hold fast. May they stand firm in confidence of what You have done for us and how You have raised us up so that we may walk in Your power and be a voice in Your Kingdom, amen."

Share this with a friend today and bless them. Let them know that God has properly positioned and promoted them in this season. Encourage them to walk it out!

TEVET 4

We are living in an exciting time! We have stepped into a season when "tests of promotion" are happening. The Lord is preparing you for what He wants to do in you during the brand-new Gregorian year. He is bringing you into a new season of great blessings!

Maybe you have been feeling as though the Lord is encouraging you to take a leap of faith. Maybe you have been under attack in different areas of your life. Whatever the case, know that God wants to promote you—but first you need to press into Him and spend quality time with Him. This empowers you to push past the pressure of your situation. It's important that you know that God is testing you for promotion. Knowing this will make the test easier to bear.

"Tests of promotion" help us to learn and better understand our identities in Christ. They bring knowledge that we can stand on, a knowledge of the authority we are walking in, and what the Lord has called us to do. This knowledge can catapult our lives into the next season. Walk through the tests of promotion with faith, and the promotion is on the other side!

TEVET 5

These tests of promotion are now and God is bringing you to a good land, a good season, a good place, a place of blessing. He is positioning you now to stand in faith and walk out your identity in Christ just as Esther did when she stood on behalf of her people, the Jews, against the plot of evil Haman. Her cousin Mordecai challenged her in Esther 4:13-14 when he said, *"Esther, 'Do not imagine that you in the king's palace can escape any more than all the other Jews. For if you keep silent at this time, liberation and rescue will arise for the Jews from another place, and you and your father's house will perish. And who knows whether you have not attained royalty for such a time as this?'"*

God wants you to walk out your destiny this month. He wants you to put your hand to the plow. *Step it up!* God has set you up, and He has put you in the proper position to walk out your destiny before Him. He has elevated you. You are promoted!

Choose today to walk in confidence by faith.

TEVET 6

Our destiny can be accomplished when we recognize God's goodness and faithfulness beyond the odds or even our adversaries. Let us keep the heart of David when, no matter our adversaries, we respond as he did in Psalm 27:11-14 (NKJV): *"Teach me Your way, O Lord, and lead me in a smooth path, because of my enemies. Do not deliver me to the will of my adversaries; for false witnesses have risen against me, and such as breathe out violence. I would have lost heart, unless I had believed that I would see the goodness of the Lord in the land of the living. Wait on the Lord; be of good courage, and He shall strengthen your heart; wait, I say, on the Lord!"*

Wait on the Lord and remain righteous and in prayer. Jesus is your Advocate as you are being promoted. He is moving you into a special position during this time of promotion.

Take time this week to ask the Lord, "What happened this past year that changed me, and what can I change in preparation for this upcoming year? What are You preparing me for? How can I get myself ready for what's coming? What is Your vision for me?" A wise person inquires of the Lord. God knows everything the enemy is plotting, and only He can prepare you for the road ahead.

I would like to pray for you today: "Father, I praise You and thank You right now, in the mighty name of Jesus. Increase the faith of my friend today. Help them begin to step into a new realm of knowing who You are today as we are close to ending one year and moving ahead to another. Father, I praise You that faith is increasing, that strength is increasing, that Your blessings are going to come forth. My friend reading this is going to step into pressing past the blockades and obstacles and into their promotion. Lord, I give You glory, honor, and praise. You are showing us what is in the way and providing us with strength for this new season. Thank You for the month of Tevet. Open up my friend to this month of goodness and teach them to rest in Your goodness, in Jesus's name, amen."

TEVET 7

When troubles come, we are more than victorious in Christ. If you find that facing the continual blockades and obstacles is wearing you down, you are not alone.

This happens to be a purposeful enemy tactic to wear down the disciples of the Lord. The very tactics of the enemy are revealed in Daniel 7:25 (KJV), *"And he shall speak great words against the most High, and shall wear out the saints of the most High, and think to change times and laws: and they shall be given into his hand until a time and times and the dividing of time."*

The enemy has a plan to weary you. He can only succeed if you lose faith and hope! Endeavor today to stand strong in the faith and do not lose your faith and hope! God is promoting you, and during this time, warfare will ensue—you can be sure of it. Warfare proves your promotion because it means that the Lord has surely purposed to do it, and this is the enemy's last-ditch effort to squelch your joy in the process.

You can stand firm in your joy and your victory over the enemy because of the shed blood of Jesus Christ! Hold fast to the confession of your faith and see the manifestation of your purpose!

TEVET 8

Historically this is the day King Ptolemy II called together 72 sages to translate the Torah into Greek. This translation is called the Septuagint. It is said that all 72 sages who worked on this in separate chambers all miraculously came up with the same Greek translation. It is a fast day because it was considered an abomination for the Torah to be translated from its original text into Greek; therefore, some fast during this day.

The Lord gave me a prophetic word for you. He said, "I am getting things into alignment with Me, though the world systems think they are aligning things for their own benefit. No, I am aligning things for My benefit."

In Exodus 14:13 (NIV), Moses spoke to the people, saying, *"Do not be afraid. Stand firm and you will see the deliverance the Lord will bring you today."* That is also a word for you today! Do not be afraid of what you see happening in the world. Stand firm and see the Lord bring your deliverance. Yes, God is bringing deliverance. We walk it out by faith in our personal lives by knowing and understanding the King is alive; He hasn't and won't abandoned us!

My challenge to you is this: Through what lens do you see the world? God's abandonment? God's omnipresence? God's love for you? No matter how difficult things get, keep your focus on the Lord through "faith" lenses. In doing this, you will see your environments change and miracles happen! He wants you to change your eyesight. You have the power to prophesy to dry bones and dead places! Speak God's Word to what is overwhelming you. Speak to what's happening in the world today with God's wisdom. God is still on the throne. Remind yourself of this truth!

TEVET 9

Jesus Christ in His death, burial, and resurrection commissioned you to be part of the army that will bring forth deliverance on earth. Pick up your sword, the Sword of the Spirit! Declare and decree! Stand firm in the place of prayer. It's in this place you will begin to see a shifting take place. God responds to faith. If you respond overwhelmed and weary, it's almost like telling Him that what He did wasn't enough for you! God's plan and purpose is that you live by faith, keeping your eyes on Him, remaining steadfast in your faith.

You, as part of the Church and a member of His Kingdom, need to arise. You are one flesh with Him. He is moving forward, making a way and putting things into perfect alignment. You need to listen and do what He says.

Truth is revealed from Heaven, we are to speak from Heaven's perspective. Do not be dismayed or discouraged. Every trial you are going through is bringing forth gold, a greater understanding of who you are in Christ and of Jesus being on His throne and you being seated with Him.

TEVET 10

Historically this is the day of *Asarah B'Tevet,* or the Tenth of Tevet, a fast day, because this is the day when Nebuchadnezzar, king of Babylon, laid siege to Jerusalem in the ninth year of Zedekiah's reign. The Bible tells us in 2 Kings 25:1 (KJV): *"And it came to pass in the ninth year of his reign, in the **tenth month, in the tenth day** of the month, that Nebuchadnezzar king of Babylon came, he, and all his host, against Jerusalem, and pitched against it; and they built forts against it round about."*

Historically this is also the day when Esther approached King Ahasuerus for the first time. You are also to come into this new year with the knowledge and understanding that God has called you to live royally, just like Queen Esther (see Esther 2)!

God says He is retrieving the orphans and He is restoring legacy. This means that if you have had an orphan spirit, it came from feeling unloved or abandoned. You may have had a sense of loneliness, a void, or questions about where you belong. But in this season, you are being retrieved! That's powerful!

Being an orphan did not stop God from using Queen Esther *"for such a time as this."* He chose her, and He chooses you. He is telling you today, "Stand up and be the royalty that you are!" You represent Jesus, the Lion of Judah. He wants you to walk royally in His resurrection power. Remember, God is restoring you to the place of royalty. Your restoration will produce a legacy!

Share this with a friend who needs to be reminded that he or she is a child of the King!

TEVET 11

Jesus, the Messiah, has arrived and offers you life everlasting! In Him is peace, rest, and joy. Spiritual blessings are yours as you are seated with Him in heavenly places. The power and the presence of the Holy Spirit is with you. Jesus is with you! He is covering you, holding you, and speaking words of truth and life to you. It doesn't matter what situation, disappointment, or difficult circumstance you're going through right now—you have the good news that Jesus is with you!

God loves you so much He sends angels to minister to you. Here in this season, the heavens are open and miracles are taking place over you. While the enemy comes to steal, kill, and destroy, God comes to give life! Do not lose heart. Your miracle is coming!

Luke 2:10-11 (NKJV): *"Then the angel said to them, 'Do not be afraid, for behold, I bring you good tidings of great joy which will be to all people. For there is born to you this day in the city of David a Savior, who is Christ the Lord.'"*

The Lord spoke to me, saying, "Tell My people to increase their faith." Even if you're experiencing fear, faith overcomes it. You may be scared that a blessing from the Lord is going to be taken away. I bind that fear, in the name of Jesus! I release a confidence in you that you have the blessings He gave you. Hold on to this assurance and fight forward in faith.

If you're dealing with a physical issue, listen, get up and start fighting! Get out of your bed and start moving! God said, "Start living by faith and step out!" I know chronic issues are hard, but God is empowering you now to take a leap of faith, to have His faith for your healing. Know that He is willing and able to heal you. God loves you more than anything. He sent His Son Jesus Christ as your Gift!

TEVET 12

January is the Gregorian calendar month when we offer our first-fruits unto the Lord. It's a foundational month often referred to as "the month of firstfruits." What is firstfruits? It's the promise to come (Proverbs 3:9-10). In Tevet, we learn the principle of giving, which brings power!

Now is your time of preparation. What a special time! Many are already praying, fasting, giving, and living set apart from the world. If you have been preparing like this, you have positioned yourself and laid a foundation for the months to come. You are about to step into all the promises of God for your life, to walk in your destiny and abide in His hope.

When it comes to wanting to see prosperity and abundance in your life, you have to give above and beyond. You do this by faith! You do this by understanding the realm of Heaven, that you are seated with Christ in heavenly places. You don't give from a place of lack. That is an earthly perspective. You give from your heavenly perspective.

Don't forget to bless the Lord this month with firstfruits offering! Give the Lord your best as this offering is a *whole* of a gift. The whole of your hourly wage, first sale of month. This is not the tithe, it is an offering for a foundation on which all tithes and offerings are blessed for the remainder of year. Go back to the beginning and review Chapter 2 again, "Sowing in the Right Season for Blessing," and you will be encouraged in the principle of firstfruits.

I also hear God saying, "There are people who want to give; there are people who want to give to others but feel like they don't have enough." I'm asking God to shower you with blessings from Heaven. When you receive, you will turn around and bless somebody else with what you received. The true meaning of life is to be a giver and not a getter.

TEVET 13

Let me speak over you: "The Lord says right now, 'I am taking care of your issue. I took care of it on the cross. I took care of it through the death, burial, and resurrection of Jesus. I am increasing your faith now to believe for the great things that I have called into being for you.'"

I hear Him saying specific things: He is calling out silver and gold to be released, new job opportunities, new divine relationships and alignments. He is calling new spiritual gifts to come forth. God is calling forth new apostles, prophets, five-fold ministry leaders, and marketplace ministry leaders. I'm speaking to the entrepreneur spirit right now: I want you to rise up, in the mighty name of Jesus. Begin to work with the entrepreneur ideas that are flowing from Heaven to you. I see creative ideas coming from Heaven. Just lift up your hands and grab hold of one of those right now. These will help bring you income this new year.

The revelatory Word of God is coming to you that you would have heavenly encounters and see angels. You will know for sure the power and presence of God is with you and you will step out in "Godfidence," which is God-confidence, knowing that if God sent you, it is already accomplished. You are a sent one.

This whole season is about the life that Jesus Christ gave us. We speak life and not death. We speak power and not poverty. We speak provision and increase. We speak encouragement. Any depression, anxiety, and fear plaguing you or your family, we command to leave in the name of Jesus, and we speak that your mind will shift and new brain cells will begin to grow, and you will start to flow with the power of the Spirit. You will feel and experience the joy of the Lord! May the joy of the Lord and may heavenly habitations bind to your soul, in the name of Jesus. I speak joy to you! laugh! A merry heart does the bones good. Your bones are glowing right now. You are a light in the darkness.

TEVET 14

Tonight there is a full moon in the night sky.

In this month of Tevet, we usually enter the Gregorian calendar month of January. It is a time of consecration and to fast, pray, and reset your focus. It's a time to eliminate all distractions and align yourself with Christ. A vital key to resetting focus is keeping our eyes and our heart fixed on Jesus, the Author and Protector of our faith. God has created a special plan for each of us. Ephesians 2:10 (NKJV) says, *"For we are His workmanship, created in Christ Jesus for good works, which God prepared beforehand that we should walk in them."* God has ordained a plan in advance for every person. He wants the best for us!

I'm believing great things for you in the spirit realm as a result of you participating in this month of firstfruits. God has great plans! He wants you to build a strong foundation, starting right here at the beginning of the year. Do you want to receive a greater revelation from Heaven about who you are in Christ and what He's positioned you to do this year? It's done through prayer, fasting, consecration, setting apart, and evaluation.

What is fasting? To me, fasting simply means that you miss a meal a day. Some may purpose to miss two meals and others may drink only liquids for the time they set aside. During this time, you evaluate what you are putting in your mouth so your flesh can be under complete control of the Holy Spirit. "Feeding" your spirit the Word of God places you in a position to recognize the substance God has already given you. Your spiritual touch, taste, smell, sight, and sound will be opened and alert. You're going to enter a new place of heavenly blessings.

God wants to build you strong and sturdy. He wants to advance and expand you. How can that happen unless you consecrate yourself, unless you come into the place of fully honoring God with your substance and the firstfruits of all of your increase? It's after you do those things that His Word says you will enter the overflow, your barns will be filled and new wines will burst forth.

TEVET 15

Ask God today to ignite your spiritual senses and to empower you for the journey ahead. Stay vigilant. The enemy is coming hard to distract your focus and take you off course. You must stand firm, hold your position, continue to wear His righteousness and advance. Do not allow the enemy any footholds. Let go of all offenses and forgive those who have hurt you. Forgiveness brings healing to your life; and when we are completely aligned with Christ, blessings will come forth.

The plan God has for you is mighty. You are important. Be encouraged! God wants you on His team. He wants to use you, and there is much to be done! Let me pray for you today: "Father, I praise You and thank You that my friend is going to get things in order in life and will put You first. Father, I thank You that a powerful overflow anointing is coming to this reader's life. It's going to pour in and through them, and their life is going to make a difference for the Kingdom of God. Amen."

You have come through a time of testing for promotion. Yes! I can see it happening in the heavenly realms! The Lord is pouring out grain, wine, and oil upon you (Hosea 2). The vats of Heaven are open. I see gold and silver from Heaven being poured down upon you. The resources of Heaven are coming to touch you right now, to aid in this promotion. Lift up your hands and shout, "Amen!"

TEVET 16

God is aligning your life with a divine setup for the new Gregorian calendar year! God causes all things for your good and is properly positioning you.

You are a voice of the Kingdom, and God wants to use you in a mighty way. Just like when Esther came into King Ahasuerus's house, not only was she prepared, but she was promoted. She was called to save her nation. She stepped up to the task and stood up to the king. She became a voice in her Kingdom and everything she needed was provided. She protected her people from evil Haman and became close with King Ahasuerus. She passed the test of loving the people more than herself.

Your promotion time will put you in places you have never even imagined, with people you have never seen! It will cause you to press in for them and save your family, workplace, and nation! Embrace your divine connections! Get excited that God is properly positioning you! He is preparing you to minister to people who will show up in your life. You will have the resources you need to complete every task.

There is a greater release of finances coming to you. *"He who sows sparingly will also reap sparingly, and he who sows bountifully will also reap bountifully"* (2 Corinthians 9:6 NKJV). Choose to sow bountifully today. This is the month we practice the principle of firstfruits giving.

Share this with friends, and let them know that they have been properly positioned for promotion!

TEVET 17

You will walk in the resurrection power of Jesus Christ this year. You are the adopted child of the Lord.

Romans 8:15-17 (KJV) says, *"For ye have not received the spirit of bondage again to fear, but ye have received the Spirit of adoption, whereby we cry, Abba! Father. The Spirit itself beareth witness with our spirit, that we are the children of God: and if children, then heirs; heirs of God and joint-heirs with Christ, if so be that we suffer with him, that we may be also glorified together."*

You probably know the story about how Mary and Joseph could not find Jesus for a few days when He was an adolescent. Finally, they found Him in the temple. Luke 2:49 (NKJV) says, *"And He said to them, 'Why did you seek Me? Did you not know that I must be about My Father's business?'"* Jesus had an earthly mother and father, Mary and Joseph, and He obeyed them and went to Nazareth with them. But this verse shows us that He was drawn to His Father God, the Father's Kingdom, and the business of His Father's Kingdom. Even though Mary didn't understand all that Jesus was saying, she kept what He said in her heart.

As you enter the new year, you need to know that you are an adopted son or daughter of Father God. Through Jesus's death, burial, and resurrection, He has united you with the Father. You are His royal child, with His royal inheritance and a royal Kingdom mandate. Claim your inheritance today!

TEVET 18

You are called to live in Jesus's resurrection power. You are called to live with the knowledge that *Jesus is the Life and the Light of the world*—every day!

You could be tested by the Holy Spirit in the resurrection power that you have been given. But remember, you have all the power in the world. You are connected to God by the Holy Spirit who lives inside you! You are seated with Him in heavenly places as a royal child of the King. You can call Him "Abba Father"!

With these blessings and benefits, you are called to march forward in the new year. You need to make sure as a royal child of the Kingdom of Heaven that the Kingdom is manifest on earth this year. Think about what kind of impact you are going to make this year. You need to be about your Father's business.

It's time to stand up and be a warrior for the Kingdom!

Share this with a friend and let them know you both have a roar just like the Lion of Judah! Enter this new year with courage and joy!

TEVET 19

God is distributing new mantles. What is a mantle? A mantle is a covering or cloak. It is a drape that positions you to walk in the authority God has given you and with the spiritual gifts He has assigned to you. A mantle is something you carry no matter what's going on around you or how you're feeling. It determines your level of authority and the office that you have been called to. You must learn to walk in your mantle. Some mantles are given individually, some corporately. Today, let's examine the corporate mantle.

Jesus told His disciples corporately what *they* should do when facing a problem. Matthew 14:15-16 (NIV) says, *"As evening approached, the disciples came to him* [Jesus] *and said, 'This is a remote place, and it's already getting late. Send the crowds away so they can go to the villages and buy themselves some food.' Jesus replied, 'They do not need to go away. You give them something to eat.'"*

Jesus turned the whole issue around. He told the disciples that they were the sent ones. He needed them to exercise their authority in this area. Likewise, you are a *sent one* in the Kingdom of God—exercise your authority today and *go!*

TEVET 20

Feeding the crowd is an example of miraculous working. When Jesus said, *"They do not need to go away. You give them something to eat,"* He wanted the disciples to supply the food, but all they had were five loaves of bread and two fish. The disciples didn't think that small amount would feed the multitude listening to Jesus teach. But with God a miracle happened! Jesus took the bread and fish, blessed it, and it multiplied! More than 5,000 people were fed that day by just that little lunch!

This is exactly what God is calling you to do this year. You have been given a mantle assignment in the Kingdom of God. You are a sent one; God is sending you out. You are in an ascension place with Christ and you have all the fullness you need to bless others. If Jesus calls you to feed the sheep, to go out and help or bless others, He will bring all provision necessary to complete what He asks of you.

When Jesus lifted up the bread and fish and prayed, it was as if He was lifting Himself up, offering Himself as food for the people. The five loaves symbolize grace and the two fish symbolize "double grace." The grace of God leads to multiplication. There is a double portion coming! Notice how the fish as well as the Church of Jesus Christ multiplied that day!

The great awakening is coming! It's our job to tell people about Jesus. Jesus didn't take people out of their desolate places—He met them there. God wants you to carry your mantle assignment and be the disciple who takes provision to others. You will carry the Word and bless people because you are full in spirit, soul, and body! More people are going to come into the Kingdom of God because of this power inside you!

TEVET 21

You're going to be full of God's power, because you know that the work was complete when Jesus died, was buried, then was resurrected and ascended. You have everything you need to be a disciple who looks to Heaven, gives thanks, and then sees miracles take place.

Everywhere God sends you the work is already complete, and great and mighty things are going to happen. You just need to show up. He'll show up with the miracle necessary to meet the needs of the people. Just walk in the mantle and the authority that comes with it, and He will bring about the result.

Know this today: You are living in green pastures. You are full. God is going to take that fullness and bless others through you. As part of the Kingdom of God, He has given you a mantle to go into desolate places. God will use you in a mighty way as you position yourself with Him and extend yourself to others. You will walk in a power that will be distributed to those who need it. Receive and believe that with me, in the mighty name of Jesus.

TEVET 22

God wants His Church to begin to realize the power of being seated with Christ in heavenly places. The apostle Paul spoke of these truths as though they were to be evident by Christ's body on a daily basis. We have been crying out to God for centuries for Him to return. Well, this is a key that can catapult His return in this decade. We must live with our spiritual senses of sight, hearing, taste, touch, and smell focused on the Spirit. This enhances our ability to be remain seated with Him in heavenly places in our souls.

How then can the Church, Christ's body, prepare for Christ's return? The answer is in our ability to stay seated spiritually in the heavenlies with Christ, manifesting this by faith in our mind, will, and emotions. This means our soul needs to submit to our spirit and we must keep our minds on things above, such as our spiritual position in Christ. The apostle Paul received revelation from Heaven on his spiritual position in Christ and he had many writings on this subject.

In Ephesians 2:5-7 (NIV), he shares with the church at Ephesus that God has *"made us alive with Christ even when we were dead in transgressions—it is by grace you have been saved. And **God raised us up with Christ and seated us with him in the heavenly realms** in Christ Jesus, in order that in the coming ages he might show the incomparable riches of his grace, expressed in his kindness to us in Christ Jesus."*

We need to know we are sitting in our heavenly seat and we must stay there no matter our circumstances and distractions from the enemy. As we enter this new year, we need to keep our eyes and heart on things above where Christ is seated, at the right hand of God (Colossians 3:1).

I believe God wants His Church to prepare for His return by focusing on our spiritual position in Christ as His body. As we live by faith in this area, we are preparing His Kingdom. He will only come back when His bride is ready. That means we must live by faith in these truths now.

TEVET 23

The Lord also says clarity is coming to your soul this year. Clarity involves your spiritual sight. This includes your mental and spiritual understanding of being seated in the heavenly realms with Christ.

This year focus on receiving greater vision and clarity of your position in Christ. As clarity comes to our souls—mind, will, and emotions—we will be preparing ourselves to speak with our mouths.

Psalm 34:8 (KJV) says, *"O taste and see that the Lord is good: blessed is the man that trusteth in him."* The New International Version puts it this way, *"Taste and see that the Lord is good; blessed is the one who takes refuge in him."*

Therefore, activate your spiritual taste and speak with your mouth. The greater clarity we have in our souls, the greater alignment with the heart of God to speak in faith. God is preparing His people to live seated with Him in heavenly places in the here and now, and you will gain clarity of this in your soul this year.

He made a way through our death, burial, and resurrection in Him; now it is time to stay positioned, in our seats on His lap, at the royal table and remain there, regardless of enemy distraction. It is here you will manifest the presence of God for overflow.

TEVET 24

Let's remember that the goodness and mercy of the Lord follow us all the days of our lives (Psalm 23:6). The Lord is pouring out His goodness from Heaven upon us!

In Exodus 33:18 (NKJV), Moses says to the Lord, *"Please, show me Your glory."* The Lord responded to him in verse 19, saying, *"I will make all My goodness pass before you, and I will proclaim the name of the Lord before you. I will be gracious to whom I will be gracious, and I will have compassion on whom I will have compassion."*

What is His goodness? *Goodness* in the Hebrew is the word *tub,* and it means His goodness, His beauty, His gladness, His welfare, and His joy! Did you know the word *tevet* is *tuv,* which means good.

Do you need the joy of the Lord today? Do you want to start walking in the joy of the Lord? Praise the Lord! God wants to reveal His joy, His beauty, and His gladness to you! When you walk in the joy of the Lord, in His beauty and His gladness, then His glory will come forth.

Manifestations of His glory can come in the form of laughter, fire, or healing. It may even come in the *kabad* glory, which is a weightier and heavier glory that is part of the character of God. I know I want to carry this *kabad* glory!

When God shows you His goodness, He is sharing His honor, authority, and character with you. How blessed it is when God reveals Himself to us.

TEVET 25

Do you want to see more of the glory of the Lord in your life? Do you want to be a glory carrier? Then you need to know and understand God's goodness and how He proclaims His name before you.

Take a self-evaluation. How good is God? Do you feel that God is good in your life? Is God good in everything He does? Or do you have a theology that says God is only good when He does this or that?

Open yourself to the goodness of the Lord. Proclaim His name! Habakkuk 2:14 (NKJV) says, *"For the earth will be filled with the knowledge of the glory of the Lord, as the waters cover the sea."* This is an element that will come before the revealing of the *kabad* glory.

Since God's character is one of goodness and joy. When you stand in His joy, honor, and authority, you become a glory carrier. This allows the Lord to release His glory into your home, work-place, city, state, and nation.

You are called to be a glory carrier! Take time today to ask the Lord to show you His goodness which fuels the glory.

Share this with a friend who needs to see that God's goodness is present in their life!

TEVET 26

As this new year begins, God really wants you to *rest* in the realms of His Kingdom. He is positioning you now through a higher level of faith to enter His Kingdom realms of prosperity and ascension. This is so important. Why? Because you need to get to where you can receive an impartation in the realms of the Kingdom so you can truly impact the earth!

You must understand the rulership and authority in the Kingdom of faith that you have been given. This will allow a rest to settle in your heart and mind. This is done through a purification process. When you take time to allow God to purify, consecrate, and sanctify you, it will change your mindset from a victim mentality with thoughts of lack to a royalty mindset with expectation for increase.

The world will constantly tell you that you don't have enough or that you aren't enough. But I'm here to tell you that you have been given authority, you are positioned for greatness, and all the blessings of the Kingdom are yours!

You are a child of the Kingdom of Heaven and you have a royal inheritance! Just like Queen Esther entered a place of royalty, you have too. Your heavenly Father, Abba Father, has made a way through the shed blood of Jesus Christ. You have gone from orphan to son or daughter. You are part of the royal family!

One way to walk this out is to apply Matthew 6:33-34 (NIV) to your life every day: *"But seek first his kingdom and his righteousness, and all these things will be given to you as well. Therefore do not worry about tomorrow, for tomorrow will worry about itself. Each day has enough trouble of its own."*

TEVET 27

You don't need to worry about anything. When Jesus came to earth He said, *"The Kingdom of heaven has arrived."* As a son or daughter of the King, know that in the realms of royalty is the realm of the Kingdom of Heaven. You have a legacy you are called to carry out! You lack nothing. Don't be afraid!

Proverbs 3:9-10 (NIV) shows us another way that we can honor God: *"Honor the Lord with your wealth, with the firstfruits of all your crops; then your barns will be filled to overflowing, and your vats will brim over with new wine."*

This year you are going to rule and reign in faith and in the earth. As you gain this revelation, your capacity to believe for miracles to take place in your life will grow. Increase and blessings are yours!

Choose today to walk in sonship and practice the power of firstfruits. Sow in faith the Word and prayerfully consider sowing a financial seed before the month is complete.

This is the Month of Firstfruits—let's give Him honor in giving! Share this with friends who need to be reminded that they are royalty.

TEVET 28

This is the month we remember the celebration of firstfruits. Firstfruits are "chief, principal things, a first thing, whole thing or beginning." This celebration of giving is established in Proverbs 3:9-10 (KJV), which tells us to *"Honour the Lord with thy sub-stance, and with the firstfruits of all thine increase: So shall thy barns be filled with plenty, and thy presses shall burst out with new wine."*

We are to honor the Lord with our substance, which starts at the core with our faith. Our substance is two parts: internal faith and external resources. What has God deposited inside you? Do you have fullness, satisfaction, and an understanding of who He is? What external resources has God given you? What wealth, abundance, and possessions do you have? Now is the time to begin assessing your substance and positioning your heart.

God has given you great substance by His *dunamis* power, His Holy Spirit, and His *exousia* power (delegated authority to you). You should honor God with your wholeness and the resources He has given you. It blesses the Lord when you bless Him with your increase. Every year as you increase, it's important to not only bless Him with your substance but also with the additional fruit God has provided for you.

I declare over you right now that your spirit, soul, and body will be filled with the strength of God. Your bones will be healed. You will be a light to the darkness. God is bringing creative ideas from Heaven to you now. You will live in the overflow. You will stop letting tsunamis overtake you. Instead, you will get on the top of the waves and start surfing. Watch and see God do amazing things for you this year!

TEVET 29

I believe this is a year of new wineskins and a new "mind skin." In Matthew 17, the disciples had been trying to cast a demon out of a man, and they were unsuccessful. They wanted to know why. Verse 20 (NKJV) says, *"Jesus said to them, 'Because of your unbelief; for assuredly, I say to you, if you have faith as a mustard seed, you will say to this mountain, "Move from here to there," and it will move; and nothing will be impossible for you.'"* We need to have a faith mindset focused on the goodness of God and His love for us.

The devil is a liar. He comes with thoughts of doubt, fear, anxiety, and depression. He wants you to hold back your faith, to think that you can do it on your own or to believe that God's promises are for everyone, except you.

God wants to do a miracle for *you!* His love for you is so great. He wants to come into every situation of your life and do a miracle. He wants you healed and whole in your body and soul, to walk in blessings and not debt, and for you to move through life with clarity instead of fear. Do you believe this? This year, you *must* believe that God wants His best for you.

Let me pray over you right now: "Lord, I thank You in the mighty name of Jesus that You are speaking to my friend. Enlighten their hearts and open their spiritual eyes so that they might see You— Your glory, beauty, majesty, and Your plan for them this new year. Heal the wounds from the past and launch this reader with a new vision, new goals, and a new position in You. Help my friend walk in step with You on the path that You have commissioned them to walk. Help them to walk in the footsteps of Jesus as they enter the new year. In Jesus's mighty name, amen."

Get ready for the month of *Shevat* as this new month will be a release of the angelic hosts in your life! Are you ready for more of the supernatural?

THE MONTH
OF SHEVAT

Shevat means strike or lashing which can be attributed to the heavy rains that come this time of year in Israel.

This is the fifth month on the civil calendar and the eleventh month on the religious calendar.

This is a month of angelic release on earth and continued practice of the principle of firstfruits.

Zechariah 1:7-8 (NIV): *"On the **twenty-fourth day of the eleventh month, the month of Shebat,** in the second year of Darius, the word of the Lord came to the prophet Zechariah son of Berekiah, the son of Iddo. During the night I had a vision, and there before me was a man mounted on a red horse. He was standing among the myrtle trees in a ravine. Behind him were red, brown and white horses."*

Tribe of Israel (Conventional): Asher

Gemstone in Aaron's breastplate: Agate

Constellation in Sky/Hebrew name: Aquarius/Deli

SHEVAT 1
Rosh Chodesh Shevat

Tonight there is a new moon in the night sky.

Historically Moses taught the children of Israel the Torah and the book of Deuteronomy for 37 days. This was done to prepare them, as he passed away next month on Adar 7.

Deuteronomy 1:3 (KJV): *"And it came to pass in the fortieth year, in the eleventh month, on the first day of the month, that Moses spake unto the children of Israel, according unto all that the Lord had given him in commandment unto them."*

God is giving you eyes of spiritual clarity to see the supernatural and walk it out this month. Do not bring with you the trauma of the past, as God is doing a new thing and it requires new eyes of faith!

Isaiah 42:9 (NASB) says, *"Behold, the former things have come to pass, now I declare new things; before they sprout I proclaim them to you."* God has great things in store for you. Take time to seek Him, and He will reveal them. Once He does, write the vision down and make it plain (Habakkuk 2). This way you will accomplish the vision God has for you.

In Jeremiah 1:12, God asked Jeremiah to describe something he saw. Jeremiah told the Lord he saw the branch of an almond tree. The Lord told him that he saw correctly and declared to him that He would watch over His Word. We too need to be this intently focused on Christ and His Word so that we are confidently walking in the direction He has given us. Speak what you see! The angels hearken to the voice of the Lord, and they will hearken to you stepping into your God-given authority.

SHEVAT 2

Historically this is the day that Asher, one of the tribes of Israel, was born.

In Genesis 1:27-28, God is calling us as the Church of Jesus Christ to be fruitful, multiply, replenish the earth, subdue, it and have dominion. It's important to the Lord that you, as part of His Church, be victorious. He wants you to stand with other believers and move forward in line with His Word: be fruitful, replenish, and have dominion. Through Jesus, you have been given power to rule. Even though we're in a tumultuous time, do not be discouraged! Jesus has already said you will triumph! Your job is to declare, decree, and proclaim it!

God wants you to subdue, to positively conquer and have dominion. How do you that? You do it through prayer, fasting, and positioning yourself to be strong in the Lord. If you have not taken time here at beginning of the year to seek the Lord, pray, fast, and give. It isn't too late! This is a time of cleansing in our lives and on earth.

Let me pray for you as we begin this new month of Shevat. "Father, I thank You for my friend right now. I'm asking you to give them a supernatural impartation of faith. Let their faith in You and Your goodness be substance, so real to them that they begin to see the changes being made in and around their lives. Father, I thank You and praise You right now. Please raise the faith in this reader's heart so when they speak to the mountain that is before them, it shall be moved, in Jesus's name. Thank You, Father, that a faith impartation is coming to Your people right now, and they are being raised up to see themselves seated with You in heavenly places where there is no restriction. They have all the inheritance and everything they ask for; in accordance with Your Word, it shall be done, in Jesus's name."

SHEVAT 3

God also recently showed me an open portal in Heaven where He was dispatching angels to come down and patrol the earth. This isn't the first time God sent His angels. Zechariah 1:7-8, talks about how angels were dispatched to patrol and control the earth and to bring peace. This is a great chapter to read as we come into the Hebrew month of Shevat.

The Lord is surrounding you with angels. He has dispatched angels to go with you as you carry out Kingdom assignments this year. As said before, God is giving you new assignments and new angels to go along with them. So declare this with me: "I will rise up. God is cleansing the earth and angels are patrolling it. God is strengthening me. I will be strong and healthy. I will be ready to step into what God has for me this year. I am victorious no matter how difficult the situation. I am triumphant! Lord, open my spiritual eyes to see in the spirit realms."

SHEVAT 4

We have been learning how to walk in the faith of God and how we can step into new "mind skins" and new wineskins. We have set strong foundations in our spiritual lives that will last the rest of the year. This preparation allows us to be ready for God to pour newness into us and cultivate a manifestation of spiritual gifts.

Shevat is the eleventh Hebrew month when Moses recited the Torah (Deuteronomy 1:1-3). When we meditate on the law, we become righteous people and gain an understanding of who we are in Christ. Jesus is our great example. He fulfilled the entire law and used the Word to overcome. As we mediate on Scripture and begin to speak it over our lives, we will see the Word of God in action.

Stand firm in your faith! Live by the Word and meditate on it day and night. As you continue to walk righteously, God will reward you. He wants you to live like the tribe of Asher—full of blessing, fortune, and happiness. This is what the name "Asher" means! You are now purified, sanctified, and consecrated for a new work this year. Celebrate His righteousness and grace. Press forward. Walk by faith and not by sight. God has amazing things in store for you!

SHEVAT 5

Double glory is coming to you, and you will experience double in so many areas of your life this year!

Right now, I feel the glory of the Lord. His presence is going to be coming forth in miracles, signs, and wonders this year. God is going to use you in a mighty way for sure!

Shevat is also known as the month of trees. It stands as a reminder that you are the planting of the Lord. You need to have deep roots to stand in this new year. Your roots have to be grounded in the Father, Son, and Holy Spirit. Learn to put God first this month, to remember your foundation in Him. God wants to glory in the fruit you bear in Him!

Isaiah 61:3 (KJV): *"To appoint unto them that mourn in Zion, to give unto them beauty for ashes, the oil of joy for mourning, the garment of praise for the spirit of heaviness; that they might be called trees of righteousness, the planting of the Lord, that he might be glorified."*

SHEVAT 6

Shevat is a time when the angels patrolled the earth. Zechariah 1 tells us that angels are on patrol. Warrior angels are coming! These angels are looking for ways to advance His Kingdom and report back to the Father. They come in a variety of colors, and each color represents a different element of fire. There are red, white, and gold-colored angels. These angels can be recognized as angels of fire sent to earth.

I believe and I'm going to say this prophetically, you are going to receive a touch from the angels of fire this month. You are going to begin to understand the angels of fire and how to participate with them for Kingdom advancement.

Remember, you have the voice of the Lord, and angels respond to His voice! The Lord's voice is a spark, a fire, and a thunder! Today, activate your partnership with angels.

Step in confidence, knowing that this is your month of fruitfulness, abundancy, and increase. More importantly, take time this month to consecrate yourself for the entire year—pray, fast, and give. Purpose to remain consecrated before God. If you do not yet have a copy of my book *Angels of Fire: The Ministry of Angels in the End Time Revival,* get one today to learn about how God has given us authority to participate with angels in the Kingdom.

SHEVAT 7

The Hebrew month of Shevat is a time assigned to fruitfulness. It comes through purification and holiness. The Lord has been showing you what is hindering you from moving in the realms of Kingdom living. Have you identified what they are? Let them go, move them out of your life so you can increase in the Kingdom. When you do, you will see increase and multiplication!

It is so important for you to learn how to walk in the realms of the Kingdom. In these realms, you will bring forth fruit! Soon, it will be the day *Tu Bishvat* on Shevat 15 which is a minor new year that the Jews remember by planting trees. This month is characterized by the root of fruit-bearing and bringing forth more in the Kingdom.

Just as the Jews plant trees, you are a planting of the Lord. Your roots are supposed to go deep into the soil of faith so that you can become a tree of righteousness. Let me help you understand this concept. Hebrews 12:14 (KJV) reads, *"**Follow peace*** *with all men, and holiness, without which no man shall see the Lord."* To *"follow peace"* in the Greek really means to join together in peace and prosperity. When you join yourself with God, you come into the realms of Heaven, the realms of prosperity, and the realms of Kingdom living. You can correspond with them and have this prosperity with all people—in a place of peace and holiness.

SHEVAT 8

If you don't have holiness, you will not see the Lord. The Lord is holy and righteous—that is who He is. He wants you to follow in His footsteps. Understanding His character is part of understanding the realms of the Kingdom. In the realms of the Kingdom, the Word tells us there is holiness, righteousness, love, peace, joy—all the fruit of the Spirit! (See Galatians 5:22-23.)

The Lord takes time during January/February to chasten you and bring discipline to your life. Because you are a son or daughter of the King, He chastens whom He loves. He wants you to share in His holiness and righteousness.

This is the key! As a son or daughter of the King, you have everything as part of your godly inheritance. Your adoption came as a result of the shed blood, burial, resurrection, and ascension of Jesus Christ. Hear me again: You have *all* things that belong to Jesus. How do you step into the Kingdom realms? You do it by faith! God wants you to be in a greater, higher place of faith. Being disciplined and living according to the Word will bring forth the peaceful fruit of righteousness in your life.

This month of Shevat is about bringing the best of fruit to the Lord. It's not too late to sow a firstfruit offering for the month of January! Consider blessing the Lord today with the whole of an offering to Him! That might be an hourly wage, week's wage, month's wage, first sale of year—the best of a gift to Him! This is what you believe as a foundational gift for your promise to come in the new year! It sanctifies all other tithes and offerings that come afterward. Firstfruit means promise to come, holy and devoted, first in chief order and rank. Follow after His holiness and righteousness.

Share this with a friend who needs to be challenged to go after God in fresh ways!

SHEVAT 9

God is expanding you! He is increasing who you are. I see Him expanding your spirits, your souls, your temple, and your capacity. As God is expanding you, you will step into a larger sphere of influence, greater regions and territories. You will have tremendous growth as you step into this expanse.

Jesus is the firstfruit of many brothers. We are the "many brothers," and we put Him first by setting time to pray, fast, give, and consecrate ourselves unto to Him. When you make yourself holy, everything you touch shall be holy. *"If the part of the dough offered as firstfruits is holy, then the whole batch is holy; if the root is holy, so are the branches"* (Romans 11:16 NIV).

Greater territories are coming to you this year as you purify and consecrate yourself, as you continue in a deep abiding relationship with the Lord. Your expansion shall be great! Allow the Lord to continue to minister to you about your upcoming transitions to greater increase and multiplication. Set your foundation on God, for He is the Master Builder. He is preparing your temple, correcting, aligning, and repositioning things in your life for a season of victory!

Join your faith with Him. Let Him align everything—your spirit, soul, and body. When you position yourself to live an overcoming life with Him, you are set on the right course. God needs you on His team. He needs you to be strong. Your transition begins today.

SHEVAT 10

Be encouraged today! Angels of replenishment are being released! I can feel a move of God in the area of new wine and new opportunities. I saw a new anointing oil from Heaven pouring down over you. It is positioning you to carry a greater power for these new opportunities being placed before you. I urge you to respond. Each person's response is based on what the Lord has spoken, the direction He has given, and the calling He has on your life specifically. Don't let these opportunities slip by. Take advantage of them! Respond in *faith!*

The Lord gave me a vision today of an angel carrying a golden bowl, and this golden bowl pours out oil. This represents an angel of replenishment. God is going to ask you to take your vessel and wipe it empty so He can refill you. Just like with the widow and Elijah—when Elijah asked the widow to pour the oil, she obeyed. God used her obedience to supernaturally fill many vessels with oil, and this ultimately retired the family debt! God is sending you angels of replenishment. We can obey confidently that God will come through for us supernaturally, because Jeremiah 1:12 says that God watches over His word to perform it, to fulfill it.

Let me pray for you today: "Father, I thank You for my friend. I thank You for increasing their capacity. Lord, just as You are holy, we shall be holy. A spiritual empowerment is coming out from this reader and touching others. An increase is coming in territories, spheres of influence, and in spirit, soul, and body. Lord, You alone direct spiritual giftings. Give them guidance and help them feel Your presence and Your Spirit. Surround them with angels that will take them to the places You have prepared for them. Lord, You called this friend into this season, and You will give strength to stand firm, speak life, and declare the Word. Father, thank You for causing their spirit and soul to increase by Your Word, that they will see the multiplication. Thank You for every allowance that You made for us through Jesus, amen."

SHEVAT 11

As you start moving in the Word, speaking the Word, responding to the Word, the angels of replenishment are dispatched from Heaven to bring you what you need. They respond to the Word of God. They will bring oil, resources, finances—everything you need to fulfill the vision, plan, and purpose of God on your life! They will refill any area you have that is depleted! Praise the Lord! He is an on-time and faithful God!

Recently the Lord spoke to me, "Tell My people to have an attitude of redemption." Having an attitude of redemption means that you accept you are fully redeemed and everything around you is redeemed. The Lord placed it strongly on my heart to encourage you in this, to pursue and obtain this attitude.

Everything on earth today has been fully redeemed by the death, burial, resurrection, and ascension of Jesus Christ. He has covered all things in the eternal realms. You may be experiencing difficulties, obstacles, blockages, offenses, or sicknesses, but I'm here to tell you that no matter what you see with your natural eyes, you are *still* called to have an attitude of redemption! Keep the faith and keep pressing!

SHEVAT 12

As a Kingdom citizen, your viewpoint is supposed to be different from the world's. You are to see things as if they are complete with the fullness of Christ in every moment. When you see something broken or lacking in the natural, choose to see the fullness of Christ in that situation. This is living by faith, not by sight!

The earth realms are fact, but they aren't truth. There is a difference between fact and truth. Fact is: I see this disorder, the misalignment, the lies, the sin, the sickness, the lack and poverty in the world. But the truth of the matter comes only from what Jesus Christ says about the situation.

You are fully redeemed in the Lord. That means the brokenness you may be experiencing has been fully redeemed; and as you continue to walk Christ's way, you will open a portal that will release the blessings of Heaven on earth.

It's critical that you learn to walk as a mature Kingdom citizen. When you are mature, you are able to walk in the fullness of God, His completeness, His *shalom,* peace with nothing missing and nothing broken. I want to see you step into that place. Life may look like brokenness every day, but the "look" is fact—not the truth.

Philippians 4:7 (KJV): *"And **the peace of God**, which passeth all understanding, shall keep your hearts and minds through Christ Jesus."*

SHEVAT 13

Some people have asked me, "How do you release Heaven to earth? How do you operate in the ascension mindset? How do you live in the prosperity realms, not in the poverty realms? How do you work in miracles, signs, and wonders? How do you release the glory?" Maybe you have these same questions. I'll tell you how I do it: I obey the Word of the Lord, regardless of what I see. You can only be a glory carrier and release the glory when you properly position yourself to see from God's perspective.

Psalm 1:1-3 (NIV) says: *"Blessed is the one who does not walk in step with the wicked or stand in the way that sinners take or sit in the company of mockers, but whose delight is in the law of the Lord, and who meditates on his law day and night. That person is like a tree planted by streams of water, which yields its fruit in season and whose leaf does not wither—whatever they do prospers."*

God stretched you in the month of Tevet with purification and holiness so you could prosper beyond measure this year. In practicing firstfruits in the beginning month, you got ready for foundational giving that will take place for the rest of the year. Your seed is ready to bring to fruition the promises of God for your life! You are tapping into a time of multiplication and increase, and a greater level of faith capacity.

SHEVAT 14

Tonight there is a full moon in the night sky.

Historically today is around the time of *Shabbat Shirah* that includes *Parsha Beshalach*—the song sung by the children of Israel after they passed through the Red Sea (Exodus 15:1-18).

In January you offered your firstfruits. Firstfruits represent the promises to come. "Firstfruit" actually means chief or the chief order rank. Another way of saying this is that by giving your firstfruits, you are putting God first. The firstfruit is holy, devoted, and set apart. Firstfruits are 100 percent of something, not a portion or 10 percent. For example: a first day's wage, a first month's wage, a first hourly wage, or a first sale. It's what you received first in its entirety that you are returning to the Lord.

God is pleased with your firstfruits offering and obedience and will supply everything that you need along the way. He will put you into places where you can reap the realms of supernatural provision!

When you sow your firstfruits, you tell God, "I'm going to trust You in faith for a spiritual strategy that is going to handle my natural issue." It's never wise to handle natural issues with natural strategies. It doesn't work well, or sometimes not at all! God's way is for you to handle your issues with Kingdom strategies. You have access to the spiritual realm that will bring increase into the natural world.

SHEVAT 15

Historically this day is *Tu Bishvat,* the New Year for Trees, a minor Jewish new year holiday. It is tradition to plant a tree and some read Scriptures focusing on fruit. This is also a time to remember when the firstfruits were to be tithed to the priests.

Deuteronomy 20:19 (NKJV): *"When you besiege a city for a long time, while making war against it to take it, you shall not destroy its trees by wielding an ax against them; if you can eat of them, do not cut them down to use in the siege, for the tree of the field is man's food."*

Don't try to fix your natural issues without accessing spiritual answers! You want to first go to the holy realms and prosperous realms. When you do this, your level of faith will be increased and you will be able to respond in that faith!

Sowing opens what is in the spiritual realms so that the natural can be affected! Sowing is not just financial, it is also in the word. Galatians 6:8 (NKJV) says, *"For he who sows to his flesh will of the flesh reap corruption; but he who sows to the Spirit will of the Spirit reap everlasting life."*

Meditate day and night on God's Word and sow to the spiritual realms in faith, then watch the fruit come forth. You are a special child of God and He loves you!

Share this with a friend who needs to be encouraged to keep pressing into the realm of the Spirit!

SHEVAT 16

God is building divine relationships and making new alignments so that acceleration can take place and you can enter the new territories He has for you. I see streams that will quickly bring you to your purpose and destiny. Are you ready for what is coming?

Every blessing I have ever received is because I practiced giving God my firstfruits (praying, fasting, and financial giving) at the beginning of each year. You have to have your heart right, you have to be consecrated in prayer and fasting. These acts of faith lead to a strong and correctly laid foundation. Will you build a strong foundation? Remember, when the root is holy, the branches are holy. When the firstfruit is holy, the lump is also holy (Romans 11:16).

In the area of firstfruits as a foundation, God calls us to give of our time, talent, treasures, and testimony. God wants our first of everything, and everything else grows from that point. When we see and understand this, we come to know that God is building a foundation in us.

SHEVAT 17

Are you sensing that God wants to start establishing new relationships for you? Know this! The Lord is giving you a divine setup—so begin to move into those places.

Acceleration is coming. God has strong relationships that will help establish your destiny. As God properly positions you, you will begin to see a major acceleration. God is connecting you with people, divine alignments, and giving you new territories.

The Lord showed me that many of these new alignments aren't temporary; they are structured, permanent alignments from Him. Some of these will come even this month and carry you almost to the end of the decade.

Jesus says in John 15:9-12 (KJV): *"As the Father hath loved me, so have I loved you: continue ye in my love. If ye keep my commandments, ye shall abide in my love; even as I have kept my Father's commandments, and abide in his love. These things have I spoken unto you, that my joy might remain in you, and that your joy might be full. This is my commandment, That ye love one another, as I have loved you."*

SHEVAT 18

New territories are before you. God is setting you up for new things! You will be able to advance in the giftings He has given you. You are set up to complete the project for every Kingdom assignment that God has given you and each mantle that you are carrying for Him.

We are called to serve God and be faithful in all things.

In Luke 6:47-49 (NASB) Jesus says, *"Everyone who comes to Me and hears My words and acts on them, I will show you whom he is like: he is like a man building a house, who dug deep and laid a foundation on the rock; and when there was a flood, the river burst against that house and yet it could not shake it, because it had been well built. But the one who has heard and has not acted accordingly is like a man who built a house on the ground without a foundation; and the river burst against it and it immediately collapsed, and the ruin of that house was great."*

Act on His word so your foundation is strong and ready for growth!

SHEVAT 19

I declare over you that you are blessed to be a blessing. When you continue to bless Him with your increase, He will continue to give you more. You are trustworthy. You are honest. You are loyal. You are positioning yourself in great character to carry the capacity. Great things are coming to you. God is going to take you to the next level!

I feel the angels of replenishment still continuing to bring replenishment to those who are dry, weary, and depleted of resources. It doesn't matter what area the depletion is in, God wants you to be refreshed! He wants you to be infused with His "supernatural" to be victorious in your "natural."

Today, stand firm in the fact that He loves you and is for you. Do not shrink back. Do not allow fear to overcome you. Walk victoriously, knowing that God has heard your prayers. He knows what you need and He wants to bring you victory in every area of your life. In fact, He's going to bring that victory, but only with your acknowledgment that He has a plan, a divine "victory" set up just for you. Believe and receive today!

SHEVAT 20

God has given you victory over *all* things. God wants you to go to the next level in freedom. He desires for you to activate a heart and attitude of victory within yourself!

You will live victoriously all the time when you understand that the victory comes through knowing the Lord and understanding what He has already done for you.

Psalm 44:3 (NIV) says, *"It was not by their sword that they won the land, nor did their arm bring the victory; it was your* [God's] *right hand, your arm, and the light of your face, for you loved them."*

Victory comes because God is for us and with us. He is always bringing encouragement and fighting on our behalf. As you move into this week, walk in the confidence that God will bring you victory in every situation you face. You must believe and not doubt, understanding His love for you and the goodness of His nature. He is the God of victory and His right arm holds you up!

SHEVAT 21

Today I want to help you better understand the concept of purification. Purification, in the most basic sense of the word, is the act of removing contaminants from something. When we take time to fast, pray, and give, these are ways we purify ourselves to God. Taking time to purify yourself will set you up for godly success for the rest of the year.

Do you know that there can be no fellowship between light and darkness, none at all? In John 14:30 (NKJV), Jesus says, *"I will no longer talk much with you, for the ruler of this world is coming, and he has nothing in Me."* Jesus often encountered demonic forces and He overcame them because He was nothing like them. In other words, there is a distinction between Him and the enemy. And as God's children, there should be a distinction between us and the enemy as well.

Now I'm going to ask you a question: Is there anything that the enemy could find in you that looks or smells like him? You don't want any open doors in your life where the enemy can come in and wreak havoc. Remember, the enemy ravished Adam and Eve even when they were in the perfect place. The evil one came in and lied to them. Unfortunately, they listened to him and he took them on a path of destruction that has affected generations—all because of the wrong decisions they made. This is why it is so important to self-evaluate. Evaluate your behavior, your home life, your business life, even your church life so you can bear godly fruit this month and beyond!

SHEVAT 22

God has a great plan to use you mightily, and He doesn't want the enemy to stronghold you. We break those strongholds over your life right now, in Jesus's name.

Jesus could cast out demons because there was nothing of the enemy in Him. Now listen, the lie of the enemy is that you have something in common with him. So take a good look at yourself. Is there anything God is revealing to you that you need to give up? Is there anything that the enemy could sniff out in your life and say, "That looks a little like me?"

When you ask, "Is there anything in me that is in common with the enemy," the answer should be "No" from a spiritual standpoint, because all connection with the enemy is removed through the redemptive work of Jesus Christ. Once you become born again, your spirit becomes whole, righteous, and perfect. It's your soul that must undergo a continual process of transformation.

From a soulish standpoint, when you ask this question, the Lord can remove whatever it is in you that favors the enemy. These are things the Lord will convict you about—old habits and patterns, effects of trauma, and more that are not like God. God is properly positioning you now through repentance and faith in Him. He loves you and His plan for you is great.

SHEVAT 23

The Lord God planted a garden eastward in Eden, and there He put the man whom He had formed. And out of the ground the Lord God made every tree grow that is pleasant to the sight and good for food. ...Out of the ground the Lord God formed every beast of the field and every bird of the air, and brought them to Adam to see what he would call them. And whatever Adam called each living creature, that was its name. So Adam gave names to all cattle, to the birds of the air, and to every beast of the field. But for Adam there was not found a helper comparable to him. And the Lord God caused a deep sleep to fall on Adam, and he slept; and He took one of his ribs, and closed up the flesh in its place. Then the rib which the Lord God had taken from man He made into a woman, and He brought her to the man **(Genesis 2:8-9, 19-21 NKJV).**

God is bringing you back to your place and position with Him in the Garden of Eden. I know you look around with your natural eyes and consider what you see to be fact. You see all that's going wrong. But that's only fact and not truth! The truth of the matter is that *all* was redeemed when you were born again. Anything that was old has now become new.

You need to be the one who stands firm and says, "Enemy, there is nothing inside me that is in common with you!" This will empower you for the rest of the year to be able to cast out demons, heal the sick, and cause the lame to walk by the power of God! I know you want to walk in greater fruit and signs, miracles and wonders. God is pruning you and purifying your tree of righteousness by faith in Him!

Share this with a friend who needs to hear the good news that Jesus Christ has redeemed all things!

SHEVAT 24

Historically this is the day of Zechariah's prophecy in Zechariah 1:7-16, which in part says:

*"On the **twenty-fourth day of the eleventh month, which is the month Shebat**, in the second year of Darius, the word of the Lord came to Zechariah the son of Berechiah, the son of Iddo the prophet: I saw by night, and behold, a man riding on a red horse, and it stood among the myrtle trees in the hollow; and behind him were horses: red, sorrel, and white"* (Zechariah 1:7-8 NKJV).

Have you been experiencing warfare lately? That's because the enemy has been coming against you. He is threatened by the faith you have in God's fruit production taking place this month! He is threatened by your obedience to sow a firstfruit and also to sow in faith into the spirit realms.

Joshua 5:10-12 (NIV) says, *"On the evening of the fourteenth day of the month, while camped at Gilgal on the plains of Jericho, the Israelites celebrated the Passover. The day after the Passover, that very day, they ate some of the produce of the land: unleavened bread and roasted grain. The manna stopped the day after they ate this food from the land; there was no longer any manna for the Israelites, but that year they ate the produce of Canaan."*

God wants you to eat from the produce of the land now. We are not called to be children just waiting for manna anymore. We have entered the Promised Land by faith. All things are redeemed in Him.

SHEVAT 25

When the Israelites went from Egypt to the Promised Land, they went under the mantle of Moses. They learned to develop a relationship with God from him. God showed up in many unique ways—manna from Heaven, quail in their yards, water from a rock, their feet didn't swell, and their clothes did not wear out. All supernatural provision was made for them, and all revealed God's goodness! However, we are not called to wait for the provision. We are called to live in the daily provision of the Promised Land.

Remember, the Israelites were a bruised people. They had been held in bondage for 400 years in Egypt. They had cried out for a deliverer. All of a sudden, a deliverer named Moses came. God used him to release the people and lead them to the Promised Land.

God used their time in the wilderness to establish a relationship with them. Even though they murmured and complained, He met all of their provisionary needs. He also used this time to teach them the process of trusting Him and being obedient to Him.

And just like God wanted a relationship with them, He longs for a relationship with you! He is taking you from manna daily to multiplication monthly! He wants you to have faith in Him as a good Father who loves you and will indeed provide for His covenant child of the inheritance.

Yes, that's *you!*

SHEVAT 26

After Moses died, the Word tells us that his mantle of leadership was passed to Joshua and the Israelites went through circumcision. Circumcision is when you come to know Jesus as your Lord and Savior. It's a cutting away of the old and a birthing of the new! Circumcision represents covenant. God is the covenant-keeping God. He loves you and promises to provide for you. God wants you to rest in the fact that you are circumcised and in covenant with God.

Water baptism is an outward sign of the inward change of circumcision that happens in your life. Did you know that the unleavened bread and the roasted grain was the first produce of the land that the Israelites ate? That is when the manna stopped coming down from Heaven. Wow! Think about that. God was so faithful in providing for them!

You must receive supernatural strategies from Heaven to affect and operate in this world! God wants you to shift from being in a place of learning to hear His voice, to being in a place of hearing His voice without doubt and then trusting Him for provision.

Begin making choices today based on the fact that you trust God. He will never forsake you. He will never be unfaithful to you. He is the same yesterday, today, and tomorrow! Don't use your worldly relationships as evidence of how things work with God. You need to raise your understanding of who God is and know that He is your Provider who is in covenant with you!

Share this truth with a friend. God has promoted you. Live in His fruitfulness, not in your own provision!

SHEVAT 27

You have consecrated, prepared, and sanctified yourself. You also positioned yourself through firstfruits principles and right foundations. Now, expansion and capacity are here! God is expanding you and your soul. This allows you to increase in your capacity to take over and maintain greater territories.

We have read 3 John 2 (NIV) previously, which says, *"Dear friend, I pray that you may enjoy good health and that all may go well with you, even as your soul is getting along well."* You see, when your soul joins the process of pressing into God, He can expand you in many ways, including a heavenly expanse. God can take your mind to new places, enhancing your ability to understand who He is, what Heaven is like, and how you are seated with Christ in heavenly places. You also gain the understanding that every spiritual blessing in Heaven belongs to you!

Activate your faith today!

SHEVAT 28

When your thoughts are more focused on the Kingdom, you become a portal God can use to change your atmosphere and make a difference. Did you know that territories can expand on earth when God uses you? Yes, you! He needs you! God has given you giftings that bring about Kingdom change right here on earth.

God is walking you into new territories and divine relationships. Great things are beginning to happen for you! Have you ever watched bricks being stacked? They get stacked one by one on top of each other. This is a brand-new year, and you will watch this kind of bricklaying take place in your life.

Listen, no matter what is happening in the world today—no matter what trial, tragedy, or difficulty may come your way—do not lose your faith! Hebrews 10:38-39 (NASB) says, *"But My righteous one will live by faith; and if he shrinks back My soul has no pleasure in him. But we are not among those who shrink back to destruction, but of those who have faith for the safekeeping of the soul."*

Don't shrink back; carry forth in faith so you can realize the promises of God for you!

SHEVAT 29

You, my friend, are righteous. You have the righteousness of Christ inside you. God is setting you up right now to be used of Him for Kingdom purposes. Stand firm. Hold fast to the confession of your faith. Keep going forward. You're going to begin to walk in signs, wonders, and miracles. God is going to give you greater territories and your spiritual gifts are going to come forth with greater power! God will give you opportunities for blind eyes to see, deaf ears to hear, and the lame to walk. Fire angels are joining you on your assignments.

Love your neighbor. Do not allow division in the body. Do not participate in divisive activity. Set yourself apart with a pure heart. Do not allow yourself to have anything in common with the enemy. He only wants to gain a stronghold in your life for destruction. Don't get entangled with things of the world or people who want to argue. There are so many people who need the Lord right now, and that number will continue to grow as the days go forward. Align yourself with God and pray for people to repent. Repentance is necessary for God to break strongholds in people's lives.

Shalom peace is coming to earth. It's coming through you when you believe, stay steadfast, stand firm, and trust in what Jesus has done. Share this with a friend because someone needs to hear this word today!

SHEVAT 30

This day is *Yom HaMishpacha*. It's called Family Day in Israel and is in memory of Henrietta Szold, the American-born founder of a group, Hadassah for Women.

The Lord is shifting the atmosphere and His glory is being released in this season! You can lift your head up high, just as it says in Psalm 24:7 (NIV), *"Lift up your heads, you gates; be lifted up, you ancient doors, that the King of glory may come in."* You have been seated with Christ in heavenly places and are in the perfect position to receive His glory. Depression, anxiety, apprehension—all melt away in Jesus's name and healings and miracles begin to take place!

The Lord is with you and wants to give you direction today. Do you believe that? As you sit in communion with Him, He will speak to you. He will give you His supernatural victory that will conquer any situation you are facing. An overwhelming peace and clarity of mind will come when you rest in His glory. The gifts that are in you will come alive, and you will be empowered to use them to make a huge impact on earth.

Purpose every day to stay in this position at His table and maintain a godly attitude. Even when times get difficult, stay seated. Remember that your circumstances do not define you, but they are not going to change until you are repositioned like the Word says. There is power in His glory. We are victorious in Christ! Speak words of *great faith* and continue to *stand on the Word* of God. Intently cultivate your relationship with Christ. Open your heart to receive. Then watch your circumstances change and your mountains move!

As you have completed the month of Shevat, God is releasing you into the last month of the Hebrew calendar year—the month of Adar.

ADAR 1
(AND ADAR 2 LEAP YEAR)

This is referred to as the month of celebration and happiness.

This is the twelfth month of the religious calendar and the sixth month of the civil calendar. *Adar* is the Hebrew word *adir,* which means strength and power.

Please note: If you are reading this in a leap year where there are 2 Adars, please return to this chapter again and re-read to prepare you for the month of Nisan.

Adar 1 in a leap year is called *Adar Bet* and Adar 2 in a leap year is called *Adar Aleph.* Adar Aleph becomes the primary month in a leap year due to the fact that it holds the sacred Jewish holiday of *Purim.* The Adar that comes directly before Nisan in any year is the Adar Aleph. It is as if Adar 1 is inserted as an additional month.

If you are reading this in Adar 2, know that Adar 2 (Adar Aleph) is considered to be the thirteenth month of the religious calendar. The reason for Adar 2 is that within 19 years, there will be 7 years, usually once every three years, on a Hebrew calendar, which are considered leap years, or years in which the lunar calendar must be adjusted to add another month before the new religious month of Nisan begins. For your reading pleasure and not to confuse you with this information, *simply just read Adar two times and you will be all ready for the month of Nisan.*

Tribe of Israel (Conventional): Naphtali

Gemstone in Aaron's breastplate: Crystal

Constellation in Sky/Hebrew name: Pisces/Dagim

ADAR 1
Rosh Chodesh Adar

Tonight there is a new moon in the night sky.

Historically this was the day when the ninth plague came upon Egypt, the Plague of Darkness. Exodus 10:21 (KJV): *"And the Lord said unto Moses, Stretch out thine hand toward heaven, that there may be darkness over the land of Egypt...."*

Historically this day is around the time known as *Shabbat Shekalim* in which each Jewish male must contribute a half a shekel to the Tent of Meeting (see Exodus 30:11-16). This date floats depending on Shabbat.

Welcome to the Hebrew month of *Adar.* Let me highlight a few important aspects of the month of Adar:

- A time to recognize the completion of the temple. Ezra 6:15 (NIV) says, *"The temple was completed on the third day of the month Adar, in the sixth year of the reign of King Darius."*

- A time to dwell in the power and strength of God. Adar literally means "to dwell in His power even when there are limits around you." Adar signifies that you have entered into a place where limits are broken by the power of God.

- A time when we enter into the constellation Pisces. Pisces refers to fruitfulness and multiplication. It's actually a sign for the advancement and multiplication of the church.

- A time of great joy! Adar is actually all about a transformation and increase in joy.

Why are these four points important? Because the Lord wants to bring increase to your life. He wants to multiply you!

ADAR 2

Historically today is when Nebuchadnezzar defeated Jerusalem and Jehoiachin, the king of Judah, was overthrown. Then after 37 years, on Adar 25, Jehoiachin was released by Nebuchadnezzar's son. (See 2 Chronicles 36:8-9.)

Now the question is, have you taken the necessary steps during the past month of Shevat—praying, fasting, and giving— to enter into the fullness of what Adar brings? Consecration sets you apart. According to Matthew 6, praying, fasting, and giving establishes a foundation that everything else can be built upon. Take time today to get your heart right before God in this final month of the year before Nisan.

Proverbs 3:9-10 (KJV) has been mentioned numerous times but worth another look: *"Honor the Lord with thy substance, and with the firstfruits of all thine increase: so shall thy barns be filled with plenty, and thy presses shall burst out with new wine."* The giving of firstfruits serves as a representation of a covenant relationship with the Lord. It's a way to recognize a covenant that brings wealth and power because of your giving. You want your barns to be filled with increase and vats to overflow, so give!

ADAR 3

Historically today is when the second temple, Herod's Temple that replaced Solomon's Temple was completed.

Ezra 6:15-18 (KJV): *"And this house was finished on the third day of the month Adar, which was in the sixth year of the reign of Darius the king. And the children of Israel, the priests, and the Levites, and the rest of the children of the captivity, kept the dedication of this house of God with joy. And offered at the dedication of this house of God an hundred bullocks, two hundred rams, four hundred lambs; and for a sin offering for all Israel, twelve he goats, according to the number of the tribes of Israel. And they set the priests in their divisions, and the Levites in their courses, for the service of God, which is at Jerusalem; as it is written in the book of Moses."*

Have you been experiencing spiritual warfare lately? Does it seem there are blockades and obstacles in your way? Have things been difficult? This is happening because you have just been promoted! The temple construction had many blockades before it was complete and many people tried to stop it.

Adar means completion and is known as the month of joy. During this month, the Jewish people celebrate *Purim*, when they remember how Esther went boldly before the king to share Haman's evil plan for the annihilation of the Jewish people. Esther risked her life to properly position the Jews and their nation to be saved. God gave her favor and a plan. Just like God prepared, promoted, and put her in a place for *"such a time as this,"* He is doing the same for you, for the purpose and destiny to which He has called you.

ADAR 4

Queen Esther was promoted this month of Adar. You might think her promotion was when she entered the palace in the month of Tevet, but real promotion does not happen until you stand in your mantle. She was only promoted to the position in Tevet, but her mantle calling was in the month of Adar. You may be given a position, but until you are tested in that position you have not truly been spiritually promoted. This month Esther passes her test—and you will too!

Mordecai, Esther's cousin told her what would happen to the Jewish people if she didn't speak up. These words invited Esther to her place of promotion to save her nation. We are never truly promoted until we are faced with a situation where we have to stand for righteousness, otherwise all we hold is a title.

Esther 4:12-14 (NIV) reads, *"When Esther's words were reported to Mordecai, he sent back this answer: 'Do not think that because you are in the king's house you alone of all the Jews will escape. For if you remain silent at this time, relief and deliverance for the Jews will arise from another place, but you and your father's family will perish. And who knows but that you have come to your royal position for such a time as this?'"*

We need to remember the importance of our promotion as we see the increase in spiritual warfare and our response to it. The enemy always wants to push back whenever we get promoted. Let's not forget that in the months of Tevet and Shevat, we gave God our firstfruits and consecrated ourselves before Him. He brought us to capacity and expanded us upon a strong foundation. You've gone to the next level! This is why you feel the friction in the spirit realms. You have been given a greater responsibility than you have ever had before.

ADAR 5

God has properly positioned you, not to sit around like royals, but to minister to a remnant. He has given you a sphere of influence for you to use the power He gave you to make changes. You must open your mouth! God has given you a voice and His Word. When you speak, a spark of God releases and ignites things. You can change a nation!

Promotion comes with a test that proves we walked into the promotion. The enemy is prepared to convince you that this promotion didn't happen, that you're not good enough or that you couldn't possibly be called to do this. He tries to get involved in the things of God and the progression of the Lord. He tries to push it back by bringing hinderances. Stand strong against him!

What did Esther do next? Esther 4:15-16 (NIV): *"Then Esther sent this reply to Mordecai: 'Go, gather together all the Jews who are in Susa, and fast for me. Do not eat or drink for three days, night or day. I and my attendants will fast as you do. When this is done, I will go to the king, even though it is against the law. And if I perish, I perish.'"*

Esther asked her people to fast and pray with her for three days and nights. They joined in agreement that she would obtain the strength needed to go before the king. If she didn't go, she and her people would perish.

The secret to getting past the pushback of the enemy is to step into the heavenly places—position yourself in His presence. Remember you're a citizen of Heaven and the joy of the Lord is your strength (Nehemiah 8:10). Get in that secret place with the Lord and let Him build you up. Fasting and praying will discipline you to sit with the Lord and hear Him. He will give you strategies and show you how to navigate the sphere of influence He called you to.

ADAR 6

The Lord will promote you many times to next levels. Two times of year that regularly bring promotion are Passover and Rosh Hashanah, the two main Hebrew new years. God usually starts adjusting us for the promotion about four to six weeks before-hand. Why? Our God is cyclical. He works in cycles.

God wants you to walk in the totality of each promotion for six months. This brings strength. It helps you stay in proper position, keeps your joy steady, and allows you to carry His power until He turns the calendar again with a new promotion.

So be encouraged! You have stepped into a new season, a new time and place where God is using you in a mighty way. Do not shrink back. The righteous do not shrink back; they live by faith. No matter the opposition, press forward. The enemy cannot take your promotion or assigned mantle calling.

There is joy in His presence, and that's what it takes for you to fulfill your purpose and destiny.

ADAR 7

Historically and interestingly, this is the day when Moses was born, and 120 years later he died on this day. Prior to his death, Moses ministered to the people for 37 days from book of Deuter-onomy to prepare them for entering the Promised Land.

Every day, broken people surround you. Every day, you have the opportunity to bring life and healing. God positioned you for this purpose—to touch others today with His word! In the book of Acts, Peter and John came across a lame beggar who was des-perate for handouts. Peter said to him, *"Silver and gold I do not have, but what I do have I give you: In the name of Jesus Christ of Nazareth, rise up and walk"* (Acts 3:6 NKJV). I challenge you today to use the gifts God has given you. Each person has been freely given something, and when we use that "something," people are touched by Jesus and changed!

When we look beyond people's appearances, negative talk and anger, we see what is really going on in their hearts. Jesus was supernatural in this area of discernment. He looked at hearts and could tell instantly when someone was broken and what they needed. You can take this approach as you go about your busy life. How you love people is so important. May your heart have a burden of love for God, His people, and all those around you.

When you walk in His love and obedience, God can move through you to touch others. This will cause people to rise up and step into places where they can see themselves as Jesus sees them. You may be the only person with that word, with that touch that will make a difference in someone's life. Miracles happen when we flow in His calling on our lives.

ADAR 8

Be who God has called you to be. Stop trying to be like everyone else and embrace the destiny God has designed specifically for you! He will use you in your sphere of influence, no matter what that looks like—family, workplace, church, neighborhood, state, country, etc. We have been commissioned to carry His love wherever we go.

Know this—your journey looks different from others' journey, but we all need to build up, not tear down. Encourage; don't condemn. Pray, intercede for others, and God will change their hearts. What a great joy it is to watch Jesus move and people come to know Him as their Lord and Savior! I want you to experience this! I want you to be overwhelmed by His goodness and declare, "All glory belongs to You, Jesus!"

ADAR 9

This is the month of joy! Why do I say that? Because it was in this month when the temple was completed, and God's people celebrated its dedication with great joy. You can read the account again in Ezra 6:15-18 (NIV): *"The temple was completed on the third day of the month Adar, in the sixth year of the reign of King Darius. Then the people of Israel—the priests, the Levites and the rest of the exiles—celebrated the dedication of the house of God with joy. For the dedication of this house of God they offered a hundred bulls, two hundred rams, four hundred male lambs and, as a sin offering for all Israel, twelve male goats, one for each of the tribes of Israel. And they installed the priests in their divisions and the Levites in their groups for the service of God at Jerusalem, according to what is written in the Book of Moses."*

God is building your temple strong this month. You had a new foundation in firstfruits built during Tevet and Shevat, and now the building is being erected strong for you to wear your mantle to make a difference. Walk in your new mantle promotion today!

ADAR 10

Historically this is around the time of *Shabbat Zachor* or the Sabbath of Remembrance. It is the Sabbath before *Purim* to remember the attack by Amalek on the Jewish people, this is because Haman was a descendent of Amalek (see Deuteronomy 25:17-19).

Just as the temple in the Old Testament was completed and dedicated to the Lord, God is preparing your temple—your body, your life—for the things that are coming. You are the temple of the Lord (1 Corinthians 3:16-17). The Holy Spirit lives inside you. You are a dwelling place for the Most High God! This is so important for you to understand!

In Ezra 6:15-18, discussed yesterday, it says priests were installed into their divisions and the Levites into their groups. This is where mantle assignments come in. I believe that right now God is separating believers into divisions and groups. *He* is calling you forth. *He* is calling forward apostles, prophets, pastors, teachers, administrators, and those with healing gifts. *He* is calling forth the body for the works of service.

God is setting you apart, consecrating you, and bringing you into a new time of promotion. He is calling you to step out into His grace and His favor. What you have freely been given, He wants you to freely give back to Him and to others as well.

There is a lot of angelic activity happening right now. New mantle assignments are made this month. Receive your new mantle and new assignment with JOY! You will bear fruit that will make a difference on earth!

ADAR 11

Historically this is when Esther called her three-day fast for all the Jews of Susa. Now the fast is practiced only one day, on the eve of *Purim,* called the Fast of Esther or *Ta'anit Ester.*

As I think of Esther stepping into her promotion time for her nation, I am reminded of Yeshua and how His destiny was to die on the cross for us. He entered prayer and His soul was sorrowful unto death as we read in Matthew 26:36-39 (NKJV): *"Then Jesus came with them to a place called Gethsemane, and said to the disciples, 'Sit here while I go and pray over there.' And He took with Him Peter and the two sons of Zebedee, and He began to be sorrowful and deeply distressed. Then He said to them, 'My soul is exceedingly sorrowful, even to death. Stay here and watch with Me.' He went a little farther and fell on His face, and prayed, saying, 'O My Father, if it is possible, let this cup pass from Me; nevertheless, not as I will, but as You will.'"*

Oftentimes, the closer we get to destiny, the more our souls feel the pain of death and we must enter into a place of prayer and fasting to gain strength from Heaven. If you are stepping into something new this season, take time to gain your strength through prayer and fasting and seeking the heart of God.

ADAR 12

God wants you to operate in signs, miracles, and wonders on earth, but how? You have to change your thinking and walk in the realms of the Kingdom of God. The Kingdom is a realm where you acquire things by foot. It's here and now. In other words, while you walk in the Kingdom of Heaven on earth, Heaven walks with you everywhere you go. You are walking in eternal realms. Miracles, signs, and wonders happen when you know and believe that you are in the realm of Heaven, though you walk upon the earth. Heaven is connected to you. It's inside you and it's all around you too! You are the temple of the Holy Spirit.

Paul writes in 1 Corinthians 3:16-17 (KJV), *"Know ye not that ye are the temple of God, and that the Spirit of God dwelleth in you? If any man defile the temple of God, him shall God destroy; for the temple of God is holy, which temple ye are."*

Jesus has done everything for you, from His death, burial, resurrection, and ascension. You are seated with Him in heavenly places and everything in Heaven is yours. You simply have to activate this truth in the name of Jesus. You are called for such a time as this, just as Esther was in her day.

ADAR 13

Historically this day is the Fast of Esther, *Ta'anit Esters,* which is a one-day Jewish fast from dawn until dusk on *Purim* eve. This one-day fast commemorates the three-day fast observed by the

Jewish people in the story of *Purim*. This date changes based on the Sabbath.

Adar was Esther's month, her test of promotion. She had to take a step knowing that God had called her to live in the realm of the Kingdom. Yes, even though she was in the earthly king's house, she had to operate in her God-given royalty and exercise her faith.

You are a true citizen of the Kingdom of Heaven. God has assigned you a duty to walk faith out on earth. That means everywhere your foot treads, you will begin to see miracles, healings, transformation, revelations, and great things happening! Agree with me today. God is bringing you into a very special place. You do not acquire these places except by faith. You must believe and have childlike faith.

God wants to use you in a mighty way! Grab hold of the fact that He has surrounded you with His Spirit. I feel that the heavenly realms are surrounding you even now and that there is truly an open heaven above you. He has properly positioned you to go and change environments. He wants you to walk in these heavenly realms and learn to yield to Him (covenant) and to abide in Him. If you want know more about walking in these heavenly realms of prosperity and ascension, get a copy of my book, *Heavenly Portals: How Eternity Impacts Our Past, Present, and Future* on my website at www.candicesmithyman.com.

ADAR 14

Tonight there is a full moon in the night sky.

Historically today is *Purim* in Jerusalem or the Feast of Lots. It is the day of celebration after Esther went to see the king and the Jewish people were saved. The king was made aware of Haman's evil plot against the Jews.

This day is also called *Purim Katan,* a minor celebration on leap years.

I see you walking in signs, miracles, and wonders and being the tool God wants to use in the most difficult of circumstances. You will find that your circumstances are not so difficult even if at first they seemed life-threatening or downright awful. Right now, something has been broken in the spirit realm. Every room in your home contains the power of the Holy Spirit. Every room is another realm of Kingdom rule and leadership. As you enter your home, declare and decree that the Kingdom is here and that every room will respond just as God has called you to respond. Heaven has come to earth though Jesus Christ. He said before He died that we are to pray for the Kingdom of Heaven to come on earth.

Let me pray for you today: "Father, I thank You for my friend. Help this reader to walk in the Kingdom of Heaven here on earth. Help them yield to You. Thank You for the miracles, signs, and wonders that are going to come forth. I thank You that their body is completely healed right now in the name of Jesus. Any pressure in their head, any stress or weight that they are carrying is lifted now, in the mighty name of Jesus. They are victorious overcomers, more than conquerors, in Christ—no matter what they're faced with. Father, give them fullness in their bank account. Show them how they can access the treasures of Heaven right now. I bind spirits right now that are coming to aggravate their soul and trying to get their focus off the realm of the Kingdom and what they have been called to walk in. They will live according to Your will and do all that You have called them to do, in Jesus's name, amen."

Share this with a friend. Begin to live the life of signs, miracles, and wonders. God has great things in store for you. Be blessed. You are a Kingdom ruler!

ADAR 15

Historically this is *Sushan Purim* (different from Adar 14) in which *Purim* is celebrated within the walls of Jerusalem. It is also a minor holiday on leap years called *Sushan Purim Katan*.

Historically this is called Jerusalem Gate Day, during the time of Herod Agrippa I.

This is the twelfth month of the religious calendar year from Nisan last year. Twelve is a number of government. It is a time when God begins to set things in your life straight so that the new spring rains can come upon you and you can flourish in your calling.

Now is the time for repentance and for us to be cleansed and purified. Take time out of your busy schedule to spend time with God. Allow His water of purification to flow over your life and water you for what He has in store for you. Be like David in Psalm 42:7 (NIV) and say, *"Deep calls to deep in the roar of your waterfalls; all your waves and breakers have swept over me."*

That word *Adar* is broken down to three Hebrews letters, A, D, R. The letter "A" is *aleph* and means the power of the Lord. The letter "D" is *dalet,* and the letter "R" is *resh.* "D" and "R" together means to dwell.

Powerful! You are invited to dwell in the power of the Lord! Yes, you're still in a world that has limitations, but you are invited to limitless living in Him!

ADAR 16

Historically today is *Purim Meshulash,* a holiday where *Purim* is three days within the walled city of Jerusalem when *Shushan Purim* falls on a Sabbath. It does not happen every year, only sometimes, and is a rare occurrence. It is stated here for reference.

You now have entered the Hebrew month Adar. If you are reading this during a leap year, it is Adar 2, it is called a month of Double Joy! You will have two months of joy. Double joy!

This transformative joy is available for you, but you have to allow the Lord to move on your heart. You have to move into the realm of new wine and position yourself to allow the presence and power of the Holy Spirit to surround you. Then joy will come!

The joy of the Lord is your strength. It will carry you through any situation that you face—whatever God is doing around you. As you remain in this place of joy with Him, He will take care of your enemies. You may walk through the battlefield, but He will fight your battle for you.

Psalm 63:5 (NIV), *"I will be fully satisfied as with the richest of foods; with singing lips my mouth will praise you."*

ADAR 17

Historically today is *Yom Adar,* a day to celebrate the Jews leaving Persia.

Your heavenly Father is a loving Father. He rejoices over you! I have seen this in a vision of the heavenly realms. I saw the royal banquet table, and I saw the Lord in His glory, laughing. It was so amazing! As He laughed, glory waves went forth and everyone started laughing. I share more about this in my book, *Releasing Heaven: Creating Supernatural Environments through Heavenly Encounters*, which is found on my website at www.candicesmithyman.com.

I hear the Lord say, "It's time to move on." Let go of the things that didn't work out as you planned, the relationships, the opportunities, the expectations you've held so tightly. There was a time when the Lord had to say the same to Moses: *"Why are you crying out to me? Tell the Israelites to move on. Raise your staff and* stretch out your hand over the sea to divide the water so that the Israelites can go through the sea on dry ground" (Exodus 14:15-16 NIV).

Maybe today you're facing a seemingly insurmountable obstacle. You're bound. You're a slave in your mind, yearning for freedom on the other side of this sea of troubles. But it's the joy of the Lord that breaks off difficulties and bondages. It shifts moods and gives fresh perspective! I encourage you to move on. Take the step. Make the joy of the Lord your focus and get moving.

Practice laughing! Depression, anxiety, fear, and other strongholds in your life will begin to break. Laugh! Stop complaining, murmuring, and saying how depressed you are, how anxious and sick you are. Laugh with the joy of the Lord!

ADAR 18

Historically this is around the date of *Shabbat Parah,* or the Sabbath of the Red Heifer. This takes place on the Shabbat before the Shabbat called *Shabbat HaChodesh* in preparation for Passover. The red heifer *(parah adumah)* was an animal known to the Jewish people as a pure sacrifice on Passover.

Numbers 19:1-4 (NIV): *"The Lord said to Moses and Aaron: 'This is a requirement of the law that the Lord has commanded: Tell the Israelites to bring you a red heifer without defect or blemish and that has never been under a yoke. Give it to Eleazar the priest; it is to be taken outside the camp and slaughtered in his presence. Then Eleazar the priest is to take some of its blood on his finger and sprinkle it seven times toward the front of the tent of meeting.'"*

God has called you to this position in Him. Ezra 6:15-18 shares that after the temple was complete, they broke down into groups or divisions, special groups to perform special services.

There were leaders in charge of specific things, and their assignments reflected their sphere of influence. The same goes for you. God has released your mantle and properly positioned you. Now, there must be a purification. Take time to purify yourself today in the choices you make, what you think, eat, watch, listen to.

You are a temple of the Holy Spirit and your sacrifice that is pure and holy is the shed blood of Yeshua Messiah. Hebrews 10:1-7 reveals Yeshua as the One who has finally met all requirements of the sacrificial system of sacrifices. He has propelled us into a relationship with the Father. Because of the sacrifice He satisfied, we have confidence to enter the Most Holy Place daily. We are now properly positioned as children of the King.

Ponder today what Jesus has done to fulfill the old covenant. How does this effect your life today and the mantle you carry?

ADAR 19

If you look back at Moses in the book of Exodus, you can see that the Israelites were facing limitations before they crossed the Red Sea. But God moved them past their limitations when Moses obeyed the Lord, stretched forth his staff by faith, and the waters parted. They went across on dry land! A miracle deliverance! Moses used the authority He had been given by God to lead the people in faith.

God is saying, "Now is the time to activate your mantle!" God is stretching you and causing His will to come out of you to act upon. Rise up! Now is the time to step into what God has called you to do. You are being called out. I know you may feel tired and helpless, but you need to shrug off those feelings and get up and move.

God is moving upon you, and the warfare is revealing that you need to step up to the plate. When you speak, when you move, the warfare will end. Shout hallelujah! Share this word of encouragement with a friend who needs someone to stand with them through their test.

God wants you to stretch forth your faith and open your heart to Him this month. You are called to do mighty exploits for Him!

ADAR 20

Do you believe that you have received a mantle? An assignment from God? Are you going to carry out His assignment?

You may be afraid—but receive courage from what Mordecai told Esther: *"Do not think that because you are in the king's house you alone of all the Jews will escape. For if you remain silent at this time, relief and deliverance for the Jews will arise from another place, but you and your father's family will perish. And who knows but that you have come to your royal position for such a time as this?"* (Esther 4:13-14 NIV).

Esther had to face the fear that came with the assignment she had been given. Her mantle was tested. She needed to be called forth to enter the king's presence, to be able to share Haman's wicked plans—but the king had not called for her. She had to seek the Lord and fast to gain the strength to move past her fear. She was appointed for her time.

You too have been appointed and put into a certain place for a moment such as this!

ADAR 21

Now that your mantle has come, there may be pushback from the enemy. It's common for an enemy to test your faith's capacity. I feel that satan is testing a lot of people right now in the area of finances. I see that there have been tests springing up in many different places. Know this, these tests are helping to raise you up, to cause you to become who God has called you to be in this moment!

Tests put pressure on a mantle that causes the mantle to respond. Your mantle advances the Kingdom. When your faith is being tested, your mantle is beginning to operate for you. I feel that so strongly from God right now.

Esther's mantle was tested. She was already queen, but her first great test was if she was willing to put her life on the line for her people. Mordecai, her uncle, said if she remained silent, although relief and deliverance would arise for the Jews from another place, she and the Jews in the kingdom would die. He told her God had positioned her at this time and in this place to save her people, God's chosen people (see Esther 4:13-14).

Esther was an orphan. Her uncle Mordecai took care of her in the natural as a father would. But Mordecai also represented her spiritual father when he spoke into her life. His words caused her to call a fast so she would know how to handle the test.

Listen to your heavenly Father and He will lead you with His word!

ADAR 22

Right now, God is revealing to you who you are, who He has called you to be, what is getting ready to come up, and how you fit into that plan. Your purpose and destiny are being revealed.

I want to encourage you that you have been promoted. God Himself has promoted you and properly positioned you for greatest impact. The shed blood of Yeshua gives you access to the Most Holy Place all the time.

Now that your mantle has come, there may be pushback from the enemy. As mentioned previously, it's common for an enemy to test your faith's capacity. Watch carefully where tests of faith may be coming against you. Know this, these tests help to raise you up, to cause you to become who God has called you to be in this moment! Without a test, you don't know your faith capacity, and you don't know how God has equipped you through faith and the mantles He has assigned you.

I know you are being tested, but rest assured, your mantle is operating for you. Rest in the mantle and watch God come to the rescue!

ADAR 23

God is moving upon you, and the warfare is revealing that you need to step up to the plate. When you speak, when you move, the warfare will end. Shout hallelujah!

Paul writes in 1 Corinthians 15:57 (NIV), *"But thanks be to God! He gives us the victory through our Lord Jesus Christ."*

Because of what Jesus did when He died, was buried, resurrected, and ascended, you now have the victory all the time—not just when days are bad, but when they are good too. Make it a point to live in heavenly places as the apostle Paul admonishes us in Ephesians 2:5-6 (KJV). *"Even when we were dead in sins, hath quickened us together with Christ, (by grace ye are saved;) and hath raised us up together, and made us sit together in heavenly places in Christ Jesus."*

Yeshua made a way for *your victory every day!*

Bless the Lord today with a special love offering to say, "God, I believe in the mantle You've called me to, and I'm going to walk in it!"

ADAR 24

The Lord has been showing me some amazing things from a heavenly perspective. Things about subduing the earth, having power, dominion and authority, and the provision God has given to His children. You have Heaven at your fingertips. You are in heavenly places although your body is in the earth realm. These are the secrets of the Kingdom that Jesus Himself knew. It's how He walked in such incredible signs, miracles, and wonders. He never left His heavenly seat even though His body was here on this planet!

Jesus died, was buried, resurrected, and ascended from this earth to Heaven. The resurrection is evidence that sin, death, and the grave have been overcome. Ascension is evidence that you are seated with Him in heavenly places. You don't have to wait until you die to access everything that Heaven has for you. You can access it today in faith, understanding that it's all yours. This is God's great kindness toward you in these end times—everything Heaven has is accessible to you right now, no more time restrictions.

For more information on how to live in heavenly places on earth, get a copy of my book, *Heavenly Portals: How Eternity Impacts Your Past Present and Future.*

ADAR 25

Historically some sources say Nebuchadnezzar died on this day.

Historically this day is around *Shabbat HaChodesh* or the Sabbath of the Month. This is the last Sabbath before the month of Nisan. Exodus 12 shares how the month of Nisan is to be properly accounted for with the new moon. Exodus 12:1-2 (NKJV), *"The Lord spoke to Moses and Aaron in the land of Egypt saying, 'This month shall be your beginning of months; it shall be the first month of the year to you.'"*

One of the reasons this was the first month of the religious calendar year is that it was to be a new beginning for the Israelites to worship God without the bondage of Pharaoh.

Jesus fulfilled everything for you on the cross. All you have to do is live like you have it all in this moment. You might be saying, "I don't have what it takes; have you seen my life? You don't know what's going on in my family." Listen, you have all that you need in the here and now. When you believe that, you will see the overflow from heavenly vats. Those vats are promised you in Hosea 2: grain, wine, oil, gold, silver, water, fire, wool, and flax are all yours!

God is properly positioning you to step into the very things He has called you to do. Everything you need will be fully supplied. It's found in the storehouse of Heaven, and it's reposited into your heart when you put heavenly things first. This is why Matthew 6:19-21 (NASB) says, *"Do not store up for yourselves treasures on earth, where moth and rust destroy, and where thieves break in and steal. But store up for yourselves treasures in heaven, where neither moth nor rust destroys, and where thieves do not break in or steal; for where your treasure is, there your heart will be also."*

The Lord wants you to know your greatest treasure is what you already have access to in the heavenly realms.

ADAR 26

Today, the Lord is asking you to put your heart where your treasure is—in Heaven. You are a citizen of Heaven, which comes with heavenly privileges and provision. The apostle Paul knew he was a citizen of Heaven, even while being imprisoned and flogged. His perspective changed how he saw his circumstances, and I know it will do the same for you today!

This is good news! Tell someone today that you have changed citizenship. You can now correspond with Heaven on a daily basis. You don't have to fill the void or deal with things in the earthly realms. Just simply be seated in heavenly places and allow God to bring the rest into alignment.

Living from this position will cause you to step in faith and turn your needs over to the Lord.

ADAR 27

Purim is the time we remember God had the right person in the right place, and that He used her to save a nation. God raised up Queen Esther as an advocate for the Jews to escape the evil plot of Haman to annihilate the nation. This opportunity was her test of promotion.

Just like Esther, your test of promotion has been taking place. You're doing great and passing the test! Keep using your faith. Keep preparing for the great things God has in store for you.

I challenge you as Adar is coming to a close to think about how Esther faced the king. How has God been promoting you in this season? What tests have you undergone to prove your mantle calling?

You will soon be entering the month of Nisan. It's the first month on the Hebrew calendar and a very power-filled time. Stand firm. If you do, you will be blessed with an overflow of His anointing, revelation, and new opportunities!

ADAR 28

I heard the word of the Lord for you today, which was just one word: *advance*. We are getting close to Nisan, the first month on the Jewish calendar. I feel the Lord saying that the shift that has been taking place is gathering momentum right now. You may have felt a stirring. This shift is meant to *advance* you, to move you forward into all God has for you.

This period between Nisan and Rosh Hashanah is the time of spring rains. It is a time when God begins to build and bring increase. Make sure you are in the proper position before the double portion comes at Rosh Hashanah this autumn.

In Philippians 3:13-14 (NKJV) the apostle Paul tells us, *"Brethren, I do not count myself to have apprehended; but one thing I do, forgetting those things which are behind and reaching forward to those things which are ahead, I press toward the goal for the prize of the upward call of God in Christ Jesus."*

God is adjusting things in your life. Trust Him in this! Embrace the process! Be confident and know that He is preparing the way for you, moving you into great things this year.

ADAR 29

Today is a beautiful day in the Lord! We are getting ready to step into the month of Nisan. This is the first month on the Hebrew calendar and thought of as the month of redemption, salvation, and deliverance. During this time of approaching the end of the month of Adar, purpose to set yourself apart in consecration.

In Deuteronomy 26:8 (NKJV), we read, *"The Lord brought us out of Egypt with a mighty hand and with an outstretched arm, with great terror and with signs and wonders."* This month, God is preparing to bring you out of places where you are held in bondage and need deliverance. He is the God of promise, and He wants to take you into the Promised Land. He will do it with His outstretched arms as Jesus did when He outstretched His arms on the cross for us and shed His blood for our salvation and deliverance.

During Passover week, let's remember Jesus's great act of love. His death, burial, resurrection, and ascension provide for you the foundation of how to live as His child. Not only are you resurrected from the dead places, but you are also properly positioned to walk in the heavenly realms right here on earth.

ADAR 30

Adar 1 is usually 30 days; if there is a leap year, Adar 2 will have only 29 days.

I see your capacity increasing! You are getting ready to step into something BIG! The Lord showed me that your capacity is maxing out. When you reach this point, God is going to reveal to you what needs to be changed in your life. You will feel a breaking, but I want you to allow God to show you what is holding you back. When you respond through confession and repentance, God will mend you and expand your capacity again. The expansion comes when you say, "Jesus, I want more of You. Increase my capacity where nothing is missing or broken. Position me to go to the next level."

We are starting new. It's spring. I feel in the spirit that spring is abounding! Spring forward. Move beyond where you are currently. God is doing something new. He is preparing you for greatness. When you walk in heavenly realms on earth, you will walk in completeness and fullness of life. Our Father is so good and awesome!

Before you go, let me pray over you: "Father, thank You for giving my friend courage. You are giving them courage as You pull them out of Egypt and move them to the promised land. You are showing them Your greatness in every way, in signs, miracles, wonders, might, and outstretched arms. They will see and revere you, Father, and know by Your goodness and love for them You are taking them to a better place. You want them to experience more of You, so You are working on them. Let them be coura-geous and stand forth and do what it is that they need to do to step into that place. Father, I thank you for blessing my friend. In Jesus's name, amen."

Share this with a friend. God is getting your heart ready. He is doing great things! Be blessed!

You have now completed a whole year from Nisan and it is time to enjoy again this devotional and begin with the first month of the religious calendar. Turn the page to start fresh for a new year. God will speak differently to you this next year then He did last year, as you have grown in the foundations of the Hebrew calendar. Now you will have greater encounters prophetically because of your faithfulness last year to do all the readings. I am excited for you!

Please contact my ministry and share with me how you enjoyed this devotional and what you personally experienced. I would love to have you join my monthly live mentoring group or any of my School of the Supernatural classes, please go to www.candicesmithyman.com.

APPENDIX

I cited dates from the Hebrew calendar using the following sources:

- www.hebcal.com

- www.Chabad.org

- www.hebrew4christians.com

- www.aish.com

- https://www.britannica.com/topic/Gregorian -calendar

- Wikipedia. I realize Wikipedia is not a strong reference, but the general information led me to other sources. Each Wikipedia citation linked to other sources where I collected more data.

To further your advancement regarding the Hebrew calendar and events, I encourage you to research for yourself. There are many good resources that will help you grow in your knowledge of the Hebrew calendar.

ABOUT
THE AUTHOR

Dr. Candice Smithyman is an international prophetic revivalist and healing minister. She is the founder of Dream Mentors International and retired cofounder and pastor of Freedom Destiny Church in Orange Park, Florida, with her husband, Adam. She is also host of the Glory Road Television broadcast that showcases international prophetic voices and can be seen on worldwide networks. Her programs are translated into Urdu to reach Muslim populations through satellites and other outlets.

Dr. Smithyman hosts *Your Path to Destiny* on Sid Roth's It's Supernatural Network (ISN). She is the host of the *On the Glory Road* podcast with Destiny Image Publishers and *Manifest His Presence* podcast with *Charisma Podcast Network*. She has been a guest on: Sid Roth's *It's Supernatural, Today with Marilyn and Sarah, The Paula White Today Show,* Jim Bakker Show, and many others.

She has authored multiple books on soul transformation, healing, heavenly encounters, and curriculum for secular and Christian coaching organizations. She is also a residential faculty instructor with Wagner University. She writes for multiple online prophetic news magazines including *Elijah List, Charisma, CBN News, God TV, Global Prophetic Voice, Prophetic 365,* and *Spirit Fuel.*

FOR MORE INFORMATION
VISIT HER WEBSITE AT

www.candicesmithyman.com

AND

www.dreammentors.org

Check out
our **Destiny Image**
bestsellers page at
destinyimage.com/bestsellers

for cutting-edge,
prophetic messages
that will supernaturally
empower you and the
body of Christ.

YOUR
Prophetic
COMMUNITY

Sign up for a **FREE** subscription to the Destiny Image digital magazine and get awesome content delivered directly to your inbox!

destinyimage.com/signup

Sign up for Cutting-Edge Messages that Supernaturally Empower You

- Gain valuable insights and guidance based on biblical principles
- Deepen your faith and understanding of God's plan for your life
- Receive regular updates and prophetic messages
- Connect with a community of believers who share your values and beliefs

Experience Fresh Video Content that Reveals Your Prophetic Inheritance

- Receive prophetic messages and insights
- Connect with a powerful tool for spiritual growth and development
- Stay connected and inspired on your faith journey

Listen to Powerful Podcasts that Propel You into God's Presence Every Day

- Deepen your understanding of God's prophetic assignment
- Experience God's revival power throughout your day
- Learn how to grow spiritually in your walk with God